Social science and
the ignoble savage

Cambridge Studies in the History and Theory of Politics

Social science and the ignoble savage

RONALD L. MEEK
Tyler Professor of Economics
University of Leicester

CAMBRIDGE UNIVERSITY PRESS

CAMBRIDGE

LONDON · NEW YORK · MELBOURNE

H 51. M44.

Published by the Syndics of the Cambridge University Press
The Pitt Building, Trumpington Street, Cambridge CB2 1RP
Bentley House, 200 Euston Road, London NW1 2DB
32 East 57th Street, New York, NY 10022, USA
296 Beaconsfield Parade, Middle Park, Melbourne 3206, Australia

© Cambridge University Press 1976

Library of Congress catalogue card number: 75–22985

ISBN: 0 521 20969 2

First published 1976

Printed in Great Britain by
Western Printing Services Ltd
Bristol

Contents

Introduction   *page* 1

1   The four stages theory and its prehistory   5

2   'In the beginning all the World was *America*'   37

3   The French pioneers of the 1750s   68

4   The Scottish pioneers of the 1750s   99

5   The ignoble savage and 'the history of rude nations'   131

6   Revisionists, poets, and economists   177

     Afterword   230

     Index   244

Introduction

What was it which gave unity to the ideas about the structure and development of society generated in Europe during that incredible century between the English and French revolutions – the century traditionally described as the Enlightenment? Basically, I suppose, it was a common *concern*: to apply to the study of man and society those 'scientific' methods of enquiry which had recently proved their worth and importance in the sphere of natural science. The leading assumption of the French and Scottish *philosophes* was that everything in society and history, just like everything in the physical realm, was bound together by an intricate concatenation of causes and effects which it was the main task of the student of man and society – i.e. the social scientist – to unravel.

But this, of course, was only the beginning. There were certain other rather more specific ideas which were almost universally held. Among these, perhaps the most pervasive was a sensationalist psychology or theory of knowledge derived in one way or another from Locke. Associated with this, and just as important, was the so-called 'law of unintended consequences' – i.e. roughly, the idea that what happened in history was (to quote Ferguson) 'the result of human action, but not the execution of any human design'.[1] Finally, and perhaps most important of all, there was another associated idea which in effect added a new dimension to the problem of man and society. Man, it was postulated, not only *made himself* and his institutions: he and his institutions in an important sense *were themselves made* by the circumstances in which from time to time and from place to place he happened to find himself.

Perhaps the most typical and far-reaching product – or expression, or embodiment, for it was all three – of this set of

[1] Adam Ferguson, *An Essay on the History of Civil Society* (6th edn, London, 1793), p. 205.

1

notions, at any rate in the latter half of the century, was the particular theory of socio-economic development which is the main subject of the present book. This theory, in its most general form, was simply that the key factor in the process of development was the mode of subsistence. As William Robertson put it in his *History of America,* 'In every inquiry concerning the operations of men when united together in society, the first object of attention should be their mode of subsistence. Accordingly as that varies, their laws and policy must be different.'[2] In its most specific form, the theory was that society 'naturally' or 'normally' progressed over time through four more or less distinct and consecutive stages, each corresponding to a different mode of subsistence, these stages being defined as hunting, pasturage, agriculture, and commerce. To each of these modes of subsistence, it came to be argued, there corresponded different sets of ideas and institutions relating to law, property, and government, and also different sets of customs, manners, and morals. For better or for worse, this 'four stages theory', as I shall from now on call it for short, was destined not only to dominate socio-economic thought in Europe in the latter half of the eighteenth century, but also to become of crucial significance in the subsequent development of economics, sociology, anthropology, and historiography, right down to our own time. It is therefore a matter of some importance to investigate its origins and early development; and this is the first main task undertaken in the present book.

Many different influences no doubt contributed to the making of the four stages theory. In this book, however, I shall be directly concerned with only one of these – that of the contemporary literature about savage[3] societies, and in particular about the American Indians. It is well enough known that contemporary notions of savagery influenced eighteenth-century social science by generating a critique of society through the idea of the *noble* savage. It is not quite so well known, I think, that they also stimulated the emergence of a new theory of the development of society through

[2] William Robertson, *Works* (Edinburgh, 1890), Vol. II, p. 104.
[3] Here and in most subsequent contexts the word 'savage', and also the word 'civilised', should be read as if they were in quotation marks.

2

the idea of the *ignoble* savage. The contemporary literature about the American Indians, I shall claim, played an important part in determining some of the leading emphases of the four stages theory, and the form of a number of its chief propositions. The substantiation of this claim is the second main task undertaken in the present book.

Let me make it quite clear from the outset that this is in fact *all* that I shall be claiming. I would not, of course, wish to argue that the general framework of 'philosophical' ideas within which the four stages theory was set was significantly influenced by the studies of the American Indians. Even if America had not by that time been discovered, European writers in the eighteenth century would no doubt still have started talking about the progress and perfectibility of society; they would still have begun trying to apply to the study of society and its history the new methods of enquiry which had proved so fruitful in the field of the natural sciences; and their studies would still have been predominantly 'materialist', even if only in the attenuated sense of being bound up with a Lockean theory of knowledge. And so far as the four stages theory itself is concerned, even if the studies of the American Indians had not been available, there was a great deal of literature about other relatively primitive peoples upon which the new social scientists could have drawn – and did in actual fact draw – for the same or similar purposes. The fact that most of them drew so heavily upon the American studies and constantly emphasised their significance, however, seems to indicate that they may well have played a rather special role, perhaps going beyond that of a catalyst and approaching that of an independent primary cause.

In Chapter 1, the prehistory of the four stages theory is surveyed, the general conclusion being that the anticipations of the theory in the literature prior to Montesquieu, Smith, and Turgot were so scarce and scattered that the true origins of the theory must up to a point be sought in sources outside the literature itself. In Chapter 2, I try to trace the gradual emergence of the crucial notion that (as Locke put it) 'in the beginning all the World was *America*'.[4] Chapter 3 discusses

---

[4] John Locke, *Two Treatises of Government* (Mentor edn, ed. Peter Laslett, New American Library, New York, 1965), p. 343.

in detail the work in this field of the French pioneers of the 1750s, and Chapter 4 the work of the Scottish pioneers in the same decade. Chapter 5 is mainly concerned with the contributions of a number of French and Scottish followers who used the four stages theory between 1760 and 1780 to illuminate what Ferguson called 'the history of rude nations'.[5] In Chapter 6, the story of the development of the theory from 1780 to 1800 is told, with particular reference to a number of 'revisionist' contributions which appeared during that period. Finally, in a brief Afterword, I say a little about the elements of truth and falsity in a number of modern assessments of the socio-economic thought of the Enlightenment.

[5] 'Of the History of Rude Nations' is the title of Part II of Ferguson's *Essay on the History of Civil Society*.

The four stages theory and its prehistory

Semyon Efimovich Desnitsky, one of the two Russian students who came to Glasgow University in 1761 to sit at the feet of Adam Smith and John Millar, delivered a lecture at Moscow University twenty years later in which the following statement occurs:

We cannot measure the various successes of the human race, its risings and falling, on the basis of its imputed childhood, youth, maturity, and old age . . . Fortunately for our times, the newest and most assiduous explorers of human nature have discovered incomparably better means for studying nations in their various successes according to the circumstances and conditions through which those peoples, starting from their primordial society with wild animals, rose to the highest degree of greatness and enlightenment. Even ancient writers suggested four such conditions of the human race, of which the most primitive is held to be the *condition* of peoples living by *hunting* animals and feeding on the *spontaneous fruits* of the earth; the second is the *condition* of peoples living as shepherds, or the *pastoral*; the third is the *agricultural*; the fourth and last is the *commercial*. In accordance with these conditions, the most famous Roman writers, Julius Caesar, Tacitus, and Sallust measured the success not only of their own people, but of many others . . . Such an origin and rising of human society is common to all the primitive peoples, and in accordance with these four conditions of peoples we must deduce their history, government, laws, and customs and measure their various successes in sciences and arts.[1]

Here we have not only an unequivocal statement of the four stages theory, not only an affirmation of its essential novelty

[1] Desnitsky's speech, entitled 'A Legal Discourse about the Different Ideas which People have concerning the Ownership of Property in Different Conditions of Society', will be found reprinted in S. A. Pokrovsky (ed.), *Yuridicheskie proizvedeniya progressivnykh russkikh mysliteley: vtoraya polovina XVIII veka* (Moscow, 1959). I owe this reference, and also the translation of the extract from the speech which is reproduced in the text, to Mr A. H. Brown, of St Antony's College, Oxford. The italics are all Desnitsky's.

and its superiority to previous analytical frameworks of a stadial type, but also – and this is what most concerns us here – a suggestion that certain anticipations of the theory are to be found in the work of 'even ancient writers'.[2] The question we must now ask is whether such suggestions as this – which are by no means uncommon in the contemporary literature – indicated anything more than attempts to provide a new theory with a respectable pedigree. In other words, did the four stages theory have a *history* before the 1750s, or merely a *prehistory*?

To answer this question, we must first decide what we are going to count as true anticipations of the theory. The essential idea embodied in the theory is that societies undergo *development* through successive *stages* based on different *modes of subsistence*. In looking for anticipations of this idea, we should presumably not worry too much if the development which is postulated does not clearly imply progress in the eighteenth-century sense; or if the number of stages concerned is less than (or indeed greater than) four; or if the order of the stages is rather different. The important point is that the stages should be based on different *modes of subsistence*, rather than on (for example) different modes of political organisation, or different phases of some kind of 'life cycle' based on the analogy of human life; and that these different modes of subsistence should be recognised, even if only vaguely, as in some sense *determining* elements in the total situation. Men, after all, have been speculating about the development of human society ever since they first consciously began to speculate, and there were of course a great number of attempts before the eighteenth century to analyse the process of development in terms of one or another kind of stadial framework. Many of these contributions no doubt helped to put the problem of development on the agenda and to keep it there, and also to familiarise men with the notion that some kind of stage-oriented methodology might help in solving this problem. But unless the postulated stages are fairly firmly based on the mode of subsistence, such contributions should not in my opinion be regarded as anticipa-

---

[2] In the original, *i drevnie pisateli*, an alternative translation of which would be 'Ancient writers also . . .'

tions of the eighteenth-century four stages theory. To take the contrary view would be virtually equivalent to claiming not only that there was nothing new in the Enlightenment, but also that there was nothing new under the sun.

What can we find by way of anticipations in the defined sense, then, in the work of those 'ancient writers' to whom Desnitsky referred in his speech? The answer, broadly, is that we can indeed find something, but that it is much less than we might have expected, and (with one or two exceptions) not very easy to find unless we know what we are looking for and are fairly adept at reading between the lines. A non-classicist such as the present writer can never be sure, of course, that he has not missed something; but he can at least read – even if only in English translation – the major sources referred to by the eighteenth-century social scientists themselves, and he can be greatly aided by the availability of two splendid collections of readings – *The Idea of Progress*[3] and *Primitivism and Related Ideas in Antiquity*.[4] The latter volume is particularly helpful in the present connection, for although its compilers have cast their net primarily with the aim of catching ancient 'primitivists', they have in fact cast it widely enough to catch any ancient anticipators of the four stages theory as well.

Reading through these sources, one finds a number of intellectual constructs and ideas which are as it were peripheral to the four stages theory: the legend of the Five Ages, for example, as recounted by Hesiod and interpreted in different ways by later writers; various versions of the theory of recurrent world-cycles; a number of stage-oriented theories of the course of *political* history; many theories involving the idea of the gradual degeneration of society, a few involving the idea of its gradual progress, and one or two containing vague hints of its infinite perfectibility; various examples of the use of the concept of geographical or climatic determinism; and, last but not least, several attempts to reconstruct the chain of individual technological discoveries characteristic of the

[3] *The Idea of Progress: a Collection of Readings*, selected by Frederick J. Teggart (revised edn, with an introduction, by George H. Hildebrand, University of California Press, Berkeley and Los Angeles, 1949).

[4] *Primitivism and Related Ideas in Antiquity*, by Arthur O. Lovejoy and George Boas (Octagon Books, New York, 1965).

period of prehistory.[5] Substantive anticipations (in our sense) of the four stages theory, however, are very much harder to find. Plato's account in *The Laws* of 'the first beginning of a State', for example, presents us with a picture of a small number of 'mountain shepherds' who have escaped from Deucalion's Flood and who obtain their subsistence in the first instance not only from their flocks and herds but also from hunting. Later, significantly enough, when their numbers increase, they 'turn to agriculture', and we then find the beginnings of legislation and the enclosure of land.[6] This is encouraging, of course, but the general impression one gets is that the rise of the city, political sovereignty, and legislation – with which Plato is here primarily concerned – was regarded by him as being determined by the mode of subsistence only in very early times, and then only in part. In Aristotle's *Politics*, again, there is an interesting account of the 'differences of life among mankind' in which a distinction is made between the lives of the herdsman, the husbandman, the brigand (*sic*), the fisherman, the hunter, those who 'procure their food by barter and trade', and those who 'live pleasantly by combining some of these pursuits';[7] and towards the end of the book there is an equally interesting discussion of the relation between 'democracy' and communities based respectively on agriculture and pasturage.[8] Once again this is encouraging; but nowhere in Aristotle, so far as I am aware, is there any clear suggestion that the *development* of society goes hand in hand with a more or less orderly succession of any or all of these different modes of life. For real anticipations of the four stages theory, the only individual writers of antiquity whom we can properly single out are Lucretius and Dicaearchus, although as we shall see there were also a number of important hints of the basic under-

---

[5] These last constitute one of the main subjects of Thomas Cole's *Democritus and the Sources of Greek Anthropology* (American Philological Association, 1967). Of the authors of the five 'ancient histories of technology' considered by Professor Cole at the beginning of this remarkable book, Lucretius is the only one whose work can in my opinion be considered as containing anything in the nature of *real* anticipations of the four stages theory.

[6] Plato, *The Laws* (Everyman edn, tr. A. E. Taylor), pp. 55–61.

[7] Aristotle, *Politics* (Loeb edn, tr. H. Rackham), p. 35.

[8] *Ibid.*, pp. 497ff.

8

lying idea of the theory in some of the studies by other classical writers of the primitive peoples of their times.

The remarkable and influential account of the development of human society given by Lucretius towards the end of the fifth book of his *De Rerum Natura* certainly deserves separate consideration. The first race of men, the poet claims, included 'no study guider of the curved plough'. In the early ages, men simply appropriated 'what the earth had produced of her own accord', and 'hunt[ed] the woodland tribes of beasts with volleys of stones and ponderous clubs'. Next, 'when they had got them huts and skins, and fire, and woman mated with man was appropriated to one . . . neighbours began eagerly to join friendship amongst themselves to do no hurt and to suffer no violence'; language arose and developed; 'kings began to found cities'; 'they divided cattle and lands, and gave them to each according to beauty and strength and genius'; later 'wealth was introduced and gold was discovered, which easily robbed both the strong and the handsome of their honour'; this led to the rise of ambition and the desire for power; and out of the resultant strife and confusion there arose 'established law', to which men 'tired of living in violence' were readier to submit. At this point in Lucretius's narrative a detailed discussion of the origin of religion is interpolated; and he then goes on to describe the discovery of metals, which came about accidentally when forest fires had melted them – for example, when men 'wished to clear the fat fields and make the place fit for pasturage'. With bronze, men 'tilled the soil', but with it, too, they 'stirred up the waves of war' and 'seized cattle and lands'. Then iron was substituted for bronze in 'break[ing] the soil of the earth', and also in the waging of war, in which tamed animals were also widely employed. So far as agriculture was concerned,

the pattern of sowing and the beginning of grafting first came from nature herself the maker of all things, since berries and acorns falling from trees in due time produced swarms of seedlings underneath; and this also gave them the whimsy to insert shoots in the branches and to plant new slips in the earth all over the fields. Next one after another they tried ways of cultivating the little plot they loved, and found that the earth could tame wild fruits by kind treatment and friendly tillage. Day by day they made the forests climb higher up the mountains and yield the place below to their tillth . . .

Men gradually learned to sing and dance; the range of their wants and needs increased; 'the earth was divided up and distributed for cultivation'; and all the arts of life were taught by practice and experiment 'as men progressed gradually step by step'.[9]

This account is certainly impressive, and it is quite possible to read into it, at any rate if one knows what one is looking for and tries hard enough, a theory of socio-economic development which is not too dissimilar from the eighteenth-century theory. But no more than this can properly be claimed for it. The summary I have just given deliberately places rather more weight on the different modes of subsistence mentioned by Lucretius than is really warranted by the context. As Lovejoy and Boas note, in Lucretius's account 'there are several manifest contradictions, and the chronological order of the origins of the several arts, and of the stages of "social evolution", remains in part obscure'.[10] Pasturage and agriculture are not clearly distinguished from one another, and there is little evidence that Lucretius regarded changes in the mode of subsistence as the main determining factor in the process of development.

The vagueness of Lucretius's account becomes all the more apparent when we compare it with the much more precise statement apparently given in the fourth century B.C. by Dicaearchus, a Peripatetic philosopher whose work seems to have been read and utilised by quite a number of later classical writers. Lovejoy and Boas reproduce two very interesting extracts from the summaries of Dicaearchus's theory which were given respectively by Porphyry and Varro.[11] The latter's summary, in which the primitivist strain is less apparent than in Porphyry's, is as follows:

Therefore, I say, that since it is necessary in the nature of things that men and flocks have always existed . . . it must be true that step by step from the most remote period human life has come

[9] Lucretius, *De Rerum Natura* (Loeb edn, tr. W. H. D. Rouse), pp. 407–43.
[10] Lovejoy and Boas, *op. cit.*, p. 222.
[11] *Op. cit.*, pp. 93–6 and 368–9.

down to this age, as Dicaearchus writes, and that the earliest stage was a state of nature, when men lived on those things which the virgin earth bore; from this life they passed into a second, a pastoral life, and as they plucked from the wild and untrimmed trees and bushes acorns, arbute-berries, blackberries, apples and gathered them for their use, in like manner they caught such wild animals as they could and shut them up and tamed them. Among these, it is reasonable to think, the first to be caught were sheep, both because of their utility and their placidity. For they are by nature especially tame and most useful for human life. For food they supply milk and cheese, for clothing the body they furnish skins. Finally in the third stage, from the pastoral life they attained the agricultural, in which they retained many of the features of the two earlier periods, and from which they continued for a long time in the condition which they had reached until that in which we live was attained.[12]

This is certainly the clearest and least equivocal statement of a stadial theory of development based on different modes of subsistence which has come down to us from antiquity.[13]

Before leaving antiquity, however, we must note the important fact that a number of classical writers, when they were considering particular primitive peoples of their times and comparing them both with neighbouring primitive peoples and also with more civilised peoples, laid a certain amount of stress on their mode of subsistence. Herodotus, for example, noted that the Scythians lived 'not by agriculture but from their cattle'.[14] Caesar, again, said of the Suebi that 'they have no private or separate holding of land, nor are they allowed to abide longer than a year in one place for their habitation. They make not much use of corn for food, but chiefly of milk and of cattle, and are much engaged in hunting.'[15] Of the 'inlanders' of Britain, he wrote that 'most do not sow corn, but live on milk and flesh and clothe themselves in skins';[16] and of the Germans he said that 'their whole life is composed of hunting expeditions and military

---

[12] Lovejoy and Boas, *op. cit.*, pp. 368–9.
[13] Cf. Thomas Cole, *op. cit.*, pp. 54–5, where the contrast between Dicaearchus's 'preconceived' scheme and the five 'ancient histories of technology' mentioned in footnote 5 above is heavily emphasised.
[14] Lovejoy and Boas, *op. cit.*, p. 322.
[15] Caesar, *The Gallic War* (Loeb edn, tr. H. J. Edwards), p. 181.
[16] *Ibid.*, p. 253.

Social science and the ignoble savage

pursuits'.[17] And Tacitus's *Germania*, of course, contains quite a few statements of this type, upon which the eighteenth-century writers were to draw heavily, and from which some of them were to conclude that according to Tacitus the relative degree of civilisation of the different German tribes depended upon the extent to which agriculture and pasturage, rather than hunting, preponderated in their mode of subsistence. This view, which men like Desnitsky were later to father upon the classical historians, was in fact by no means as clearly expressed as they liked to make out. It is true that one sometimes gets a hint of the idea that the mode of subsistence of a people is largely instrumental in determining its character and customs; but in most contexts the particular mode of subsistence of the people concerned is simply listed alongside other characteristics such as the way its warriors wear their hair or the nature of its sexual or religious conventions, without much indication of the relevant order of determination. It was only when the eighteenth-century writers knew what they were looking for – or when, as we shall see later, they wanted to compare accounts of the primitive tribes of *their* day with those of classical times – that the existence of these significant overtones was discovered.

It is with Grotius's *The Law of War and Peace*, published in 1625 – almost 2000 years after Dicaearchus – that we take up the story again. By that time, of course, the ground had already up to a point been prepared for the cultivation of a number of those notions about the progress of society which were to come into full flower in the eighteenth century. Machiavelli and others had revived the old idea of cycles in political history; and Bodin had not only suggested that there might be an upward trend in these cycles but had also to some extent paved the way for a 'materialist' explanation of this trend by his emphasis on the influence of geographical and climatic conditions on the character of a people. A few years before 1625, Francis Bacon had published his *Novum Organum*, with its stress on the importance of the growth of scientific knowledge; and not very many years after 1625, Descartes was to publish his *Discourse on Method*, with its

[17] *Ibid.*, p. 347.

12

emphasis on the principle of the uniformity of natural laws and its immense faith in the powers of reason. By 1625, too, the powerful intellectual effects of the great overseas explorations and discoveries had begun to make themselves felt. Montaigne, for example, had already drawn attention to the fact that 'each several nation hath divers customs, fashions, and usages which to some others are not only unknown and strange but savage, barbarous, and wondrous'.[18] He had also remarked that 'our world hath of late discovered another . . . so new and infantine that he is yet to learn his A B C', thereby helping to popularise the idea that contemporary savagery could be regarded as a kind of model of the first ages of the world. And in one place he had noted that the absence of agriculture was a feature both of the New World and of antiquity:

There is neither corn, nor wine, no, nor any of our beasts seen in that new corner of the world which our fathers have lately discovered; all things differ from ours. And in the old time, mark but in how many parts of the world they had never knowledge nor of Bacchus nor of Ceres.[19]

Bacon, again, in his *Novum Organum*, had said that 'by the distant voyages and travels which have become frequent in our times, many things in nature have been laid open and discovered which may let in new light upon philosophy'.[20] And, even more significantly, he had been stimulated by the startling difference between 'the life of men in the most civilised province of Europe, and in the wildest and most barbarous districts of New India', to postulate that 'this difference comes not from soil, not from climate, not from race, but from the arts'.[21]

Grotius's *The Law of War and Peace*,[22] however, is of

18 *Selected Essays of Montaigne* (ed. Walter Kaiser, Houghton Mifflin Company, Boston, 1964), p. 355.
19 *Ibid.*, pp. 283 and 168–9.
20 *The Works of Francis Bacon* (ed. J. Spedding, R. L. Ellis, and D. D. Heath), Vol. IV (London, 1875), p. 82. Cf. also p. 73.
21 *Ibid.*, p. 114.
22 The quotations from this work in the text below are taken from pp. 186–90 of Book II of the translation by Francis W. Kelsey, published by the Carnegie Endowment for International Peace, Washington. I have used the reprint of 1964 (Oceana Publications, New York).

special significance in the development of the four stages
theory. It is true that there are only a few pages of this work
(at the beginning of the chapter in Book II entitled 'Of Things
which belong to Men in Common') which include anything
of direct relevance to the theory, and that the passages concerned do not add up to anything like a specific statement of
it: they contain nothing, indeed, which approaches in clarity
an inspired aside which had been made by Louis Le Roy
almost half a century earlier.[23] But these few pages of
Grotius's book are nevertheless important, because the views
on the historical origins of property which he expressed in
them were destined to be developed by Pufendorf, Locke,
and others into a 'stream of thought' on this subject which,
when it eventually came into the hands of men like Smith
and Kames, was to be associated very closely with the four
stages theory.

The 'first men', Grotius writes, 'lived easily on the fruits
which the earth brought forth of its own accord, without
toil'.[24] Men did not, however, 'continue to live in this simple
and innocent life, but turned their thoughts to various kinds
of knowledge, the symbol for which was the tree of knowledge of good and evil'. To the men who came after the first,
Grotius proceeds, 'the craft and various inventions devised
for the advantage of life proved not to be very useful; for
men devoted their talents not so much to the cultivation of
bravery and justice as to devising means of enjoyment'.[25]

23 The work I am referring to is *De la Vicissitude ou Variété des Choses en
   l'Univers*, by Louis Le Roy (Paris, 1576). The passage in question, which
   appears on p. 26, reads as follows: 'Or comme la nourriture ayt esté
   plustost prise des animaux priuez que des grains & fruicts n'y à doubte
   que le pasturage & Bergerie n'ayt esté auant l'Agriculture: comme il
   appert par les plus anciennes nations lesquelles ayans ainsi vescu du
   commencement en ont prins leurs noms, comme les Hébrieux & les
   Italiens, c'est à dire pasteurs, & qu'en vsent encores auiourd'huy plusieurs
   gens exerceans par maniere de dire [*sic*] vne agriculture viue. Le labour-
   age des terres nues & plantees a esté inuenté apres le pasturage, & aux
   deulx ont esté adioustees la venerie, faulconnerie, pescherie.' The passages
   on pp. 25–6 immediately preceding this one are also very interesting; and
   the classification on p. 13 of different "maniere de viure", each based
   on a different mode of subsistence, is quite advanced for its time.
24 Grotius at this point refers the reader in a footnote to 'the excellent passage of Dicaearchus on this subject'.
25 In the course of this passage, which Grotius is apparently quoting from
   Dio of Prusa, the reader is advised in a footnote to read Seneca on the

Cain and Abel pursued 'the most ancient arts, agriculture and grazing', and 'from the difference in pursuits arose rivalry, and even murder'. Then, after the confusion of tongues,

> men divided off countries, and possessed them separately. Afterward, nevertheless, there remained among neighbours a common ownership, not of flocks to be sure, but of pasture lands, because the extent of the land was so great, in proportion to the small number of men, that it sufficed without any inconvenience for the use of many . . . Finally, with increase in the number of men as well as of flocks, lands everywhere began to be divided, not as previously by peoples, but by families.

All this, says Grotius, we learn from sacred history. But the account is quite in accord with what we learn from 'philosophers and poets':

> From these sources we learn what was the cause on account of which the primitive common ownership, first of movable objects, later also of immovable property, was abandoned. The reason was that men were not content to feed on the spontaneous products of the earth, to dwell in caves, to have the body either naked or clothed with the bark of trees or skins of wild animals, but chose a more refined mode of life; this gave rise to industry, which some applied to one thing, others to another.

Things became subject to private ownership by 'a kind of agreement, either expressed, as by a division, or implied, as by occupation'. When the ancients called Ceres a lawgiver, Grotius concludes, 'they implied that out of the division of lands a new law had arisen'.

It will be clear, I think, that a number of component ideas of the four stages theory are hinted at in these interesting passages. Grotius's main concern, it is true, is not with the question of the origin and development of society as such, but with the question of the origin and development of the right of private ownership of property. His emphasis, however, is on the fact that things come into private ownership not all at once but *successively*, depending in part upon the size of the population and the nature of the terrain, but also

subject, 'and also Dicaearchus in the writers already cited' [i.e. Varro and Porphyry].

upon the nature of the particular 'arts' (agriculture and pasturage, for example) and species of 'industry' which men adopt in order to lift themselves out of their original primitive condition. Obviously this notion was potentially capable of extension. If changes in the mode of subsistence are the chief cause of changes in property rights, may they not also be the chief cause of changes in *society as a whole*, the latter being conceived as an integrated collection of conventions and institutions (including those relating to property rights)? This idea must have begun to appear more plausible when people came to assert that (as Smith was to put it) 'property and government very much depend on one another'.[26] It should be emphasised, however, that Grotius himself did not indicate the possibility of such an extension of his argument. Nor, in spite of his admiration for Dicaearchus, did he give any hint at all that the modes of subsistence which followed the first might usefully be conceived as succeeding one another in some kind of regular or normal sequence. We are still a very long way from the four stages theory in the form in which it was to dominate European social science in the latter half of the eighteenth century.[27]

'The next writer of note after Grotius', Smith was to tell his Glasgow students, 'was Mr. Hobbes.'[28] From the point of view of the development of the four stages theory, the most important contribution made by Hobbes was his well-known description in *Leviathan* (1651) of the 'naturall condition of mankind' as a 'condition of warre', and his rather less well-known use of 'the savage people in many places of *America*' as an example of this condition:

Whatsoever therefore is consequent to a time of Warre, where every man is Enemy to every man; the same is consequent to the time, wherein men live without other security, than what their own strength, and their own invention shall furnish them withall.

26 *Lectures on Justice, Police, Revenue and Arms* (ed. Edwin Cannan, Oxford, 1896), p. 8.
27 Before leaving Grotius, it is worth noting that in the course of the argument summarised in the text he cites 'certain tribes in America' as an example of 'community of property arising from extreme simplicity', alongside a number of references to classical accounts of the manners and ways of life of the Scythians, Getae, Scrithiphini, etc.
28 *Lectures on Justice, Police, Revenue and Arms*, p. 2.

16

In such condition, there is no place for Industry; because the fruit thereof is uncertain: and consequently no Culture of the Earth, no Navigation, nor use of the commodities that may be imported by Sea; no commodious Building; no Instruments of moving, and removing such things as require much force; no Knowledge of the face of the Earth; no account of Time; no Arts; no Letters; no Society; and which is worst of all, continuall feare, and danger of violent death; And the life of man, solitary, poore, nasty, brutish, and short . . . It may peradventure be thought, there was never such a time, nor condition of warre as this; and I believe it was never generally so, over all the world: but there are many places, where they live so now. For the savage people in many places of *America*, except the government of small Families, the concord whereof dependeth on naturall lust, have no government at all; and live at this day in that brutish manner, as I said before.[29]

The significance of this influential statement lay not only in the fact that it encouraged the further development of the idea that America was a kind of living model of the first state of mankind; not only in the fact that according to Hobbes this state was characterised first and foremost by the absence of agriculture and commerce; but also in the fact that the memorable phrase with which Hobbes described 'the life of man' in this state made its *idealisation* rather more difficult than it might otherwise have been. The four stages theory in its eighteenth-century form, it will be recalled, usually implied that society in some sense *progressed* as it moved from the earliest stage to the later ones; and this concept of progress was (at any rate up to a point) inconsistent with any 'primitivist' idealisation of the first stage.

Pufendorf's great classic *The Law of Nature and Nations* (1672),[30] while owing much to Grotius's *The Law of War and Peace*, went beyond the latter work in a number of important respects. Of particular interest in the present connection is Pufendorf's treatment of the state of nature and the origin of private property. The 'natural state of man' is defined by

[29] Thomas Hobbes, *Leviathan* (Everyman edn), pp. 64–5.
[30] The quotations from this work in the text below are taken from Book I of the translation by C. H. and W. A. Oldfather, published by the Carnegie Endowment for International Peace, Washington. I have used the reprint of 1964 (Oceana Publications, New York).

Pufendorf as 'that condition for which man is understood to
be constituted, by the mere fact of his birth, all inventions
and institutions, either of man or suggested to him from
above, being disregarded'.[31] If such a state had ever in fact
existed, Pufendorf argues, it would have been a very miser-
able one, and the unhappy picture drawn of the primitive
state of man by pagan writers would have been a more or
less accurate representation of it.[32] But, says Pufendorf,

we maintain that the race of man never did live at one and the
same time in a simple state of nature, and never could have, since
we believe on the authority of Holy Writ, that the origin of all
men came from the marriage of a single pair . . . Therefore, a
state of nature never actually existed, except in some altered form
or only in part, as when, indeed, some men gathered together
with others into a civil state, or some such body, but retained a
natural liberty against the rest of mankind; although the more
groups there were in this division of the human race, and the
smaller their membership, the nearer it must have approached a
pure state of nature. So when at the first mankind separated into
different family groups, and now have divided into states, such
groups live in a mutual state of nature, in so far as no one group
obeys another, and all the members have no common master.[33]

The state of nature, therefore, at any rate in the 'altered form'
of which Pufendorf speaks in this passage, is by no means
incompatible with the private ownership of property.

How, then, does the private ownership of property
('dominion' in Pufendorf's terminology) actually arise? In the
first period after the Creation, Pufendorf asserts, there existed
what he calls a 'negative community' of all things – meaning
by this simply that all things 'lay open to all men'[34] and were
'not yet assigned to a particular person'.[35] There was no need
for 'distinct dominions', he argues,

so long as Adam's offspring, still of tender years, had to be supported by their parent, or were still under the fatherly authority.
For it was due to the force of the father's authority, and not that
of dominion, that for a time his children had to accommodate
their use of things to the will of their father. Therefore, distinct
dominions came into force only when, with the consent of their

[31] *Op. cit.*, p. 154.   [32] *Ibid.*, pp. 154–5.   [33] *Ibid.*, pp. 162–3.
[34] *Ibid.*, p. 537.   [35] *Ibid.*, p. 532.

18

father, children commenced to set up separate establishments, which was undoubtedly caused by the ancient rivalry of the brothers, as well as by the consideration that each one's industry might be his own gain and his idleness his own burden. Yet it should not be held that the whole earth was at once divided between that handful of mortals, or that all things once and for all passed under proprietorship. It was enough at first that those things should be made property which are either immediately and indivisibly of use to several persons, such as clothing, habitations, and fruits gathered for food, or which require some labour and care, such as implements, household furnishings, herds, and fields. Little by little what remained came under proprietorship, according as the inclination of men or their increasing numbers directed. Thus for a long time pasture lands remained in primitive community, until, as herds multiplied and quarrels arose, it was to the interest of peace that they also be divided.[36]

The basic idea expressed in this passage – that 'not all things passed into proprietorship at one time, but successively'[37] – had already been adumbrated by Grotius. But Pufendorf treats it at much greater length, illustrating it with (for example) the case of the Scythians who allowed 'property in flocks and household goods' while at the same time 'their fields were held in original community'.[38] He also tries on a number of occasions to explain 'the causes for things passing into proprietorship', and 'the order which they followed'.[39]

So far as the causes are concerned, the emphasis is usually placed on the growth of population and the increase in 'refinement' or 'industry', as in the following interesting passage:

It is certain that the more the number of men increased, and the more refined life became, the greater necessity there was for things in increasing numbers to pass under proprietorship. Those people who to this day are but little removed from primitive community, are somewhat barbarous and simple; such, for instance, as exist on herbs, roots, the natural fruits of the earth, by hunting, and fishing, with no other property than a shed and some rude furniture.[40]

So far as the order is concerned, the general impression Pufendorf gives is that the first things likely to be taken into

36 *Ibid.*, pp. 550–1. 37 *Ibid.*, p. 551. 38 *Ibid.*, p. 539.
39 *Ibid.*, p. 539. 40 *Ibid.*, p. 554.

proprietorship would be the sheds and 'rude furniture' of the hunters and fishers; that flocks and herds would probably follow; and that the land itself would be the last thing to come under private ownership. This view, in the eighteenth century, was to become associated with the notion that an original mode of subsistence based on hunting and fishing gave way to one based on pasturage, and this in turn to one based on agriculture. It is important to note, however, that Pufendorf himself did not adopt this notion. Before we decide to father a stadial theory of development of the eighteenth-century type upon him, we should recall that he firmly believed, on the authority of Genesis, that all three of these modes of subsistence had in fact coexisted in society from very early times.[41]

We turn now to the great figure of John Locke. His immense influence on the social science of the Enlightenment was of course exercised not only through his theory of property, but also through the doctrines of his *Essay Concerning Human Understanding*. Enlightenment thought was indeed to become pervaded with Locke's idea that there were no such things as innate principles, either 'speculative' or 'practical'; that the mind of man at birth was to all intents and purposes a piece of 'white paper'[42] or an 'empty cabinet';[43] that morality was essentially relative;[44] and that differences between groups were culturally determined.[45] If we are seek-

---

[41] Cf. *ibid.*, p. 157: 'We know that primitive man by the aid of God learned very early the most necessary arts (see *Genesis*, iii. 21, 23; iv. 2, 17, 22), to which the sagacity of men added a considerable number of others.'

[42] *An Essay Concerning Human Understanding* (Everyman edn, ed. John W. Yolton), Vol. I, p. 77.

[43] *Ibid.*, Vol. I, p. 15.

[44] *Ibid.*, Vol. I, pp. 31–2: 'He that will carefully peruse the history of mankind, and look abroad into the several tribes of men, and with indifferency survey their actions, will be able to satisfy himself that there is scarce that principle of morality to be named, or *rule* of *virtue* to be thought on (those only excepted, that are absolutely necessary to hold society together, which commonly too are neglected betwixt distinct societies) which is not, somewhere or other, *slighted* and condemned by the general fashion of *whole societies* of men, governed by practical opinions and rules of living quite opposite to others.'

[45] Cf. *ibid.*, Vol. I, p. 50: 'Had you or I been born at the Bay of *Saldanha*, possibly our thoughts and notions had not exceeded those brutish ones of the *Hottentots* that inhabit there. And had the *Virginia* king *Apochan-*

ing for anticipations of the four stages theory as such, how-ever, there is no doubt that it is to Locke's theory of property in his *Two Treatises on Government* (1690) that we should mainly look.

Locke's account of the state of nature and the original community of goods has so much in common with Pufen-dorf's that we need not pay any special attention to it here. Where the two men diverge more seriously is in their accounts of the origin of property: whereas Pufendorf saw separate ownership as arising through the medium of some kind of 'pact', Locke saw it as arising when a man 'mixed his *Labour*' with a thing.[46] Nevertheless, the kind of general picture of the 'causes' and order' of the passing of things into private ownership which we get from Locke is not essentially dissimilar from that which we get from Pufendorf, as will be seen from the following passage:

Before the Appropriation of Land, he who gathered as much of the wild Fruit, killed, caught, or tamed, as many of the Beasts as he could; he that so employed his Pains about any of the spon-taneous Products of Nature, as any way to alter them, from the state which Nature put them in, *by* placing any of his *Labour* on them, did thereby *acquire a Property in them* . . .

The same *measures* governed the *Possession of Land* too: What-soever he tilled and reaped, laid up and made use of, before it spoiled, that was his peculiar Right; whatsoever he enclosed, and could feed, and make use of, the Cattle and Product was also his . . . Thus, at the beginning, *Cain* might take as much Ground as he could till, and make it his own Land, and yet leave enough to *Abel's* Sheep to feed on; a few Acres would serve for both their Possessions. But as Families increased, and Industry inlarged their Stocks, their *Possessions inlarged* with the need of them; but yet it was commonly *without any fixed property in the ground* they made use of, till they incorporated, settled them-selves together, and built Cities, and then, by consent, they came in time, to set out the *bounds of their distinct Territories*, and

cana been educated in *England,* he had perhaps been as knowing a divine and as good a mathematician as any in it: the difference between him and a more improved *Englishman* lying barely in this, that exercise of his faculties was bounded within the ways, modes and notions of his own country and never directed to any other or further inquiries.'

46 *Two Treatises on Government* (Mentor edn, ed. Peter Laslett, New American Library, New York, 1965), p. 329.

agree on limits between them and their Neighbours, and by Laws within themselves, settled the *Properties* of those of the same Society. For we see, that in that part of the World which was first inhabited, and therefore like to be best peopled, even as low down as *Abraham*'s time, they wandred with their Flocks, and their Herds, which was their substance, freely up and down; and this *Abraham* did, in a Country where he was a Stranger. Whence it is plain, that at least, a great part of the *Land lay in common*; that the Inhabitants valued it not, nor claimed Property in any more than they made use of. But when there was not room enough in the same place, for their Herds to feed together, they, by consent, as *Abraham* and *Lot* did, *Gen.* xiii. 5. separated and inlarged their pasture, where it best liked them.[47]

It will be noted that in this passage Locke seems to assume, as Pufendorf had done and for the same reason, that hunting, pasturage, and agriculture had coexisted in the first ages of society. A little later in the chapter, however, Cain and Abel appear to be forgotten, and are in effect replaced by the American Indian – that same Indian of whom Locke has already told us that he is nourished by 'Fruit, or Venison', and that he 'knows no Inclosure, and is still a Tenant in common'.[48] The first men, Locke now informs us, 'for the most part, contented themselves with what un-assisted Nature Offered to their Necessities' – which Cain and Abel could hardly be said to have done.[49] The things which 'the necessity of subsisting made the first Commoners of the World look after', says Locke, are the same as those which the present-day American Indians are concerned with.[50] 'In the beginning all the World was *America*',[51] Locke tells us; and again, later in the book, he remarks that '*America* . . . is still a Pattern of the first Ages in *Asia* and *Europe*'.[52] This extremely influential notion, which was anticipated by a few of Locke's predecessors but which Locke himself did more than any other writer of his time to popularise, will be discussed in more detail below. At this juncture, let us merely note one of its more important implications: that hunting, pasturage, and agriculture did *not* in fact coexist in the 'first ages' of Asia and Europe, as Genesis had led so many to believe. The

[47] *Ibid.*, pp. 336–8. [48] *Ibid.*, p. 328. [49] *Ibid.*, p. 341.
[50] *Ibid.*, p. 342. [51] *Ibid.*, p. 343. [52] *Ibid.*, p. 383.

way was thus for the first time really laid open for the emergence of the idea of an orderly sequence or succession of different modes of subsistence through which societies could be conceived as progressing over time.

These writings on the historical origins of property, taken together, constituted the first of three important seventeenth-century traditions or 'streams of thought' which directly or indirectly contributed to the eventual emergence of the four stages theory in the middle of the following century. The second of these 'streams of thought' consisted of the work of a number of historians who adopted the so-called 'providential' theory of history, the most influential example being Bossuet's famous *Discours sur l'Histoire Universelle*, which appeared in 1681.

Some modern commentators have suggested that the historical importance of Bossuet's book lay solely in the fact that it provided something for Voltaire and Turgot to react against. It did indeed fulfil this useful function: the *philosophes* could scarcely have been expected to look with great favour upon a book in which events such as the Creation, the Flood, and the confusion of tongues were all given precise dates, and in which it was assumed throughout that history was made by God in accordance with a pre-ordained plan for the purpose of preserving his people, spreading his religion, and promoting his glory.[53] A true 'science' or 'philosophy' of history, in the sense in which the *philosophes* came to understand these terms, was obviously inconsistent with the acceptance of such an assumption. But when we look more closely at Bossuet's account of the *methods* by which God allegedly controlled the historical development of the human race, we see that he made a number of significant bows in the direction of the 'modernist' trends which it was one of his main purposes to oppose, and that his book in fact prepared the way for the new philosophy of history of the Enlightenment much more directly than he himself would have desired or indeed thought possible. The point is that according to Bossuet, although God certainly 'made history',

[53] *Oeuvres de Bossuet* (Bibliothèque de la Pléiade edn, ed. B. Velat and Y. Champailler, Tours, 1961), pp. 950–1.

he did not make it by means of constant and direct supernatural interventions in the affairs of men. 'Except for certain
extraordinary strokes, where God wished his hand alone to
show itself', Bossuet wrote, 'there has never been any great
change which has not had its causes in the preceding centuries.'[54] God had established in his wisdom a 'marvellous
concatenation' whereby things were interconnected and
bound up with one another in an orderly way.[55] But to have
said that God had *merely* established the laws of cause and
effect would of course have been gross heresy, which Bossuet
was certainly not the man to commit. The important point
for him was that God had 'prepared the effects in the most
remote causes'.[56] Thus the historian who sought for these
'remote causes' of historical changes was in effect seeking for
the 'secret dispositions' of God:

As in all affairs there is something which prepares them, something which determines that they are undertaken, and something
which causes them to succeed, the true science of history is to
note in each period those secret dispositions which have prepared
the great changes, and the important combinations of events
[*conjonctures*] which have made them happen.[57]

Clearly this was a view of the 'true science of history' which
was potentially capable of secularisation – a fact which
Turgot was quick to appreciate. The parallels between
Turgot's work and Bossuet's are certainly striking enough.
Bossuet had talked in terms of a succession of religious
'epochs'; Turgot talked in terms of a succession of socio-
economic 'stages'. Bossuet had emphasised the way in which
God worked through individual law-givers and conquerors,
so that although they made history they did not make it as
they wished and always felt themselves 'subject to a superior
force';[58] Turgot emphasised the way in which certain historical laws and necessities worked through them, with much
the same kind of result. Bossuet had proclaimed that 'all the
great empires which we have seen on earth have led in

---

[54] *Ibid.*, p. 953.   [55] *Ibid.*, p. 768; and cf. p. 953.
[56] *Ibid.*, p. 1025; and cf. p. 953.   [57] *Ibid.*, p. 953.
[58] *Ibid.*, p. 1026. The whole of the passage in which this phrase occurs is
worth reading, as a classical statement of what may perhaps be called the
providential version of the law of unintended consequences.

24

different ways towards the good of religion and the glory of God';[59] Turgot proclaimed that through all its vicissitudes mankind in the long run advanced towards greater perfection.

In addition to this, Bossuet's work contained certain rather more specific anticipations of elements of the four stages theory. Consider, for example, the following passage which occurs in his description of the second (Noachian) epoch:

The human race emerges little by little from ignorance; it is taught by experience, and the arts are invented or perfected. To the extent that men multiply, the earth is peopled from place to place: mountains and gorges are crossed; rivers and eventually seas are traversed, and new settlements are established. The earth, which in the beginning was nothing but a huge forest, takes on another form; the woods are cleared and give place to fields, to pastures, to hamlets, to small towns, and eventually to cities. People learn how to catch certain animals, to tame others, and to train them for service. At first savage beasts had to be fought: the early heroes distinguished themselves in these struggles; they caused arms to be invented, which men later turned against their fellows: Nimrod, the first warrior and conqueror, is described in the Holy Scriptures as a mighty hunter. With animals, moreover, men were able to improve the cultivation of [*adoucir*] fruits and plants; they bent the very metals to their purposes, and little by little they made all nature serve them.[60]

This is all very vague, no doubt, when compared with the mature four stages theory. As we have already noted, the idea of a sequence of socio-economic stages based on different modes of subsistence could hardly have been put forward clearly by one who, like Bossuet (or Pufendorf), took it as a literal historical truth that 'Abel was a shepherd and Cain a tiller of the soil'.[61] But once this difficulty had been overcome, Bossuet's emphasis on (for example) the pastoral way of life of the Patriarchs,[62] and his 'materialist' explanation of

[59] *Ibid.*, p. 951.
[60] *Ibid.*, p. 672.
[61] Genesis, iv. 2. Cf. Bossuet, *op. cit.*, p. 670: 'The first arts which men learned in the beginning, evidently from their Creator, were agriculture, the pastoral art, that of clothing themselves, and perhaps that of housing themselves.' A number of specific references to Genesis are given by Bossuet to support these statements.
[62] *Op. cit.*, pp. 673–4 and 781.

the origin of astronomy and geometry in ancient Egypt,[63] may well have taken on a new significance.

The third 'stream of thought' was constituted by the so-called 'battle of the ancients and the moderns'. The way in which the contributions of the supporters of the 'moderns' in this controversy challenged the idea of degeneration and thereby prepared the ground to some extent for the emergence of the eighteenth-century concept of progress has been familiar ever since Comte drew attention to it. The only point which really requires emphasis here is that the battle was waged on a fairly narrow front: the main question at issue, at any rate ostensibly, was simply whether contemporary literature, philosophy, and arts and sciences were or were not 'better' in some meaningful sense than those of classical times. All that the participants were really obliged to do, therefore, was to make a comparison of a better-or-worse type between a range of products of the European mind in two discrete historical periods. If some of the supporters of the 'moderns' in fact put forward what amounted to a theory of the natural progress of knowledge in order to support their case, this was essentially a bonus – one which no doubt indicated that more was actually at stake than met the eye, but a bonus none the less; and it was not to be expected that much in the way of a theory of the progress of *society* would emerge as a by-product.

Certainly, at any rate, the battle produced very little in the way of direct anticipations of the four stages theory. One of the participants, Sir William Temple, did indeed approach the theory, albeit rather vaguely, in the following passage:

In the first and most simple Ages of each Country, the Conditions and Lives of Men seem to have been very near of Kin with the rest of the Creatures; they lived by the Hour, or by the Day, and satisfied their Appetite with what they could get from the Herbs, the Fruits, the Springs they met with when they were hungry or dry; then, with what Fish, Fowl, or Beasts they could kill, by Swiftness or Strength, by Craft or Contrivance, by their Hands, or such Instruments as Wit helped or Necessity forced them to invent. When a Man had got enough for the Day, he laid

[63] *Ibid.*, pp. 960–1.

26

up the rest for the Morrow, and spent one Day in Labour, that he might pass the other at Ease; and lured on by the Pleasure of this Bait, when he was in Vigour, and his Game fortunate, he would provide for as many Days as he could, both for himself and his Children, that were too young to seek out for themselves. Then he cast about, how by sowing of Grain, and by Pasture of the tamer Cattle, to provide for the whole Year. After this, dividing the Lands necessary for these Uses, first among Children, and then among Servants, he reserved to himself a Proportion of their Gain, either in the Native Stock, or something equivalent, which brought in the Use of Money . . .[64]

This is certainly interesting, but in assessing its significance it should be remembered that Temple was an adversary, and not a supporter, of the 'moderns'; and that the statement just quoted was in fact made, not in either of his two essays on the 'ancients and moderns' issue, or even in his essay on *The Original and Nature of Government*, but in the opening section of an influential essay on (of all things) gardening.

Of more interest, although perhaps of less direct relevance, is Fontenelle's rather neglected essay on *The Origin of Fables*. In the first ages of the world, Fontenelle argues, men must have been plunged in the same depths of ignorance and barbarism as 'the Kaffirs, the Lapps, or the Iroquois today'.[65] The early fables, and the divinities who populate them, are essentially a product of this state of barbarism – and not, Fontenelle adds in a significant aside, of the particular climate concerned.[66] Now there is an 'astonishing conformity', Fontenelle says, 'between the fables of the Americans and those of the Greeks';[67] and in the course of his discussion of this point the following interesting passage occurs:

According to the traditions of Peru, the Inca Manco Guyna Capac, Son of the Sun, found the means, through his eloquence, to draw out of the depths of the forests the inhabitants of the country who lived there like beasts, and enabled them to live under

---

[64] *The Works of Sir William Temple* (2nd edn, London, 1731), Vol. I, pp. 170–1.
[65] *Oeuvres de Monsieur de Fontenelle* (Paris, 1752), Vol. III, p. 271. It should be remembered, Fontenelle adds, that since these peoples are already old, 'they must have achieved some degree of knowledge and civilisation which the first men did not possess'. Cf. *ibid.*, p. 277.
[66] *Ibid.*, pp. 287–8.   [67] *Ibid.*, p. 288.

rational laws. Orpheus did the same thing for the Greeks, and he also was the Son of the Sun. This shows that the Greeks were for a time savages as well as the Americans, and that they were drawn out of barbarism by the same means; and that the imaginations of these two peoples, so distant from one another, were in agreement in believing that those who had extraordinary talents were Sons of the Sun. Since the Greeks, with all their intellect, when they were a new people did not think any more rationally than the barbarians of America, who were according to all appearances a fairly new people when they were discovered by the Spanish, there is cause to believe that the Americans would in the end have come to think as rationally as the Greeks, if they had been allowed the time to do so.[68]

The significance of this passage, as we shall see more clearly later, lies in the fact that Fontenelle adduced cultural similarities between the early Greeks and the American Indians, *not* as evidence that the latter were genetically descended from the former, but as evidence that both peoples had the same barbarous and ignorant way of life – out of which, he added, they were eventually drawn 'by the same means' to a higher stage. This is all very imprecise, of course, but one can surely say at any rate that the rudiments of a stadial theory of socio-economic development could be found here by anyone who happened to be looking for it.

Turning now to the eighteenth century, the remarkable thing which one notices about the period prior to the appearance of Montesquieu's *The Spirit of Laws* is the absence of any substantial elaboration of the rudimentary notions concerning socio-economic development which the seventeenth century had thrown up. With hindsight, of course, one can see clearly enough that all roads were in fact leading in the direction of the new social science which was to emerge in the 1750s: they were simply taking a more circuitous route – via, for example, biblical criticism and discussions of the nature of man and the moral sense. But there was very little which pointed directly towards the view that the mode of subsistence was the key factor in socio-economic development, and still less which pointed towards the account of

[68] *Ibid.*, pp. 288–9.

he actual stages of development which we associate with
he mature four stages theory. Nowhere do we find any real
anticipations of the theory, even in those places where we
might very reasonably have expected to find them.

Take, for example, three prominent thinkers of the first half
of the century with whose work most of the pioneers of the
1750s were thoroughly familiar – Mandeville, Hutcheson, and
Cantillon. Mandeville had a great deal to say about the
origin and growth of society from its savage beginnings, and
indeed spoke of three 'Steps to Society' which were successively taken by men in the early ages.[69] But these 'steps'
were far removed from those which were later to be delineated by Smith and Turgot: they were, in fact, the association of men to protect themselves from wild animals, their
association to protect themselves from one another, and the
invention of letters. It is true that Mandeville occasionally
discusses the role of certain 'economic' factors in social
development – for example, the division of labour,[70] the
introduction of money,[71] and the invention of implements[72]
– but nowhere are these threads drawn together in anything
like a coherent way. Hutcheson, too, is disappointing, even
when he is writing, more or less in the Grotius–Pufendorf–
Locke tradition, about the origin of property. All we find are
a few vague hints, thrown out in the course of his discussion
of man's rights over animals,[73] and in his account of the
original means of acquiring property – 'viz. occupation, and
labour employed in cultivating'.[74] And Cantillon adds surprisingly little, in spite of his interest in the socio-historical
roots of modern institutions. We do find, it is true, a distinction between 'wandering Societies like Hordes of Tartars and
Camps of Indians' and 'more settled societies';[75] we hear
about 'the country of the Iroquois where the inhabitants do

69 Bernard Mandeville, *The Fable of the Bees* (ed. F. B. Kaye, Oxford,
   1924), Vol. II, pp. 261, 266, and 269.
70 *Ibid.*, pp. 141–3.   71 *Ibid.*, pp. 348–50.   72 *Ibid.*, pp. 319–20.
73 Francis Hutcheson, *Collected Works* (facsimile edn, Georg Olms, Hildesheim, 1969), Vol. IV, pp. 147–8.
74 *Ibid.*, Vol. V, p. 324. Cf. Vol. IV, pp. 163–4. Cf. also Hutcheson's statement (Vol. V, p. 283) that the 'state of natural liberty' still 'subsists in
   some ruder parts of the world'.
75 Richard Cantillon, *Essai sur la Nature du Commerce en Général* (ed.
   Henry Higgs, London, 1931), pp. 3–5.

not plough the Land and live entirely by Hunting';[76] and
there is one interesting passage, which is worth quoting in
full, concerning the relation between population and the
mode of subsistence in America:

> On the other hand there is no Country where the increase of
> Population is more limited than among the Savages in the interior
> parts of America. They neglect Agriculture, live in Woods, and on
> the Wild Beasts they find there. As their Forests destroy the
> Sweetness and Substance of the Earth there is little pasture for
> Animals, and since an Indian eats several Animals in a year, 50
> or 100 acres supply only enough food for a single Indian.
>
> A small Tribe of these Indians will have 40 square leagues for
> its hunting ground. They wage regular and bitter wars over these
> boundaries, and always proportion their numbers to their means
> of support from the chase.[77]

But that is virtually all we can get from Cantillon; and we
look in vain for anything more in the work of men like Petty,
Beccaria, and Bolingbroke.

Even in Hume, whose clarion calls for the building of a
new 'science of man' on a secular and sociological basis were
so tremendously influential, we find much less than we might
have expected. Although one perceptive scholar has contrived
to piece together a three stages theory from Hume's scattered
statements on early civilisation,[78] I do not myself think that
they really warrant this. There are in fact very few statements
of any real relevance, most of these being concentrated in
his essay *Of Commerce*;[79] and in other places in his work
where we might have looked for some recognition of the
importance of the mode of subsistence – the essays *Of
National Characters* and *Of the Rise and Progress of the Arts*

[76] *Ibid.*, p. 39.
[77] *Ibid.*, p. 69.
[78] John B. Stewart, *The Moral and Political Philosophy of David Hume*
(Columbia University Press, New York and London, 1963), pp. 161ff.
[79] See, for example, *Essays Moral, Political, and Literary by David Hume*
(ed. T. H. Green and T. H. Grose, London, 1889), Vol. i, p. 289. There
are a few references in Hume's *History of England* (on pp. 19, 33, and
219 of Vol. i of the 1825 edn of the work) to the mode of subsistence of
certain early tribes, but these are no more than echoes of the writings of
the classical historians upon whom Hume is relying, and no special attention is paid to them.

nd Sciences, for example – the absence of any such indica-
ion seems almost studied.[80] And even – most surprisingly of
ll – in the great masterpiece of Vico[81] there is little of rele-
ance to be found. In spite of his immense concern with
ecurring socio-cultural changes, his frequent use of the
:ustoms of contemporary savage peoples to throw light on
hose of ancient peoples,[82] his interesting 'agricultural' interpretation of ancient symbolism,[83] and his extremely striking
espousal of the law of unintended consequences,[84] we find
only a few vague and scattered hints of the idea we are look-
ng for.[85] In Book IV of *The New Science*, entitled 'The Course
he Nations Run', Vico argues that nations develop through
hree kinds of natures (divine, heroic, and human), from
which arise three kinds of customs, three kinds of natural
aws, three kinds of civil states, three kinds of languages,
:tc., etc.[86] – three kinds of almost everything, in fact, *except*
nodes of subsistence.

Montesquieu's *The Spirit of Laws* (1748), however, is a
norse of a different colour – even if not quite so different as
s sometimes pretended. The aim of Montesquieu's work, at
any rate as he himself expressed it at the end of Book I, was
o investigate the relation between the 'political and civil
aws' of a country on the one hand and the particular 'order
of things' in that country on the other. The laws, he wrote,

---

[80] Attention should be drawn, however, to the first two paragraphs of
Section VIII, Part II, Book III of Hume's *Treatise of Human Nature*, in
which it seems to be assumed that the way of life of 'the American
tribes', who apparently live by 'hunting and fishing', can be taken as
typical of 'the infancy of society'.

[81] *The New Science of Giambattista Vico* (ed. T. G. Bergin and M. H.
Fisch, Cornell University Press, Ithaca, New York, 1968).

[82] See, for example, *ibid.*, p. 158: 'Tacitus in his account of the customs of
the ancient Germans relates that they preserved in verse the beginnings
of their history, and Lipsius in his notes on this passage says the same of
the American Indians. The examples of these two nations, of which the
first was known only to the Romans, and to them very late, and the
second discovered but two centuries ago by our Europeans, give us a
strong argument for conjecturing the same of all other barbarous nations,
both ancient and modern . . .' *The New Science* contains a large number
of specific references to the customs and observances of the Americans.

[83] See, for example, *ibid.*, pp. 188ff. and 279–80.

[84] *Ibid.*, p. 425.

[85] See in particular *ibid.*, pp. 89, 171, 181, 188, 279, 401, and 420.

[86] *Ibid.*, pp. 335ff.

should be adapted in such a manner to the people for whom the
are framed that it should be a great chance if those of one natio
suit another.

They should be in relation to the nature and principle of eac
government: whether they form it, as may be said of politic laws
or whether they support it, as in the case of civil institutions.

They should be in relation to the climate of each country, t
the quality of its soil, to its situation and extent, to the principa
occupation of the natives, whether husbandmen, huntsmen, o
shepherds: they should have relation to the degree of libert
which the constitution will bear; to the religion of the inhabitants
to their inclinations, riches, numbers, commerce, manners, an
customs. In fine, they have relations to each other, as also to the
origin, to the intent of the legislator, and to the order of thing
on which they are established; in all of which different light
they ought to be considered.

This is what I have undertaken to perform in the following
work. These relations I shall examine, since all these togethe
constitute what I call the Spirit of Laws.[87]

The sections of the work which are most directly relevant t
the development of the four stages theory are those in Boo
xviii where Montesquieu deals with the relation between th
laws and what he calls in the passage just quoted 'the prin
cipal occupation of the natives, whether husbandmen, hunts
men, or shepherds'.

Let us note in passing, however, that Montesquieu's genera
methodology was probably just as influential as his treatmen
of this specific problem. Men like Smith and Turgot were t
see *The Spirit of Laws* as providing a kind of green light, a
ex cathedra 'go ahead', for the new social science. Montes
quieu, they believed (as Dugald Stewart was later to put it
had 'attempted to account, from the changes in the condition
of mankind, which take place in the different stages of thei
progress, for the corresponding alterations which their insti
tutions undergo'.[88] Whether Montesquieu himself would hav
agreed with this interpretation of his book is perhaps rathe
doubtful: the important point, however, is that this is wha
the pioneers of the four stages theory saw fit to read into it

[87] Montesquieu, *The Spirit of the Laws* (Hafner Library of Classics edr
tr. Thomas Nugent, Hafner, New York, 1949), Vol. i, pp. 6–7.
[88] Dugald Stewart, *Account of the Life and Writings of Adam Smith, LL.D
Kelley reprint, 1966), p. 35.

Book xviii is actually entitled 'Of Laws in the Relation they bear to the Nature of the Soil', but Montesquieu's discussion of this topic soon merges into an account of the relation of the laws to the mode of subsistence. The laws, he writes,

have a very great relation to the manner in which the several nations procure their subsistence. There should be a code of laws of a much larger extent for a nation attached to trade and navigation than for people who are content with cultivating the earth. There should be a much greater for the latter than for those who subsist by their flocks and herds. There must be a still greater for these than for such as live by hunting.[89]

He then goes on to discuss the relation of population to the mode of subsistence, in the following terms:

Let us see in what proportion countries are peopled where the inhabitants do not cultivate the earth. As the produce of uncultivated land is to that of land improved by culture, so the number of savages in one country is to that of husbandmen in another: and when the people who cultivate the land cultivate also the arts, this is also in such proportions as would require a minute detail.

They [i.e. the peoples who do not cultivate the land] can scarcely form a great nation. If they are herdsmen and shepherds, they have need of an extensive country to furnish subsistence for a small number; if they live by hunting, their number must be still less, and in order to find the means of life they must constitute a very small nation.[90]

He then makes a distinction between 'savage' and 'barbarous' nations, the first generally being hunters and the second 'herdsmen and shepherds'; and on this basis he accounts for the fact that savages are 'dispersed clans' and barbarians commonly 'small nations'.[91] There follows a remarkable, if rather fragmentary, account of the ways in which the law of nations, the civil laws, and the political state of savage and barbarous nations differ from those of nations which cultivate the land and 'know the use of money',[92] and an equally interesting explanation of the way in which the Salic law

[89] Montesquieu, *op. cit.*, Vol. i, p. 275.
[90] *Ibid.*, Vol. i, p. 275. Cf. Letter cxx of the *Lettres Persanes*.
[91] *Ibid.*, Vol. i, p. 276.
[92] *Ibid.*, Vol. i, pp. 276–81.

relates to 'the institutions of a people who do not cultivate the earth, or at least who cultivate it but very little'.[93] The American Indians, the Arabs, and the Tartars are adduced as illustrations of the various propositions put forward, and in relation to the Germans considerable reliance is placed on the accounts of their mode of subsistence given by Caesar and Tacitus. Montesquieu's sustained use, in these particular sections of his book, of the notion that differences in manners and social institutions are related to differences in the mode of subsistence has no parallel in any of the earlier literature we have been considering, and there would seem to be little doubt that this part of *The Spirit of Laws* was of considerable importance in the subsequent development of the four stages theory.

But there was still some distance to go. As his own statement about the aim of his work which I have quoted above clearly indicates, Montesquieu was concerned to investigate the relation between the 'laws' and a whole number of different aspects of the condition of society – of which the mode of subsistence was only one, and in his opinion by no means the most important one. Nor is Montesquieu's view of the *nature* of the relation between the 'laws' and these different aspects of the condition of society free from ambiguity. Sometimes he seems to be saying that a society possessing certain characteristics will as it were autonomously generate 'laws' of a certain type, whereas at other times he seems to be saying merely that these are the 'laws' which that kind of society ought properly to have bestowed upon it by the law-giver. And in whichever of these two ways we interpret him, there is certainly no indication in *The Spirit of Laws* that Montesquieu regarded the mode of subsistence as being in any sense the *key* factor in the total situation. There is indeed a great deal about the mode of subsistence in Book xviii; but there is very little about the mode of subsistence – and a great deal about climate, government, etc. – in the other thirty books.[94] Moreover, while Montesquieu certainly distinguished more precisely than any of his predecessors between societies based on hunting, pasturage,

[93] *Ibid.*, Vol. I, pp. 281ff.
[94] See, however, *ibid.*, Vol. II, pp. 172 and 175–7.

griculture, and commerce, there is no clear indication in *'he Spirit of Laws* that he visualised these different modes of ubsistence as marking *successive stages of development* hrough which societies normally progressed over time.

t first sight, the anticipations of the four stages theory which ve have culled from the literature of the period before 1750 1ay seem to be quite extensive, and to contain (even if only 1 embryo) most of the basic elements of which the mature heory was to be composed. When we recall the vast field rom which they have been gathered, however – the work f a very large number of writers stretching over a period f more than 2000 years and embodying dozens of different pproaches to the problem of the development of society – it 5 surely the extreme meagreness of the harvest which is so triking. Taking them as a whole, the anticipations are indeed o scarce and scattered, and in most cases so vague, that men ike Smith and Turgot could hardly have discovered them (in o far as they did in fact do so) if they had not known what hey were looking for. Or, to put the point in another way, if hey were struck by these particular passages in the earlier iterature they must have had a *predisposition* to be struck y them – a predisposition whose origin must up to a point e sought for outside the literature itself. Why did Millar eize so eagerly upon the classical historians' references to he mode of subsistence of primitive peoples, whereas Vico ad virtually ignored them? Why did Smith pay so much ttention to the references to the mode of subsistence in the vorks of Grotius, Pufendorf, and Locke, whereas Hutcheson ad scarcely noticed them? Why was the nature of Turgot's eaction to Bossuet so different from that of Voltaire's? And f all the pioneers of the 1750s were influenced by Montes- uieu, as the timing of the relevant events would certainly eem to suggest, why did they react so favourably to the solated passages in Book XVIII where he dealt with the mode f subsistence, and so critically to the very much larger umber of passages in the remainder of the work where he lealt with climate?

There is never any single or simple solution to problems of his kind. The sudden emergence of the four stages theory in

France and Scotland in the 1750s, and its widespread accep
tance and popularisation in the following decades, can hardl
have been an accident: the time must in some sense and fo
some reason have been ripe for these events, and the wa
must have been prepared for them by certain earlier event
But to analyse the complex interaction between past and pre
sent, between preconditions and causes, and between socio
logical and psychological determinants which brought abou
the rise of the four stages theory to the surface at this time is
task not lightly to be undertaken – and certainly not one fo
which the writer of this book is equipped. His aim, as alread
explained, is a much more modest one: to tell the story c
the emergence and development of the theory, and to dra
special attention to the influence exercised upon it by th
contemporary literature about the American Indians. Hi
hope, however, is that this mode of approach may prov
capable of throwing at least a little light upon the grea
question of 'causes' which has just been broached.

2

'In the beginning all the World was *America*'

One of the most interesting features of the seventeenth- and eighteenth-century 'anticipations' of the four stages theory which we have just surveyed is that the authors of the majority of them evidently felt that a study of the way of life of the American Indians could help to illuminate certain aspects of the problem of the development of man and society. In particular, a number of them believed, such a study might be able to throw light on the condition of mankind in the 'first' or 'earliest' period of its development. This view was crystallised in the remarkable statement by Locke which forms the title of the present chapter. In the pages which follow, we examine the genesis of this view in more detail, and from a rather different angle.

The information about the American Indians (hereafter, in most places, 'the Americans') which was available to the mid-eighteenth-century social scientists was embodied in an extremely bulky and heterogeneous collection of writings, few if any of which had been composed primarily with the aim of advancing anthropological research.[1] Almost all the writers of these works had had axes to grind. They had been concerned, to a greater or lesser extent, either to defend or to attack the colonial conquests in America, orthodox Christianity, and/or contemporary European society; and the observations they had made concerning the Americans' way

---

[1] For useful surveys of these writings, see Don Cameron Allen, *The Legend of Noah* (University of Illinois Press, Urbana, 1949), pp. 119–37; Kenneth E. Bock, *The Acceptance of Histories* (University of California Press, Berkeley and Los Angeles, 1956), pp. 68–75; Lee Eldridge Huddleston, *Origins of the American Indians* (University of Texas Press, Austin and London, 1967), *passim*; J. S. Slotkin (ed.), *Readings in Early Anthropology* (Methuen, London, 1965), *passim*; Margaret T. Hodgen, *Early Anthropology in the Sixteenth and Seventeenth Centuries* (University of Pennsylvania Press, Philadelphia, 1964), *passim*; and (for the early voyage literature as a whole) Michèle Duchet, *Anthropologie et Histoire au Siècle des Lumières* (François Maspero, Paris, 1971), *passim*.

of life had often been quite heavily influenced by the particular side on which they happened to find themselves in relation to contemporary issues such as these. Their work nevertheless contained a large amount of basic factual information about the Americans, and also a great deal of what might be called today comparative anthropological material, which could often – even if only with some difficulty – be detached from the ideological framework within which the author concerned had chosen to set it.

This literature was bound increasingly to open up new intellectual horizons – and to do so, I think, to a much greater extent than most of the literature about other relatively primitive peoples which was also available at this time. The point here is that the way of life of the Americans seemed to contemporaries to be much more remote from that of Europe than that of almost any other extant primitive people, and this very remoteness, in itself, was bound to offer a challenge to many of the prevailing ideas about religion, government, and social organisation.[2] It is rather difficult to think of a possible modern parallel. If a race of little green men were to be discovered tomorrow on Mars, this would hardly cause much of a flutter in our intellectual dovecotes. After all, we have long been accustomed to the idea that there may possibly be little green men living on Mars, and that they may have ways of life extremely different from our own. Moreover, the problem of reconciling the existence of the little green men with our sacred texts would not be a particularly difficult one. Intellectually speaking, we have as it were already discounted for the future discovery of such beings. But this was precisely what the Middle Ages had not done.

[2] Cf. J. H. Elliott, *The Old World and the New, 1492–1650* (Cambridge University Press, Cambridge, 1970), pp. 6–7: 'Its discovery [that of America] had important *intellectual* consequences, in that it brought Europeans into contact with new lands and peoples, and in so doing challenged a number of traditional European assumptions about geography, theology, history and the nature of man. America also constituted an *economic* challenge for Europe, in that it proved to be at once a source of supply for produce and for objects for which there existed a European demand, and a promising field for the extension of European business enterprise. Finally, the acquisition by European states of lands and resources in America was bound to have important *political* repercussions, in that it affected their mutual relations by bringing about changes in the balance of power.'

Suddenly, a new race of men was discovered, in a country whose very existence had not hitherto been suspected and which was apparently separated by a vast ocean from the continent where according to the sacred texts all men had originated. Not only did these newly-found men live in a region which had hitherto been widely assumed to be un-inhabitable (at least in part), but many of them also appeared to be managing to get along quite well – even if only at a very low material level – without religion, laws, government, or private property, or at any rate without any familiar and easily identifiable forms of these institutions. It is no wonder that it should have taken contemporary patterns of thought in Europe so long to absorb and adjust to this startling new phenomenon.

It was inevitable that the men of the Renaissance should not only observe and describe this phenomenon, but also that they should make some kind of moral judgement concerning it. And it was inevitable, too, that the main basis for this moral judgement should be a comparison of one sort or another between American society and contemporary European society. The judgements which were actually made fell as it were at some point between two extreme poles, approaching nearer to the one pole or the other in accordance with the particular interests and prepossessions of the writer concerned. On the one hand, those writers who were dis-satisfied with certain aspects of European society – its over-refinement, for example, its hypocrisy, or its system of ranks – could emphasise the simplicity, honesty, and equality of American society, holding the latter up (to a greater or lesser extent) as an ideal to be aimed at by Europe. On the other hand, those who admired contemporary European society – its diversity, the high level of its intellectual attainments, or its high material standard of living – could emphasise the dullness and uniformity of American life, the stupidity and cruelty of the savages, and their extremely low standard of living.

What we must now try to trace out is the way in which contemporary discussions of these and other issues relating to the Americans gradually led towards the seminal idea that 'in the beginning all the World was *America*'. One of the main points we have to remember here, I suggest, is that the mere discovery of the coexistence of an uncivilised American society alongside a civilised European society was not in itself sufficient to generate the view that societies of the European type had normally *started out as and developed from* societies of the American type. Indeed, the resistances to the emergence of such a view must have been quite considerable in the early sixteenth century, when Europeans were still relatively unaware of their own past history, and when the concept of development (let alone that of progress) had not yet been clearly formulated. It certainly could not have been much easier for men of the sixteenth century to accept the view that they were descended from tribes of naked savages than it was for men of the nineteenth century to accept the notion that they were descended from creatures resembling apes. And the authority of Genesis, at any rate as that book was traditionally interpreted by the Church, was of course fairly decisive against any such view.

Even when Europe began to acquire, or regain, a sense of its own history, certain resistances to the adoption of this view must still have remained. I agree, a sceptical seventeenth-century observer might argue, that contemporary European society may well have evolved over time from certain lower forms, about which at the moment we know very little. I also agree that the Americans appear for some reason or other to have got stuck in a very low form indeed. But these two facts (if such they be) are in all probability separate and unrelated: at any rate they do not *in themselves* enable us to draw the conclusion that 'in the beginning all the World was *America*'. To arrive at the latter conclusion, the sceptic might continue, we would need in addition concrete evidence to the effect that 'in the beginning' (whenever that was) the ancestors of present-day Europeans lived in much the same manner as the American savages do today. And where can such evidence be found? Certainly not in Genesis, at any rate: all the early societies of men described in that book seem to have been appreciably more advanced than present-day American society. Would it not be just as plausible, then, to argue that the Americans have in fact degenerated from some earlier and higher state – or even

40

perhaps to assume (as Bossuet did in 1681) that God has put
savages on earth in order to make plain to us the profound
corruption of our nature and the depth of the abyss from
which Christ has rescued us?[3]

Before the hypothesis that 'in the beginning all the World
was *America*' could hope to secure any substantial measure
of acceptance, then, what was clearly required, in addition
to the two facts just mentioned, was some kind of empirical
or 'historical' demonstration that the basic characteristics of
contemporary American society were essentially similar to
those of the very early types of society from which contemporary Europe had evolved. And it was precisely this
kind of 'historical' demonstration that literature about the
Americans was itself eventually to lead to, and indeed up to
a point itself to embody.

In this connection, it was the discussions about the historical origins of the Americans which were of particular
importance and relevance. European observers, almost from
the moment of the discovery of the New World, had begun
pondering over this problem. From which European or Asian
people or peoples were the Americans descended, and when
and how did they come over from the Eurasian to the American continent? These were rather delicate questions, because
to answer them inevitably involved one in putting something
of a gloss on the Scriptures; and then as now they were
questions which for some curious psychological reason
seemed to attract large numbers of cranks and zealots.
The important point, however, was that in order to give
a plausible answer to them one had to make some kind
of *comparison* between the Americans and the particular
European or Asian nation or people from which one was
claiming that the Americans were descended. One had to
demonstrate that the Americans looked like these people, or
spoke like them, or had similar institutions, ideas, and ways
of life, before one could even begin to claim that the Americans were descended from them. It was quite largely as a
result of 'historical' comparisons of this kind between the
Americans and various ancient peoples that the idea that 'in

[3] *Oeuvres de Bossuet* (ed. B. Velat and Y. Champailler, Bibliothèque de la
Pléiade, Tours, 1961), pp. 944–5.

41

the beginning all the World was *America*' eventually
emerged.

To document the emergence of this idea is by no means an
easy task. The relevant literature, taken as a whole, is so
voluminous, so complex, so overlaid with those ideological
considerations of which mention has already been made, and
so incapable of useful classification by period, theme, or
country of origin, as to be virtually unmanageable. What I
propose to do, therefore, is to try to cut through this difficulty by concentrating on the contributions of three authors
from three different countries – Acosta, Ogilby, and Lafitau
– whose works between them span a period of almost a century and a half. I have chosen Acosta partly because his book
was extremely influential, and partly because its strengths
and weaknesses were rather typical of those of the more in-
telligent of the early contributions to the debate. I have
chosen Ogilby not so much because of his own personal contribution, which was not particularly striking, but rather
because he provided an admirable summary of the state of
the debate at the time he wrote, including an account of
some of the main seventeenth-century highlights. And finally
I have chosen Lafitau because his book seems to me to have
played such a special role in the development of the four
stages theory that it requires separate consideration.

Father Joseph de Acosta's *Natural and Moral History of the
Indies* was first published in 1589, with an English translation by Edward Grimston following fifteen years later.[4] The
coverage of the book was very wide indeed, treating as it did
(to quote the sub-title) of 'the remarkeable things of Heaven,
of the Elements, Mettalls, Plants and Beasts which are
proper to that Country: Together with the Manners, Ceremonies, Lawes, Governements, and Warres of the Indians'.
Books i–iv, comprising the 'natural history', deal with matters concerning cosmography and terrestrial geography (Book
i); the climatic conditions in the 'burning zone' (Book ii);

---

[4] The edition I have used is the Hakluyt Society reprint from the English
translated edition of Edward Grimston, 1604, with notes and an introduction by Clements R. Markham (London, 1880). The Hakluyt text has
been checked independently against that of the 1604 edition, and a
number of corrections made.

other geographical and climatic features (Book III); and metals, plants, and animals (Book IV). Books V–VII, comprising the 'moral history', deal with the 'religion, or superstition' of the Americans (Book V); their 'customs, policy and government' (Book VI); and 'the beginning, proceedings and notable deedes of the Mexicaines' (Book VII).[5]

It will be gathered from this summary of its contents that the book was not intended primarily as a contribution to the origins debate, about which Acosta in fact says relatively little. He has no specific theory of his own to expound concerning the genetic origin of the Americans, and he does not often go very far out of his way to attack the theories of others. He does, however, make a number of perceptive statements about the problem of *how* men first came to America, and the few direct comments which he does allow himself to make on the origins question proper are quite interesting from a methodological viewpoint. In addition, he has something of significance to say about the probable mode of subsistence of the early inhabitants of the country; and the comparisons he makes between the religious beliefs and practices of the Americans and those of various ancient peoples are also of much more than passing interest.

It is about half-way through Book I, shortly after having disposed of the then commonly held belief that Peru was Ophir, that Acosta first broaches the problem of the means by which the first men came to America:

Seeing on the one side wee know for certaine, that many yeeres agoe there were men inhabiting in these parts, so likewise we cannot deny but the scripture doth teach vs cleerely, that all men are come from the first man: without doubt we shall be forced to beleeve and confesse, that men have passed hither from *Europe*, *Asia or Affricke*, yet must wee discover by what meanes they could passe.[6]

If they passed by sea, Acosta argues, it seems very unlikely that they came 'of purpose, by a determined voiage',[7] since the ancients had no lodestone or compass. And if, as would seem much more likely, they in fact came 'by chance, or by

[5] Quotations from *ibid.*, title page; tables of contents; and Vol. II, pp. 295, 390, and 449.
[6] *Ibid.*, Vol. I, p. 45. [7] *Ibid.*, Vol. I, p. 47.

force of weather',[8] this leaves unsolved the vexing problem of how the animals could have got there. On the authority of the Scriptures, Acosta says, 'we must necessarily referre the multiplication of all beastes to those which came out of the Arke of *Noe*, on the mountaines of *Ararat*, where it staied'.[9] And who can imagine, he asks, 'that in so long a voyage, men would take the paynes to carrie Foxes to Peru . . .? Who woould likewise say, that the[y] have carried Tygers and Lyons? Truely it were a thing worthy the laughing at, to thinke so.'[10] If these beasts came by sea, it could only have been by swimming, which would have been possible only over short distances. 'I coniecture then', Acosta presciently concludes,

by the discourse I have made, that the new world, which we call *Indies*, is not altogether severed and disioyned from the other world: and to speake my opinion, I have long beleeved, that the one and the other world are ioyned and continued one with an other in some part, or at the least, are very neere. And yet to this day, there is no certain knowledge of the contrary. For towards the Articke or Northerne Pole, all the longitude of the earth is not discovered, and many hold, that above *Florida*, the Land runnes out very large towards the North, and as they say, ioynes with the *Scithike* or *Germaine* Sea . . . If this be true . . . the answere is easie to the doubt we have propounded, how the first Inhabitants could passe to the *Indies*: For that wee must beleeve they could not so conveniently come thither by Sea, as travelling by Land, which might be done without consideration, in changing by little and little their lands and habitations. Some peopling the lands they found, and others seeking for newe; in time they came to inhabit and people the *Indies*, with so many nations, people, and tongues as we see.[11]

Acosta then proceeds to review two alternative theories about the coming of the original inhabitants to America. First, there is the theory that they came via Atlantis – but Plato's famous account of this island, Acosta argues, 'cannot be held true, but among children and old folkes'.[12] Second, there is the theory that they came to America under the direct protection of God, in the manner described in the

[8] *Ibid.*, Vol. i, p. 54.   [9] *Ibid.*, Vol. i, p. 57.
[10] *Ibid.*, Vol. i, p. 59.   [11] *Ibid.*, Vol. i, pp. 60–1.
[12] *Ibid.*, Vol. i, p. 65.

Second Book of Esdras[13] – in other words, that they were the Ten Lost Tribes of Israel. This theory, says Acosta, is strengthened in some people's minds by certain apparent similarities between the Americans and the Jews:

[Some say] that there are great signes and arguments amongst the common sort of the *Indians*, to breed a beleefe, that they are descended from the *Iewes*: for commonly you shall see them fearefull, submisse, ceremonious and subtill in lying. And moreover they say, their habites are like vnto those the *Iewes* vsed; for they weare a short coat or waste-coat, and a cloake imbroidered all about; they goe bare-footed, or with soles tied with latchets over the foot, which they call *Oiotas*. And they say, that it appears by their Histories, as also by their ancient pictures, which represent them in this fashion, that this attire was the ancient habite of the Hebrewes . . .[14]

Acosta's critique of this particular argument from similarities is very interesting. The first point he makes, in effect, is that the argument glosses over the existence of certain patent *dis*similarities between the Jews and the Americans:

For wee know well, that the Hebrewes vsed letters, whereof there is no shew among the *Indians*; they were great lovers of silver, these make no care of it: the Iewes, if they were not circumcised, held not themselves for Iewes, and contrariwise the *Indians* are not at all, neyther did they ever vse any ceremonies neere it, as many in the East have done. But what reason of coniecture is

---

[13] The relevant passage will be found in the Second Book of Esdras in the *Apocrypha*, xiii. 39–47. In the translation in *The New English Bible: The Apocrypha* (Oxford University Press, Cambridge University Press, 1970) the passage appears on p. 63 and reads as follows: 'Then you saw him [i.e. the man in your vision] collecting a different company, a peaceful one. They are the ten tribes which were taken off into exile in the time of King Hoshea, whom Shalmaneser king of Assyria took prisoner. He deported them beyond the River, and they were taken away into a strange country. But then they resolved to leave the country populated by the Gentiles and go to a distant land never yet inhabited by man, and there at last to be obedient to their laws, which in their own country they had failed to keep. As they passed through the narrow passages of the Euphrates, the Most High performed miracles for them, stopping up the channels of the river until they had crossed over. Their journey through that region, which is called Arzareth, was long, and took a year and a half. They have lived there ever since, until this final age. Now they are on their way back, and once more the Most High will stop the channels of the river to let them cross.'

[14] Acosta, *op. cit.*, Vol. I, pp. 67–8.

there in this, seeing the Iewes are so carefull to preserve their language and Antiquities, so as in all parts of the world they differ and are known from others, and yet at the *Indies* alone, they have forgotten their Linage, their Law, their Ceremonies, their *Messias*; and finally, their whole *Iudaisme*.[15]

His second point is that some of the traits ascribed to 'the Indians' are by no means characteristic of all Indians, and that others are in fact shared by all primitive peoples:

And whereas they say, the *Indians* are fearefull cowards, super-stitious, and subtill in lying; for the first, it is not common to all, there are some nations among the *Barbarians* free from these vices, there are some valiant and hardy, there are some blunt and dull of vnderstanding. As for ceremonies and superstitions, the Heathen have alwayes vsed them much; the manner of habites described which they vse, being the plainest and most simple in the world; without Arte, the which hath been common, not onely to the Hebrewes, but to all other Nations.[16]

The basic assumption which lay behind the kind of argument which Acosta is here criticising was, of course, that *cultural similarities* between some ancient people and the Americans, if their existence could be demonstrated, were to be regarded as indications of the *genetic descent* of the latter from the former. This assumption had been more or less un-critically accepted by the majority of writers in the field up to Acosta's time, and it is important to note that Acosta himself did not question the assumption as such. All he did, in effect, was to add two provisos – viz., that the similarities in ques-tion should be truly characteristic and distinctive, and that they should not be counterbalanced by too many dissimilari-

---

[15] *Ibid.*, Vol. i, p. 68.

[16] *Ibid.*, Vol. i, p. 68. The chapter concludes as follows: 'Seeing that the very History of *Esdras* (if wee shall beleeve the Scriptures that bee *Apocrypha*) make more against them then for their purpose: for hee saith in that place, that the ten tribes went from the multitude of the Heathen, to keepe their faith and ceremonies, and we see the *Indians* given to all the Idolatries in the world. And those which holde this opinion, see well if the entries of the River *Euphrates* stretch to the *Indies*, and whether it be necessary for the *Indies* to repasse that way, as it is written. Besides, I know not how you can name them peaceable, seeing they be alwaies in warre amongst themselves. To conclude, I can-not see how that *Euphrates* in *Esdras Apocrypha*, should be a more con-venient passage to goe to the new world, then the inchanted & fabulous *Atlantike* Iland of *Plato*' (*ibid.*, Vol. i, pp. 68–9).

ties. Acosta would certainly not have denied that if a large enough number of real, important, and specific similarities between the Americans and some ancient people could in fact be demonstrated, it would be reasonable to infer genetic descent. He did feel, however, that it was very unlikely that the use of this method – or indeed of any other – would ever lead to a definitive solution of the origins problem. Since the Americans had no written records, he argued, 'nor any certaine remembrances of their founders', and since the ancients had made no mention whatever of the New World, 'hee should seeme rash and presumptuous, that should thinke to discover the first beginning of the *Indians*'.[17]

These considerations, however, did not inhibit Acosta from making a number of generalisations – perceptive enough for their time – about 'the Originall of the Indians', and in particular about the mode of subsistence and manner of life of the first inhabitants:

The true and principall cause to people the *Indies*, was, that the lands and limits thereof are ioyned and continued in some extremities of the world, or at the least, were very neere. And I beleeve, it is not many thousand yeeres past, since men first inhabited this new world and West *Indies*, and that the first men that entred, were rather savage men and hunters, then bredde vp in civill and well governed Common weales: and that they came to this new world, having lost their owne land, or being in too great numbers, they were forced of necessitie to seeke some other habitations; the which having found, they beganne by little and little to plant, having no other law, but some instinct of nature, and that very darke, and some customes remayning of their first Countries. And although they came from Countries well governed, yet it is not incredible to thinke, that they had forgotten all through the tract of time and want of vse; seeing that in *Spaine* and *Italie* we find companies of men, which have nothing but the shape and countenance onely, whereby we may coniecture in what sort this new world grew so barbarous and vncivill.[18]

It will be noticed that although Acosta appears to admit as a possibility that the Americans may have degenerated after their arrival in the new world, his main emphasis is on the probability, as he sees it, that they were originally 'savage

17 *Ibid.*, Vol. I, p. 69.   18 *Ibid.*, Vol. I, pp. 69–70.

men and hunters' who came from uncivilised countries.
'There are great and apparent coniectures', he says,

that these men for a long time, had neither Kings nor common
weales, but lived in troupes, as they do at this day in *Florida*, the
Chiriquanas, those of *Bresill*, and many other nations, which have
no certaine Kings, but as occasion is offered in peace or warre,
they choose their Captaines as they please.[19]

It was only gradually, according to Acosta, that some out-
standing individuals began 'to rule and domineere as *Nem-
broth* [i.e. Nimrod] did',[20] eventually erecting the kingdoms
of Peru and Mexico which the Spaniards found. Acosta
returns to the same theme towards the end of his book when
he is treating of the early history of Mexico. 'The antient and
first Inhabitants of those provinces, which wee call New
Spaine', he writes, 'were men very barbarous and savage,
which lived onely by hunting . . . They did neither sowe nor
till the ground, neither lived they together; for all their exercise was to hunt.'[21] And in this respect, Acosta says, they
were similar to the inhabitants of 'other Nations and Provinces of the *Indies*, who at the first were savage men . . . living
onely by hunting . . . without tilled landes, without cattell,
without King, Law, God, or Reason'.[22]

Although Acosta, as we have seen, was critical of some
contemporary attempts to ascribe a particular genetic origin
to the Americans on the basis of a selective list of cultural
similarities, he himself – for reasons quite unconnected with
the problem of origins – was concerned to draw a whole
number of parallels between the culture of the Americans
and that of a group of ancient societies. Most of these parallels relate to religious beliefs and practices.[23] 'If any one
wonder at some fashions & customes of the *Indies*', says
Acosta, '& will scorne them as fooles, or abhorre them as
divelish and inhumane people, let him remember that the
same things, yea, worse, have beene seene amongst the

[19] *Ibid.*, Vol. ɪ, p. 72. Cf. also *ibid.*, Vol. ɪɪ, p. 410.
[20] *Ibid.*, Vol. ɪ, p. 72.   [21] *Ibid.*, Vol. ɪɪ, pp. 449–50.
[22] *Ibid.*, Vol. ɪɪ, pp. 454–5.
[23] But not all: see, for example, the parallel drawn in *ibid.*, Vol. ɪ, p. 189,
between the bartering habits of the Indians and those reported of the
ancients.

Greekes and Romans, who have commanded the whole world'.[24] In Acosta's view, these similarities had an obvious and uncomplicated explanation: they were simply the result of 'the Pride and Presumption of the Divell'.[25] The Devil, he argues, has always striven to make men worship him, inventing various forms of idolatry and seeking to imitate and pervert the religious practices decreed by God.[26] In ancient times he had held the greater part of the world in subjection; but now, his sway having been ended in the more civilised nations as a result of the coming of Christianity, 'he hath retired himself into the most remote parts'.[27] Thus we find '[the] manner which the Divell hath vsed to deceive the Indians, to be the same wherewith hee hath deceived the Greekes and Romans, and other ancient Gentiles, giving them to vnderstand that these notable creatures, the Sunne, Moone, Starres, and Elements, had power and authoritie to doe good or harme to men'.[28] Nor does it come as any surprise that the Americans should have had a large number of ceremonies and customs which 'resembled to the ancient law of *Moses,* and some to those which the Moores vse, and some approached neere to the law of the Gospel'.[29] In the beginning, it appeared, all the world was indeed America – even if this was ascribed by Acosta to the machinations of the Devil rather than to the fact that the inhabitants of the ancient world, in the beginning, were all 'savage men and hunters' like the Americans.

John Ogilby's *America: Being the Latest, and Most Accurate Description of the New World* (London, 1671) begins with a long discussion of various aspects of the origins problem, in which a number of the main solutions which had by then been propounded are critically reviewed. The first question Ogilby asks is whether America was known to the ancients – a question he has little difficulty in answering in the negative. The second question he asks, however – that concerning 'the Original of the *Americans*' – is not so easily disposed of, since, as he puts it,

---

[24] *Ibid.,* Vol. II, p. 296.   [25] *Ibid.,* Vol. II, p. 298.
[26] *Ibid.,* Vol. II, pp. 299 and 324–5.
[27] *Ibid.,* Vol. II, p. 299.   [28] *Ibid.,* Vol. II, pp. 305–6.
[29] *Ibid.,* Vol. II, p. 369.

the Learned Dispute so much, that they find nothing more difficult in Story, than to clear that Point; for whether inquiry be
made after the time, when the *Americans* first settled themselves
where they now inhabit, or after what manner they came thither,
either by Shipping or by Land; on purpose, or accidentally;
driven by Storm, or else forc'd by a more powerful People, to
remove from their old Plantations, and seek for new? or if any
one should be yet more curious, asking the way that directed
them out of another Countrey to this New World? or else enquire
for those People, from whom the *Americans* deriv'd themselves?
He will find several Opinions, and the Learned still jangling.[30]

So far as the *time* of the first settlement is concerned, says
Ogilby, some commentators (such as Samuel Purchas) claim
that '*America* hath been but lately Planted', and urge in
favour of this view that the 'Countrey or Pastoral Life' of the
Americans,[31] their lack of knowledge of commerce, and their
mean clothing and housing, all indicate them to be new-
comers. Ogilby, arguing against this view, points out (*inter
alia*) that 'if the *Americans* live a Rude Life, go meanly
Habited, be without stately Houses; such Customs are even
among us observ'd by several People; as the *Tartars, Numidians*, and others, which made their Antiquity be call'd in
question'.[32] And the Americans' relatively advanced level of
knowledge of the 'Arts and Mechanick Sciences', Ogilby
adds, is inconsistent with their having been in the country
only a few hundred years.[33]

So far as the *manner* of the first settlement is concerned,
Ogilby broadly speaking follows Acosta's line; but when it
comes to the question of 'those People, from whom the
Americans deriv'd themselves', he is quite prepared to put
forward a specific theory of his own. He does this, however,
only after a lengthy and careful review of a number of alternative theories, in the course of which he shows a degree of
awareness of certain methodological pitfalls which is not
quite as untypical of the age as some modern commentators
have suggested.

First, there is the theory that the Americans were descen-

[30] Ogilby, *op. cit.*, pp. 11–12. [31] *Ibid.*, p. 12.
[32] *Ibid.*, p. 13. [33] *Ibid.*, p. 13.

ded from the Phoenicians. '*Robert Comtaeus*',[34] writes Ogilby, '. . . with many Learned and seemingly true Arguments affirms, That the Original of the *Americans* must be sought for either among the *Phenicians, Sydonians, Tyrians,* or *Carthaginians,* being indeed all one People.'[35] Ogilby agrees that 'the *Phenicians* have every where been Admirals of the Sea',[36] but argues that there is no real evidence that America was included among the new lands which they discovered in the course of their remarkable voyages. 'Yet we will search a little further', says Ogilby, 'to see whether the People Analogize, either in their Religion, Policy, Oeconomy, or Customs.'[37]

So far as the Americans' religion is concerned, Ogilby argues (up to a point following Acosta) that 'if it agreed with the *Phenicians*, it was the same that all the World profess'd at that time, and therefore may as well be extracted from any other, as them'.[38] And so far as their 'Policy, Oeconomy, or Customs' are concerned, Ogilby emphasises that the primitive mode of subsistence of the Americans is the same as that of a number of other ancient peoples besides the Phoenicians, and, indeed, that the Phoenicians themselves had advanced to a higher stage of development by the time they were alleged to have settled America:

It is certain, that the ancient *Phenicians* liv'd in Tents, and sometimes exchang'd eaten-up Pastures for fresh, which the *Americans* to this day observe; by which it might appear, that they are of a *Phenician* Extract. But why not as well deriv'd from *Numidia, Tartary*, or the ancient Patriarchs, who all liv'd such an unsettl'd wandering Life? Besides, the *Phenicians* had a long time given over Pastoral Business, for Maritime Affairs of greater consequence, not only Merchandizing through all the World, but sending great Colonies in Ships to new Plantations: And moreover, the *Americans* could not so strangely degenerate from their Ancestors, but would have built great Cities like them; of which many were found in *Phenicia*, but none of Antiquity in *America*.[39]

Finally, Ogilby criticises Comtaeus's attempt to argue from

[34] Robertus Comtaeus was the author of *De Origine Gentium Americanarum Dissertatio* (1644).
[35] Ogilby, *op. cit.*, p. 18.   [36] *Ibid.*, p. 18.
[37] *Ibid.*, p. 22.   [38] *Ibid.*, p. 23.   [39] *Ibid.*, pp. 22–3.

the alleged 'similitude and likeness of the *Phenician* and *American* Languages':

> It is certain, that the *Phenicians* and some of the *Americans* call a Cup *Asur*, and Red Wine, *Belasa*; But does it therefore follow by this, that the one is extracted from the other? How many Names do signifie all one, amongst People that never had any Conversation together? This proceeds only from meer accident; Or else if some Words of one, sound like the same Words us'd in a remote Countrey, and be of one signification, must they therefore be deriv'd from one another?[40]

Second, there is the theory that the Americans were descended from the Jews, or the Ten Lost Tribes of Israel. But once again, Ogilby argues, the similarities adduced in support of this theory are in fact far too slender to be of any evidential value whatever:

> They conclude, that *America* was also Peopled by [the Jews and Israelites], the rather, because the antient *Jews* and *Americans* were of one Complexion, and went a like Habited, both going without Shooes, onely wearing Sandals, and an upper Coat over a shorter Linnen Vest. Both are humble, quick of apprehension, and obliging, yet Valiant: But it is certain, they cannot be like the *Jews*, because the *Americans* change their Habit, according as they live in cold or hot Countreys, and go not in the least like one another.
>
> Father *Immanuel* relates, That he saw a *Brasilian*, not onely stoutly make his party good against three *Portugal* Soldiers, but had it not been by meer chance, worsted them.[41]

And the *dis*similarities, surely, should also be brought into the account. If it was the Jews who settled America, Ogilby argues (once again echoing Acosta), 'how is it possible, that in *America* they should at once have forgotten their Extract, Laws, Circumcision, Language, and other Ceremonies, when the rest of them observ'd nothing more strictly in all parts of the Earth?'[42]

Third, there is the theory, put forward by 'the Learned *Hugo Grotius*', that the northern Americans were descended from the Norwegians, 'because something of their Languages agrees, and the Way thither easie and nearest to be found'.[43]

[40] *Ibid.*, p. 25.   [41] *Ibid.*, p. 27.   [42] *Ibid.*, p. 29.   [43] *Ibid.*, p. 29.

'In the beginning all the World was America'

Grotius, says Ogilby (largely following Joannes de Laet),
'scrues up his Arguments from the likeness of the *American*
Speech and Customs with the *Norwegian*'.[44] So far as speech
is concerned, Ogilby supports de Laet's view that 'it no ways
follows that one People take original from the other, because
here and there are several words found, that have the same
signification and sound in divers Countreys; much less when
they must either add, change, or diminish several Letters'.[45]
On the question of customs, Grotius's argument is summed
up by Ogilby (not at all unfairly)[46] as follows:

The *Mexicans* relate, that their Predecessors onely follow'd Hunting; that they divided and reckon'd the Time, not by Days, but
by Nights, and wash'd their Children as soon as they were born
in cold Water.

They are so much inclin'd to Gaming, that they venture their
Liberty at it. Every one is satisfi'd with one Wife, except some of
the Nobility, which oftentimes have more. They throw up high
Banks in several places to damm out the Sea; believe the Immor-
tality of the Soul; every one eats at a peculiar Table; most of
them go naked, onely cover their *Pudenda* with a Cloth; some
Sacrifice and eat Mans-flesh: all which, according to *Tacitus*,
Pliny, *Lucan*, and other *Roman* Writers, was observ'd by the
antient *Germans*; from whom those that inhabit between the
Norwegian Mountains were extracted.[47]

But, says Ogilby, all these comparisons signify nothing. So far
as hunting is concerned,

How many People have formerly liv'd by it? The antient *Germans*,
and to this day the *Tartars* make it their whole business, excelling
in that Art all other Nations. Besides, that the more serious sort
of the *Mexicans* many Ages since scorn'd to derive themselves
from a Hunting Ancestry, but affirm that they found the *Chichi-
mecen* in those Countreys, who were great *Venators*.[48]

---

44 *Ibid.*, p. 31.   45 *Ibid.*, p. 32.
46 Grotius's essay *De Origine Gentium Americanarum* was originally published in Paris in 1642. An English translation by Edmund Goldsmid,
under the title *On the Origin of the Native Races of America: A Dissertation by Hugo Grotius*, appeared in Edinburgh in 1884. A comparison with the latter indicates that Ogilby's summary of Grotius's
arguments is not complete, but that at the same time it is not unfair.
Most of the arguments of Grotius which Ogilby omits are fairly general
(e.g. that the Americans and the Norwegians are both monogamous), and
certainly no more convincing than those which Ogilby does quote.
47 Ogilby, *op. cit.*, p. 32.   48 *Ibid.*, p. 33.

And on all the other counts, for one reason or another, the adduced analogy is equally imperfect. The accounting of time by nights is 'observ'd by divers Eastern People'; the Mexicans never in fact washed their children in cold water as soon as they were born; the Americans are not as much addicted to gaming as other nations; a number of American peoples marry as many wives as they please; nature and necessity, rather than the Germans, have taught the Americans to make dams and banks against floods; almost everyone has always believed in the immortality of the soul; it is true that the Americans eat separately, but it is not true that they went naked; human sacrifices were almost universal in former ages; and not all the Americans by any means are guilty of cannibalism.[49] And Ogilby concludes this part of his account by summarising de Laet's arguments against Grotius's view that the Peruvians were originally extracted, not from the Norwegians, but from the Chinese.

Having disposed of these three theories, Ogilby ventures to put forward one of his own – not without some misgivings, since, as he says, 'it is something of Work, when we have beaten down a well-fortifi'd Opinion, to set up somewhat in stead thereof, to stand a permanent and undeniable truth'.[50] He is quite prepared to admit the possibility that America was 'not onely Planted from the first, but several times replenish'd since by various Nations':[51] some late-comers, he thinks, may well have come over by sea. But so far as the first-comers are concerned, his view is that 'the Planting of *America* was not onely soon after the Flood, but that they came also thither by Land'.[52] And Tartary, he believes, 'certainly was the first Nursery, from whence the *Americans* were Transplanted'.[53] It was in fact the Scythians, he opines – the ancient inhabitants of Tartary – who first settled America. The basic argument which he puts forward here 'to shut up all' is in essence an ethnological one:

It is evident, that the first Planters of *America* were not *Europeans* from the dissimilitude of the People, both in their Complexions, Language, and Persons; nor *Africans*, because that in all the far-spreading Countrey of *America*, not one *Negro* is to

[49] *Ibid.*, pp. 33–4.   [50] *Ibid.*, p. 35.
[51] *Ibid.*, p. 36.   [52] *Ibid.*, p. 37.   [53] *Ibid.*, p. 39.

be found, except a few near the River *Martha,* in the little Territory *Quarequa,* which must by Storm be drove thither from the
Guinny Coast: So that *Asia,* the Mother of all People, onely
remains to be Implanter of our *America* . . .[54]

To this argument from racial resemblances Ogilby adds a
geographical one:

Moreover, *Armenia,* out of which, by *Noah's* Progeny the whole
Earth was re-peopled, borders on *Scythia,* now call'd *Tartary,* and
Tartary faces *America,* separated onely by the *Straights* of *Anian;*
though some are of opinion, that out of the South into the Frozen
Sea, there is no passage thorow these *Straights,* else (as we have
already prov'd the contrary) how came all those Voracious and
Poysonous Beasts into *America,* if it be clearly separated from
Asia by Sea?[55]

The Scythians and the northern Americans, Ogilby argues,
resemble one another physically: among other things, they
have 'a more than ordinary and natural distance between the
Eyes . . . and [a] plumpness and swelling of their Cheeks
summits above the Cheek-bone'.[56] So far as their customs are
concerned, both the Americans and the Tartars 'differ
amongst themselves', but 'in several things they agree one
with another'. For example,

polygamy is still in use, both among the *Tartars* and *Americans;*
both acknowledge the Immortality of the Soul, both like *Canni-*
bals, Eating and Sacrificing Mans flesh . . .
   Most of the *Tartars* use no manner of Letters or Characters
. . . their bemoaning of the dead ends in one Moneth, both
by the *Tartars* and *Americans;* with a Person of Quality, the
Tartars bury a live Servant; the same Custom is observ'd by some
of the *Americans;* and so much do they agree in a salvage and
rude life, that Merchandizing and Mechanicks are little regarded.
Ayson the *American* acknowledges the *Tartars* for a rude People
in their Religion, Habits, and Dwellings, and yet in all these the
Americans differ but very little. Lastly, How common is it
amongst them to worship the Devil? . . . Others in *Virginia*
believe, That there is a great and supreme Deity, which is Ever-
lasting, and for ever. The *Tartars* also are of the like perswasion.[57]

[54] *Ibid.,* pp. 39–40.   [55] *Ibid.,* p. 40.
[56] *Ibid.,* pp. 40–1.   [57] *Ibid.,* pp. 41–2.

Several of these alleged similarities, it will be noted, are more or less identical with those upon the evidential value of which (in relation to alternative theories) Ogilby has himself just cast considerable doubt; and the new similarities which he now adduces are hardly much more impressive. The only novel point he makes is that the very diversity of practices among the Tartars on the one hand and the Americans on the other strengthens the case for the existence of a genetic relationship between them – and this is a point of which the novelty is rather more obvious than the validity. The section concludes with an argument (once again borrowed from Joannes de Laet) to counteract Grotius's view that the absence of any horses in America at the time when the Spaniards arrived proves that the Americans could not be descended from the Tartars. The answer to this, Ogilby thinks, is that although Tartary at the present day certainly abounds in horses, it did not in fact do so in the times of the ancient Scythians, by whom, shortly after the Flood, America was first peopled.

In spite of the obvious imperfections and occasional absurdities in this account, one cannot rise from a perusal of it without a feeling of surprise at the extent to which men such as Ogilby, three centuries ago, could approach as closely as they did to the solution of the problem of American origins which is generally accepted by anthropologists and archaeologists today. The obstacles with which these early enquirers had to contend were indeed formidable. It was not simply that there was no generally accepted body of scientific principles available for identifying the *relevant* facts: it was also that many of the actual facts themselves – about physical geography, for example – were still very imperfectly known, and in addition, that any conclusions reached had to be shown to be in conformity with Genesis. If under these conditions some of the enquirers achieved more than we might reasonably have expected of them, this may of course have been due in part to luck as well as to good judgement. It was lucky, for example, that the story of the Creation in Genesis should have constrained the enquirers to postulate that America was peopled from Eurasia. It was lucky, too, that the story of Noah's Ark, coupled with the current imper-

fections in geographical knowledge, should have led logically to the idea that the first migrations to America took
place by land along something like a Bering Strait land
bridge. But we should not underestimate the large element of
good judgement which also entered into the picture. At a
period when no one really knew which traits were relevant
and which irrelevant to the problem of genetic origins, men
like Ogilby gave a clear warning of the danger of relying on
superficial and non-specific similarities, and hinted at a kind
of hierarchy of relevance in which physiognomic similarities
were at the top and religious similarities at the bottom. For
its time, this was surely no mean achievement.

The third piece of origins literature which I have chosen for
particular mention, Lafitau's *Moeurs des Sauvages Ameri-
quains, comparées aux moeurs des premiers temps* (1724),
was very widely quoted by the social scientists in the second
half of the century – so widely, indeed, as to indicate that it
was regarded by them as playing rather a special role. Many
of them seem to have believed, rightly or wrongly, that
Lafitau's book had provided a convincing demonstration of
the fact that contemporary American society could be regarded as a kind of living model – conveniently laid out for
study, as if in a laboratory – of human society in the 'first' or
'earliest' stage of its development. Lafitau, in other words,
had in their view vindicated the hypothesis that 'in the beginning all the World was *America*'.

'I have not contented myself', wrote Lafitau in the introduction to his book,

with becoming acquainted with the character of the savages, and
enquiring about their customs and practices. I have sought in
these practices and in these customs for traces of the most remote
antiquity; I have read with care those of the most ancient authors
who have treated of the manners, laws, and usages of the peoples
with whom they had some acquaintance; I have compared these
manners with one another; and I must say that if the ancient
authors have helped to support certain fortunate conjectures of
mine concerning the savages, the customs of the savages have
helped me to understand the ancient authors more easily and to
explain several things in their work.[58]

[58] Lafitau, *op. cit.*, Vol. I, pp. 3–4.

One of Lafitau's main motives in undertaking this research as he candidly confesses, was to refute the atheists. Most o: the writers who have described the manners of barbarou: peoples, he says, have pictured the latter as having no reli-gious feelings, no knowledge of the Divinity, no form of wor-ship, and no laws or government.[59] Such a picture, he argues puts a powerful weapon into the hands of the atheists. The point here is that according to Lafitau one of the strongest proofs we have of the necessity of religion is the unanimous consent of all peoples to recognise a superior Being and to honour Him in some manner. But this argument from univer-sal need falls to the ground if it can be shown that there is a large number of different nations which have no idea of a God or of worship; for the atheists can then claim that in all the remaining nations religion is simply a device of human legislators, who have invented it in order to control their peoples by fear.[60] To counteract this argument, it has to be shown that there is actually no nation so barbarous as to have no religion and no manners.[61] And this, says Lafitau can in fact very readily be shown – and much more than this, too:

Not only do the peoples who are called barbarians have a religion, but this religion has relations with that of the earliest times, with what was called in antiquity the orgies of Bacchus and of the Mother of the Gods, the mysteries of Isis and Osiris – relations displaying such a high degree of conformity that one immediately feels, from this resemblance, that the basis and principles are everywhere the same.[62]

The reason why 'the basis and principles are everywhere the same', according to Lafitau's rather idiosyncratic account, is that all the religions of the world – however much they were subsequently 'corrupted' – sprang originally from one religion, 'pure and holy in itself and in its origin', which pro-ceeded directly from God and was given by Him to Adam and Eve.[63] It is for this reason, Lafitau argues, that when one looks below the surface of 'corrupted' religions, whether ancient or modern, one finds striking points of conformity

[59] *Ibid.*, Vol. I, p. 5.　　[60] *Ibid.*, Vol. I, p. 6.　　[61] *Ibid.*, Vol. I, p. 7.
[62] *Ibid.*, Vol. I, p. 7, and cf. also p. 15.　　[63] *Ibid.*, Vol. I, p. 14.

with the basic beliefs and forms of worship of 'the true religion'[64] – i.e. eighteenth-century Catholicism. Such an explanation of religious similarities, he believes, is much more plausible that that given by Acosta and others like him who ascribed them to the nefarious activities of the Ape of God;[65] and in Lafitau's eyes it has the additional advantage that it enables us to interpret pagan mythology by relating the symbols to 'the principles of our religion' rather than to 'an explanation of the physical world' – i.e. it enables us to interpret it without giving a hostage to the materialists and atheists.[66]

Lafitau is concerned, however, not only with the religion of the Americans, but also with their manners. In his description of the manners of the Americans 'the parallel with the ancients is always maintained', because, as he believes, there is not a single characteristic of the manners of the Americans which does not have its counterpart in antiquity'.[67] But there is fortunately no need for us to follow Lafitau through his very long and detailed account of the forms of government of the Americans, their matrimonial and educational arrangements, housing and clothing, war-time and peace-time occupations, illnesses, mortuary customs, languages, etc., fascinating though much of this is. All that for our purposes we need to know about Lafitau's approach can be gleaned from the relatively brief discussion of the origin of the Americans with which his account of their religion and manners is prefaced.

Like so many of his predecessors, Lafitau divides the question of American origins into three sub-questions: How and by what route was America peopled? At what period of time was it peopled? By which ancient nation or nations was it peopled? On the first sub-question Lafitau has nothing very new to say: without much discussion, he accepts what he describes as 'the most universally followed and most probable view' – viz., that all the peoples of America crossed to that continent through Asia. 'Whether these lands are contiguous or whether they are divided by a few small arms of the sea', he writes, 'it was easy to make one's way across'; and he

[64] *Ibid.*, Vol. I, p. 9. [65] *Ibid.*, Vol. I, p. 10.
[66] *Ibid.*, Vol. I, p. 16. [67] *Ibid.*, Vol. I, p. 18.

expresses the hope that the comparisons he is going to make later in his book between the manners of the Americans and those of the Asiatics and the nations comprising the peoples called Thracians and Scythians will be regarded as providing evidence in support of the view that America was peopled through the easternmost parts of Tartary.[68]

Lafitau's answer to the second sub-question is that America was peopled soon after the Flood. He makes it clear, however, that one can *not* properly infer this from the fact that the Americans are ignorant of many of the most elementary arts; for, as Genesis reveals, these arts were widely known and practised before the Flood, and Noah and his sons must have passed them on to their posterity.[69] The fact that the Americans are ignorant of them is proof of nothing more than their own idleness and apathy. His opinion that America was peopled soon after the Flood, Lafitau explains, is based on the comparison made in his book between the manners of ancient times and the manners of the Americans – the latter, according to him, not having altered as have those of the peoples of Asia and Europe.[70] The reason for this lack of alteration in the manners of the Americans, according to Lafitau, is precisely their idleness and apathy – the same cause, he asserts, which has kept certain European and Asian peoples in a state of complete barbarism in spite of their proximity to civilised nations.[71]

On the third sub-question – By which ancient nation or nations was America peopled? – Lafitau has much more of interest to say. The discovery of the East and West Indies, he argues, has enabled us to find once again the greater part of a number of ancient nations which were believed to have been completely destroyed. The problem, however, is to relate these modern survivors to 'their source and primary origin'.[72] One of the main difficulties here is that the ancient nations concerned did not constitute specific, separate, or unchanging entities. Thus, says Lafitau,

to argue that the peoples of America sprang from the peoples of Thrace, Scythia, India, Ethiopia, or Lybia is to say virtually nothing. For these names have always had a very wide significa-

[68] *Ibid.*, Vol. I, p. 34.   [69] *Ibid.*, Vol. I, p. 40.   [70] *Ibid.*, Vol. I, pp. 40–1.
[71] *Ibid.*, Vol. I, p. 40.   [72] *Ibid.*, Vol. I, p. 41.

tion, and have always been attached to countries whose boundaries were neither known nor determined; and these countries have been successively inhabited by a multitude of nations which are no longer there, which were very different from one another, and which were still more different from those which abound there today.[73]

The primary causes of these transmigrations of mankind, Lafitau argues, were economic, and he proceeds to give a brief but highly suggestive analysis of the motives which might lead to the dispersion of, first, peoples living by hunting and fishing (whom Lafitau carefully distinguishes from herdsmen), and, second, agricultural peoples such as the Egyptians, Phrygians, and Hellenians.[74] This passage must surely have caught the attention of those social scientists who drew so heavily upon his book in the latter half of the century, although it should be carefully noted that Lafitau apparently envisaged hunting, pastoral, and agricultural societies as coexisting in time rather than as succeeding one another.

Given, then, that for these and other reasons most of the ancient peoples concerned eventually came to be mixed up with one another, is it in fact possible to say anything more precise about their relation to the newly-discovered peoples of America? Lafitau seems to recognise that there are grave methodological difficulties involved here. We cannot, he says, base our conjectures on linguistic comparisons, since very few words from the original ancient languages have come down to us.[75] And if we decide to base our conjectures on comparisons of customs and manners, we must be careful to exclude those *general* customs or usages of everyday life which have been retained almost unchanged by the great majority of peoples from the very earliest times, since these obviously have no evidential value whatever.[76] 'It would only be on the basis of some distinctive and characteristic traits of

[73] *Ibid.*, Vol. I, p. 42.
[74] *Ibid.*, Vol. I, pp. 43–4.
[75] *Ibid.*, Vol. I, pp. 46–7. This consideration does not inhibit Lafitau, in the concluding section of his book (Vol. II, pp. 463ff.), from using linguistic comparisons to support his conjectures concerning the origins of the Hurons and Iroquois.
[76] *Ibid.*, Vol. I, pp. 48–9.

the newly-discovered peoples, together with those of ancient peoples of whom the histories have preserved some idea', Lafitau says, 'that we could hazard any conjectures by putting these distinctive traits side by side and comparing one set with the other.'[77] By 'distinctive and characteristic traits', Lafitau means 'certain more particular and less common usages',[78] such as, for example, the extremely singular custom of couvade[79] (by which the husband feigns illness and is put to bed during his wife's lying-in period).

In his application of this comparative method, Lafitau's purpose, as he himself explains, is a relatively modest one:

My plan is not to disentangle all these barbarous peoples [of America] in order to relate each of them to a people known in antiquity. Although one could make some fairly probable conjectures about a few of them, as I shall show in the case of the Iroquois and the Hurons, this knowledge does not seem to me to be very necessary. It is enough to show that the manners of the Americans display in every detail so high a degree of uniformity with the manners of the earliest peoples that one can infer that they all come from the same stock.[80]

The final conclusion to which Lafitau comes is that 'the greater part of the peoples of America sprang originally from those barbarians who occupied the continent of Greece and its islands . . . before those peoples who were subsequently known by the name of Greeks'.[81] These barbarians are more or less universally known under the generic names of Pelasgians and Hellenians. Although these two peoples are often mixed up together, they were in fact different in one very significant respect:

The Pelasgians were different from the Hellenians, in that the latter, who cultivated a little land, were a little more settled and established than the former, who did no sowing at all, lived only on the fruit of the trees, by hunting, by fishing, and on what chance could provide them with, dwelt only in tents, struck camp for trifling reasons, and led a wandering life by vocation and by necessity.[82]

[77] *Ibid.*, Vol. I, p. 49.   [78] *Ibid.*, Vol. I, p. 49.
[79] *Ibid.*, Vol. I, pp. 49–50.
[80] *Ibid.*, Vol. I, p. 19.   [81] *Ibid.*, Vol. I, pp. 89–90.
[82] *Ibid.*, Vol. I, p. 91. Cf. Vol. II, p. 465.

'In the beginning all the World was America'

Those who know the barbarian peoples of North America well enough, Lafitau proceeds, will recognise that the same distinction can be seen today between the Hurons on the one hand and most of the Algonquins and the savages of the north on the other; and very much the same distinction can also be found among the peoples of South America. This remarkable comparison is not pursued, and Lafitau ends this section by declaring that 'everything I have to say in what follows about the manners and customs of our savages has so great a resemblance to those of these barbarous peoples that one must conclude that the latter are to be seen in the former'.[83]

Before he goes on, however, Lafitau forewarns his readers in an important passage that the comparisons he is going to make will be more wide-ranging than they might expect. He intends, he says, to compare the customs of the Americans not only with those of the Pelasgians and Hellenians, but also with those of the later Greeks, the ancient Romans, the Iberians, and even the Gauls – the point being that 'according to the testimony of the authors, nothing was more similar than the manners of the Iberians, the Gauls, and the peoples of Thrace and Scythia, because these barbarians [i.e. the Pelasgians and Hellenians] spread out in all those directions'.[84] And in actual fact his comparisons turn out to be even wider than this: he includes for good measure a number of other peoples, and also a number of customs which are far from being 'distinctive and characteristic' in the sense in which he has defined this expression. It will not cause any difficulty, he says in one place, if I cite the customs of any people whatever, provided that I do not claim to draw any consequences from them other than 'the relation of these customs with those of early antiquity'.[85]

It was precisely this very wide-ranging character of Lafitau's comparisons, coupled with his continual reference back to the times of *early* antiquity [*la premiere Antiquité*],[86]

[83] *Ibid.*, Vol. I, p. 91.   [84] *Ibid.*, Vol. I, p. 92.   [85] *Ibid.*, Vol. I, p. 49.
[86] Margaret T. Hodgen, *op. cit.*, p. 349, states that Lafitau did not realise 'the necessity for discrimination between the varying cultural conditions which succeeded one another' in the course of the histories of the Greek and Roman civilisations. However true this may be of some of Lafitau's precursors and successors, I do not think that it can really be said to be true of Lafitau himself.

which were to attract the attention of the new social scientists. One could discount his acceptance of the time-scale of Genesis, his idiosyncratic religious views, his rather rabid anti-materialism, and even his bizarre theory of pigmentation,[87] and still recognise him as a pioneer anthropologist of high calibre who had succeeded in proving fairly conclusively that 'in the beginning' all the world really *was* America. And not only this: in some of his 'economic' *obiter dicta* he seemed to have appreciated that hunting and fishing were (as he put it in one place) 'the first occupations of the first men',[88] thereby providing an important clue as to the reason *why* 'in the beginning all the world was *America*'.

What we have so far arrived at is simply the idea that the historical starting-point in the development of European society was a very primitive form of society whose general cultural characteristics closely resembled those of the Americans – or, more accurately, those of the majority of the Americans who lived in areas other than Mexico and Peru. The next problem to be solved was that of the intermediate stages through which society had passed in order to get from this 'first' stage to its present condition. And here there were two logically separate questions which had to be answered: first, what kind of general *criterion* ought to be employed to distinguish one stage from another; and, second, what were the *actual stages* concerned? These two questions are obviously inter-connected, but at this juncture it will be convenient to discuss them separately.

So far as the question of the proper criterion of distinction between the stages was concerned, the answer eventually given by the pioneers, as we have seen, was that the stages ought to be defined in terms of different *modes of subsistence*. And here again, I suggest, the literature about the Americans played a specific and important role. The point here is not simply that some of the 'origins' writers – Acosta and Lafitau, for example – occasionally hinted at this con-

---

[87] Upon which, as is well known, Voltaire was eagerly to seize in order to denigrate Lafitau's work. Cf. Voltaire's *Essai sur les Moeurs* (ed. René Pomeau, Éditions Garnier Frères, Paris, 1963), Vol. I, p. 29.

[88] Lafitau, *op. cit.*, Vol. II, p. 337.

clusion. Rather, it is that in almost all the discussions about the origin of the Americans, at any rate up to the eighteenth century, the basic assumption made was that cultural similarities between some ancient people or group of peoples and the Americans – at any rate if they were specific enough, and thick enough upon the ground – were to be regarded as indications of the probability of the genetic descent of the latter from the former.[89] Again and again various writers tried to demonstrate that the Americans were *like* the Jews, or the Danes, or the Chinese; and the conclusion they almost invariably drew from their demonstration was that the Americans *were* Jews, or Danes, or Chinese. And the very absurdity of many of the specific ascriptions of genetic origin which were made by these writers was bound sooner or later to provoke a reaction, not only against the flimsiness and superficiality of some of the 'similarities' adduced, but also – and much more importantly – against the basic assumption that cultural similarities were evidence of genetic descent. The writers whose reaction took the latter form did not seek to deny that many important cultural similarities could in fact be observed between the Americans and at any rate certain broad groups of ancient peoples: it would not have been very easy to deny this after Lafitau's book had appeared. What they did deny was simply the validity of the assumption that such similarities were evidence of genetic descent. The similarities, they began to argue, were really evidence of the fact that 'like causes' – i.e. like *environmental* causes – always produced 'like effects'. And among these environmental causes, they began to claim, the most important was the mode of subsistence. The observed similarities, in other words, were actually evidence of nothing more than that all the peoples concerned *got their living* in the same way. This kind of reaction, as we shall see below, was expressed very explicitly by several of our writers – most notably by Robertson and de Pauw.

Turning now to the second of our two questions, concerning the actual delineation and labelling of the intermediate stages, this obviously could not have been answered on the basis of the literature about the Americans alone. The

[89] Cf. above, pp. 46–7.

important point here is that the studies of the similarities
between the Americans and the ancients were associated, as
both cause and effect, with wider comparative studies of
relatively primitive peoples (both past and present) in which
differences as well as similarities were stressed. For example,
when people began to look at the Old Testament not only as
a source of spiritual enlightenment but also as a source of
anthropological and historical data, they could hardly help
noticing that the Patriarchs, who had obviously in their time
been more advanced than the Americans were now, had got
their living not by hunting and fishing but by keeping flocks
and herds, just as the Arabs and Tartars did. Similarly, when
people began to re-read the ancient historians to find out
what they had said about the primitive peoples of their time,
they discovered (as Lafitau did) that Caesar and Tacitus, for
example, sometimes seemed to imply that the relative degree
of civilisation of the different tribes or peoples they were discussing depended upon the extent to which pasturage and/or
agriculture, rather than hunting, preponderated in their
mode of subsistence.[90] And most of the modern historians of
Egypt and Asia, as well as the ancient historians and philosophers, seemed to concur in emphasising the great importance of the invention of agriculture, which paved the way
for the subsequent development of arts, sciences, and commerce. Eventually, then, as a kind of by-product of comparative historical studies of this type, the view emerged that
society 'naturally' progressed through four distinct and normally consecutive stages – hunting, pasturage, agriculture,
and commerce – the last of these (Smith's 'commercial
society') being of course typified by modern Europe.

   In the emergence of the four stages theory, then, the contemporary literature about the Americans played an interesting and significant role. It would be too much, of course, to
say that without this literature the theory would not have
been put forward at all, but it is at any rate a distinct possibility that it would not have been put forward in quite the
same form. In particular, it would have been very difficult
for the social scientists of the mid-eighteenth century, if they
had not had the living example of the Americans before

90 Cf. above, p. 12.

them, to describe the probable characteristics of the 'first' stage of development with any degree of clarity or plausibility. There were very few other surviving examples of what Robertson called 'the rudest form in which we can conceive [man] to subsist'; and the ancient philosophers and historians (to quote Robertson again) 'had only a limited view of this subject, as they had hardly any opportunity of surveying man in his rudest and most early state'. Even the Scythians and the Germans, 'the rudest people of whom any ancient author has transmitted to us an authentic account', possessed flocks and herds and had acquired various kinds of property.[91] The Old Testament, too, was of very limited assistance so far as the 'first' stage was concerned: it had nothing very clear to say about what the ancestors of the Patriarchs had been *before* they became herdsmen, and its statement that Abel was a shepherd and Cain a tiller of the soil was (as we have already seen) an obstacle which it was not easy to avoid. One of the most important things which the studies of the Americans did, then, was to provide the new social scientists with a plausible working hypothesis about the basic characteristics of the 'first' stage. With this hypothesis in their minds, they were able to approach the sources of evidence with new eyes, and to discover in the *obiter dicta* of the ancient historians, in the myths and legends of Hesiod and Epicurus, and in the speculations of the Greek philosophers, various statements about the mode of subsistence in the earliest age of mankind whose proper significance, they came to believe, had not previously been appreciated.

It is now time to explore some of these themes further, with specific reference to the work of the pioneers of the four stages theory in the decade 1750–60.

[91] William Robertson, *Works* (Edinburgh, 1840), Vol. II, p. 90.

3

The French pioneers of the 1750s

The inventors of new paradigms, Professor Kuhn has said, have almost always been 'either very young or very new to the field whose paradigm they change'.[1] However true or untrue this may be in general, it is certainly true enough of the two earliest 'inventors' of the four stages theory – Turgot and Smith. Both men would appear to have been still in their twenties when, quite independently of one another and at almost exactly the same time, they first formulated their respective versions of the theory.

One is obliged to say no more than that this 'would appear' to have been the case because the dating of their formulations is still up to a point a matter of conjecture. Turgot's main statement of the theory is contained in an unfinished manuscript entitled *On Universal History* which was not published until many years after his death.[2] There seems, however, to be little reason to doubt Du Pont's statement that this manuscript (together with a companion work entitled *On Political Geography*) was in fact written by Turgot 'while he was at the Sorbonne, or shortly after he left it'.[3] So far as Smith is concerned, we know that he was making extensive use of the four stages theory in the early 1760s in his lectures on Jurisprudence at Glasgow University, and, as we shall see later, a strong case can be made for back-dating his use of the theory to the early 1750s or even before.[4] I shall therefore assume, in the account which follows (in this chapter and the next) of the emergence of the four stages

---

[1] T. S. Kuhn, *The Structure of Scientific Revolutions* (2nd edn, University of Chicago Press, Chicago, 1970), p. 90.

[2] It was first published by Du Pont in his edition of the *Oeuvres de M^r. Turgot*, Vol. II (Paris, 1808), pp. 209–328. Since the manuscript has not been located, it is impossible to ascertain whether there are any divergences between Turgot's original and the version published by Du Pont.

[3] *Oeuvres de M^r. Turgot*, Vol. II, p. 165. Turgot entered the Sorbonne in 1749, and left it in 1751.

[4] See below, pp. 107ff.

theory in France and Scotland in 1750–60, that the contributions of Turgot and Smith did in fact date from the early years of that decade, which would mean that they were first in the field in their respective countries.

In 1748, before he entered the Sorbonne, Turgot composed a set of notes on 'The Causes of the Progress and Decline of the Sciences and the Arts', in which a number of the views which he was later to elaborate in *On Universal History* were sketched out.[5] *The Spirit of Laws* had appeared earlier in the same year, and Turgot had apparently read it by the time he came to write the notes, since he comments in the latter on Montesquieu's theory of the influence of climate.[6] There is no trace in the notes, however, of the four stages theory, or of anything really resembling it.

The first evidence of a bow by Turgot in the direction of the four stages theory is to be found in a critique which he wrote in March 1750 of a book on the origin of languages by Maupertuis. In this critique the following statement occurs:

Thence arose the different languages, according to whether the people were hunters, shepherds, or husbandmen . . . The hunter would have few words, very vivid, not closely linked together, and progress would be slow; the shepherd, with his peaceful life, would construct a gentler and more refined language; the husbandman, one that was colder and more coherent.[7]

There would seem to be a fairly distinct echo of Montesquieu's Book xviii here.[8] But it should be noted that the passage just quoted is an isolated one, and, more importantly, that Turgot (like Montesquieu) does not specifically state – or even, perhaps, imply – that the modes of subsistence between which he distinguishes constituted different *historical stages* through which early societies naturally and successively progressed over time.

In July and December 1750, in his capacity as *prieur* at the Sorbonne, Turgot delivered his two celebrated orations, the second of which, entitled 'A Philosophical Review of the

---

[5] G. Schelle (ed.), *Oeuvres de Turgot*, Vol. i (Paris, 1913), pp. 116–42.
[6] *Ibid.*, Vol. i, pp. 139–40.
[7] *Ibid.*, Vol. i, p. 172. Cf. R. L. Meek, *Turgot on Progress, Sociology and Economics* (Cambridge University Press, Cambridge, 1973), pp. 5–6.
[8] See above, pp. 33–4.

Successive Advances of the Human Mind', is now widely (and correctly) regarded as a key document in the history of the eighteenth-century concept of progress. This remarkable piece is pervaded by the Lockean notion that 'the senses constitute the unique source of our ideas';[9] by the associated notion that 'the need perfects the tool';[10] and by the idea that mankind has passed through various 'gradations' or 'stages' in its progress 'from barbarism to refinement'. Records and remains of all these 'steps taken by the human mind', says Turgot, are spread out before us in the world today: the 'infinite variations in inequality' among the nations reflect 'the history of all the ages'.[11] But that is about as far as Turgot goes, in this particular document, towards the four stages theory. It is true that in one place he emphasises the importance of tillage, which permits the rise of towns and trade;[12] and that in another place he says, significantly enough, that after the confusion of tongues the nations 'were almost all plunged into the same barbarism in which we still see the Americans'.[13] But the idea of a normal or natural succession of specific developmental stages, each based on a different mode of subsistence, is still lacking.

In 1751, an occasion for a more detailed consideration of the 'barbarism' of the Americans, and for a direct comparison between this 'barbarism' and the 'refinement' of contemporary Europe, offered itself to Turgot in the shape of a request by Madame de Graffigny for comments on the impending second edition of her famous *Lettres Péruviennes*. Turgot's letter of reply to her[14] has frequently been cited as evidence of his advanced views on education and marriage. What has less often been commented upon is his remarkable account, in the first two or three pages of the letter, of the great economic and social advantages which a 'refined' society (like France) has over a 'barbaric' society (like America). This account, it is interesting to note, emerges in the course of what is in effect a critique of the contemporary 'primitivist' argument that the absence (or alleged absence)

[9] R. L. Meek, *op. cit.*, p. 46, and cf. pp. 42 and 45.
[10] *Ibid.*, p. 45.   [11] *Ibid.*, p. 42.
[12] *Ibid.*, p. 43.   [13] *Ibid.*, p. 42.
[14] G. Schelle (ed.), *Oeuvres de Turgot*, Vol. I (Paris, 1913), pp. 241–55.

of inequality in the conditions of life among savage peoples is a sign of their superiority over more civilised peoples. Turgot's main counter-argument is that this absence of inequality is in fact a sign not of the superiority of the savages but of their inferiority. For inequality, Turgot argues, is a necessary precondition of the extension of the division of labour, exchange, and commerce; of the accumulation of capital; and therefore of all the vast social and economic benefits which these things have brought in their train in modern Europe.[15]

Turgot was thus led by the logic of this discussion to give a more specific delineation of the basic characteristics of the stage of socio-economic development in which modern Europe found itself than he had done in any of his earlier writings. It was a society possessing these characteristics which he (and many of his contemporaries) normally had in mind when they subsequently spoke of a 'commercial society', or a 'commercial stage' in the development of society, or of 'commerce' *simpliciter*. And Turgot makes it quite clear in his letter to Madame de Griffigny that the path from a savage society to a modern 'commercial' society of this type represents an ascent rather than a descent. Although certain aspects of modern society are open to severe criticism,[16] and although savage societies have certain compensating advantages of their own,[17] it remains true, in Turgot's opinion, that 'to express a preference for the savages is ridiculous bombast'.[18]

By 1751, then, Turgot had come to be possessed of several of the main ideas of which the four stages theory was made up: the idea that societies normally progressed over time from 'barbarism' to 'refinement' in a succession of 'steps' or

---

[15] *Ibid.*, Vol. I, pp. 241–3.

[16] Notably its attitudes towards education and marriage, with which the remainder of the letter is largely concerned.

[17] 'Zilia should not be unfair', writes Turgot. 'Let her at the same time set out the compensations – unequal, it is true, but nevertheless real – which the advantages of barbarous peoples offer. Let her show that our over-arbitrary institutions have too often made us forget nature; that we have been the dupes of our own products; and that the savage, who does not know how to consult nature, often knows how to follow her' (*ibid.*, Vol. I, pp. 243–4).

[18] *Ibid.*, Vol. I, p. 243.

'stages'; the idea that a reflection of ancient 'barbarism' could still be seen today in the way of life of the peoples of America; and the idea that modern 'refinement' was based on 'commerce' in the sense in which Turgot described it in his letter to Madame de Graffigny. In addition, as we have also seen, he had on one occasion followed Montesquieu in classifying early peoples into hunters, shepherds, and husbandmen. The next step – probably the most crucial of all – was to attach these labels 'hunters', 'shepherds', and 'husbandmen' to different types of society *clearly conceived as succeeding one another over time.* This step was taken in *On Political Geography* (*c.* 1751),[19] in which Turgot, when describing the first of five projected 'political maps of the world', said that it ought to include details of (*inter alia*) the following:

The successive changes in the manner of life of men, and the order in which they have followed one another: peoples who are shepherds, hunters, husbandmen.

The causes which have been able to keep certain peoples for longer periods in the state of hunters, then shepherds. The differences which result from these three states, in relation to the number of men, to the movements of nations, to the greater or lesser degree of ease in surmounting the barriers by which nature has, so to speak, assigned to different societies their portion of the terrestrial globe, to communications, to the greater or lesser degree of ease with which peoples are intermingled.[20]

The use of the three labels in this dynamic way, and in the context of a stadial theory of development, was quite revolutionary, and was no doubt the fruit of Turgot's contemplation of much more than *The Spirit of Laws.*

In *On Universal History* (*c.* 1751–2) the four stages theory which had been gradually approached in Turgot's earlier works was brought to a quite surprising maturity, becoming in effect the basic conceptual framework within which the argument of the preliminary part (and up to a point the final

[19] *Ibid.*, Vol. i, pp. 255–74.
[20] *Ibid.*, Vol. i, p. 259. Cf. p. 260, where Turgot says that the second 'political map of the world' would contain details of 'the first formation of governments among peoples who are savages, hunters, shepherds, husbandmen', and 'the variations relative to these three manners of life'. Cf. also the interesting comments on the 'first state' of mankind on p. 259.

part) of the so-called 'first discourse'[21] was set. Turgot begins by considering the state of mankind immediately after the Flood, when the human race was 'once again reduced to a single family, and thus obliged to start afresh'. Without provisions, and in the depths of forests, says Turgot, 'men could devote themselves to nothing but obtaining their subsistence. The fruits which the earth produces in the absence of cultivation are not enough: men had to resort to the hunting of animals . . .'[22] If we take the Flood as our point of departure, then, we may postulate as the 'first' stage of development 'the state of hunters'. Men in this stage gain their subsistence primarily from the chase; they have 'no fixed dwelling-place at all'; and they 'move aimlessly wherever the hunt leads them'. In short, their basic mode of subsistence, and therefore their basic habits and customs, are much the same as those of 'the savages of America' today.[23]

Let us note in passing that Turgot, by starting the story in this way with the dispersion of mankind after the Flood,[24] and by assuming that during this dispersion 'the original traditions were forgotten',[25] was able to sidestep very neatly a number of difficulties which had bedevilled some of the earlier discussions of the development problem. In particular, this procedure enabled him to maintain that there was no real contradiction between the biblical account of man's early history and the secular account which he himself was concerned to give. The fact that 'Abel was a shepherd and Cain a tiller of the soil' no longer hindered one from postulating that the 'first' stage of socio-economic development was 'the state of hunters'.[26] And this procedure, of course, made it

---

[21] *On Universal History*, in the form in which it was published by Du Pont, consists of an introduction, a 'first discourse' on 'the formation of governments and the intermingling of nations', and a 'second discourse' on 'the progress of the human mind'.

[22] R. L. Meek, *op. cit.*, p. 65.

[23] *Ibid.*, pp. 65–6.

[24] Or, more strictly speaking, after the confusion of tongues: cf. *ibid.*, p. 42.

[25] *Ibid.*, p. 42.

[26] The same kind of procedure had been adopted much earlier by Bernard Lamy in his famous book *La Rhetorique, ou L'Art de Parler*, which certainly influenced Rousseau and may well have influenced Turgot too. In his account of 'the true origin of languages' in this book, Lamy concentrates on the developments which allegedly followed the dispersion of mankind after the confusion of tongues, and claims that since the 'first

much easier to see the life of the present-day Americans as a kind of model of that of mankind in this 'first' stage. 'Alas!', Turgot felt himself able to sigh, 'our ancestors and the Pelasgians who preceded the Greeks were like the savages of America!'[27]

From the 'state of hunters', Turgot goes on to explain, society normally moves to 'the pastoral way of life', at any rate in those countries where domesticable animals are to be found:

There are animals which allow themselves to be brought into subjection by men, such as oxen, sheep, and horses, and men find it more advantageous to gather them together into herds than to chase after wandering animals.

It did not take long for the pastoral way of life to be introduced in all places where these animals were met with: oxen and sheep in Europe, camels and goats in the east, horses in Tartary, and reindeer in the north.[28]

By making the transition to the pastoral stage conditional upon the availability of domesticable animals, Turgot was able to give a plausible answer, of breathtaking simplicity, to the obvious objection that there appeared to be little sign of any transition to the pastoral stage in America:

The way of life of hunting peoples is maintained in the parts of America where these species are lacking. In Peru, where nature has placed a species of sheep called *llamas*, the people are shepherds, and this is obviously the reason why that part of America has been more easily civilised.[29]

Given suitable animals, then, the transition to the pastoral stage will sooner or later inevitably occur, bringing with it a more abundant and more assured subsistence and a larger population. 'Herds sustained more men than were required to look after them', says Turgot, and pastoral peoples 'began

men' of these times were simple hunters their activities did not require them to have a proper language but merely a kind of jargon. The 1st edition of Lamy's book was published as early as 1676, but so far as I can ascertain from the copies of the successive editions held by the British Museum the argument just described was not introduced until the 5th edition (Amsterdam, 1712), where it appears on p. 81.

27 R. L. Meek, *op. cit.*, p. 89.
28 *Ibid.*, p. 66.
29 *Ibid.*, p. 66.

to grow richer, and to understand better the idea of property.'[30]

Eventually, argues Turgot, there is a tendency for societies
to 'move on to the state of agriculture'. 'Pastoral peoples in
fertile countries' are the first to do this; hunting peoples, who
are 'deprived of the assistance of animals to manure the soil
and to facilitate labour', are unable to arrive so soon at the
agricultural stage. As a result of the surplus which agriculture is able to generate, there gradually arise 'towns, trade,
and all the useful arts and accomplishments', together with
'the division of occupations and the inequality of men' and
'the spirit of commerce'.[31]

It is within this general conceptual framework, then, that
Turgot sets his account of wars and conquests among early
peoples, of the ways in which different nations were led to
intermingle, and of the overall effects of this intermingling.
And towards the end of the 'first discourse', when he comes
on to the subject of slavery, the distinction between hunting,
pastoral, and agricultural peoples is once again brought into
the picture as an organising principle.[32]

Turgot's formulation of the four stages theory in *On Universal History* is by no means free from ambiguity, and it is
noticeable that his argument often has a tendency to go off
at a tangent at the most interesting points. But for its time
it was a remarkable achievement: no one before Turgot, so
far as I know – with the possible exception of Smith – had
specifically formulated and illustrated the idea that 'progress'
normally took the form of the unconscious but law-governed[33]
development of society through four successive stages based
on four different modes of subsistence. Just how influential
Turgot's version of the theory was in the latter half of the
eighteenth century it is very difficult to say. *On Universal
History*, as we have seen, remained unfinished and the manuscript was not published until 1808. But there is a succinct
statement of the theory at a key point in Turgot's *Reflections
on the Formation and the Distribution of Wealth*,[34] and fairly

[30] *Ibid.*, pp. 66–7.   [31] *Ibid.*, pp. 68–9 and 73.   [32] *Ibid.*, pp. 81–3.
[33] In *On Universal History*, Turgot in one place came very close to the
idea underlying the 'law of unintended consequences'. See R. L. Meek,
op. cit., pp. 10–11.
[34] *Ibid.*, p. 148.

distinct echoes of it can be found in various other places in his published writings; and the oral tradition was of course handed on later in the century by men like Du Pont and, more importantly, Condorcet.[35] Whether Turgot's version of the four stages theory had any direct influence on the other French thinkers who promulgated the theory *in the 1750s*, however, is bound to remain an open question.

In turning now to these other French thinkers, the first question which has to be dealt with – and it is a particularly fascinating and difficult one – is whether Rousseau should properly be included among them. Rousseau's claim to rank among the early pioneers of the four stages theory must rest mainly on two of his works – his very well-known *Discourse on the Origin of Inequality*, and his very little-known *Essay on the Origin of Languages*. And in relation to each of these works certain problems arise. So far as the *Discourse* is concerned, although it certainly appeared early enough (1755) to enable Rousseau to qualify as a pioneer, there is some doubt as to whether the theory of socio-economic development which it contains ought really to be regarded as a version of the four stages theory. And so far as the *Essay* is concerned, although the theory which it contains is certainly a much closer approximation to the four stages theory, there is some doubt as to whether the relevant passages were in fact written in the 1750s. The question of the date of composition of the *Essay*, and the associated question of the nature of its relation to the *Discourse*, are still the subject of intense and intricate controversy among Rousseau-scholars. In the survey of Rousseau's contribution which follows it will not always be possible to avoid trespassing on the territory which these scholars dispute, even though our present interest in Rousseau is of course much narrower than theirs.

As everyone knows, the *Discourse* was written on a subject proposed by the Academy of Dijon – viz., 'What is the origin of inequality among men, and is it authorised by natural law?'[36] Rousseau sets out to show that inequality is not some-

---

[35] See *ibid.*, pp. 13–14.

[36] J.-J. Rousseau, *The Social Contract and Discourses* (Everyman revised edn, ed. J. H. Brumfitt and J. C. Hall, London, 1973), p. 27. This useful

thing which is 'natural' to man, but is on the contrary something which is produced by *society*. It is 'the spirit of society',
he argues, 'and the inequality which society produces,
that . . . transform and alter all our natural inclinations',
thereby causing most of our present discontents.[37] In taking
this line, Rousseau necessarily and consciously opposes himself to 'the philosophers', who, as he puts it, have constantly
'transferred to the state of nature ideas which were acquired
in society'.[38] Thus in order to prove his point, he is constrained to begin by drawing a plausible picture of the
'natural' man – of man as such, in abstraction from society
and its institutions. To know the source of inequality between
men, he says, we must begin by 'knowing mankind'. We
must try to see man 'as nature made him', and to 'distinguish
what is fundamental in his nature from the changes and
additions which his circumstances and the advances he has
made have introduced to modify his primitive condition'.[39]
Or, to put it in yet another way, we must 'distinguish properly
between what is original and what is artificial in the actual
nature of man',[40] and contemplate 'the first and most simple
operations of the human soul'.[41]

Now the great difficulty in an analytical exercise of this
nature, as Rousseau specifically recognises, is that in order to
make this kind of distinction we must somehow 'form a true
idea of a state [of "pure nature"] which no longer exists,
perhaps never did exist, and probably never will exist'.[42] That
it 'no longer exists' is demonstrated by the fact that the most
primitive peoples yet discovered, such as the 'savages of
America' who play an important part in the *Discourse*, have
evidently already advanced far beyond it.[43] That it 'perhaps
never did exist' is suggested by religion, which 'commands
us to believe that God Himself [took] men out of a state of
nature immediately after the creation'.[44] That it 'probably

edition is a revised version of the previous Everyman edition (by G. D. H.
Cole), but unfortunately it still omits the great majority of Rousseau's
footnotes to the *Discourse* – a number of which are of considerable
interest and importance in relation to the problems we are considering.
[37] *Ibid.*, p. 105.   [38] *Ibid.*, p. 45.   [39] *Ibid.*, p. 38.
[40] *Ibid.*, p. 39.   [41] *Ibid.*, p. 41.   [42] *Ibid.*, p. 39.   [43] *Ibid.*, p. 82.
[44] *Ibid.*, p. 45. 'It has not even entered into the heads of most of our
writers', says Rousseau at the end of the previous paragraph, 'to doubt

never will exist' is to be inferred, presumably, from the
extreme unlikelihood of any major retrogression towards the
primitive state on the part of contemporary peoples who are
now so far removed from that state. Thus, says Rousseau in
a key passage, 'the investigations we may enter into, in treating this subject, must not be considered as historical truths,
but only as mere conditional and hypothetical reasonings,
rather calculated to explain the nature of things, than to
ascertain their actual origin . . .'[45] What Rousseau is in effect
doing here is to warn his readers that although a number of
the things he is going to say about the state of 'pure nature'
will have the *form* of historical facts, they must not be understood as also having the *full status* of historical facts. This, I
believe, is what Rousseau really means by his much-debated
statement, which occurs immediately before the passage just
cited, that in his investigations he is going to begin 'by laying all facts aside, as they do not affect the question'.[46]

whether the state of nature ever existed; but it is clear from the Holy
Scriptures that the first man, having received his understanding and
commandments immediately from God, was not himself in such a state;
and that, if we give such credit to the writings of Moses as every Christian
philosopher ought to give, we must deny that, even before the deluge,
men were ever in the pure state of nature; unless, indeed, they fell
back into it from some very extraordinary circumstance; a paradox which
it would be very embarrassing to defend, and quite impossible to prove.'
[45] *Ibid.*, p. 45.
[46] A more fashionable interpretation of the phrase 'laying all facts aside'
maintains that the 'facts' to which Rousseau is here referring are above
all those contained in the biblical account of the origin of man and
society – about which he has indeed just been speaking at the point in
the *Discourse* where he uses the phrase. The idea lying behind this
interpretation is that Rousseau wished in the *Discourse* to put forward
his own version of the historical origins of mankind, which was inconsistent with the biblical version; that because of the censorship he could
not say clearly that this was what he was doing; and that he therefore
presented his own version in the guise of a pure hypothesis. (For
examples of this kind of interpretation, see the Everyman edition of the
Discourse, p. 313, note (b) to p. 45; and the Pléiade edition of Rousseau's
Oeuvres Complètes, Vol. III (1964), p. 1302.) Such an interpretation, in my
opinion, attributes to Rousseau a degree of deviousness of which he was
probably incapable. It was not his aim in the *Discourse* to present *any*
version of the historical origins of mankind, whether his own, or Moses's,
or anyone else's. What he was trying to do in the first part of that work
was to present a picture of the 'natural' man, of man in abstraction from
society, of the human race as it would have been 'if it had been left to
itself' (Everyman edn, p. 46). There is no evidence that I am aware of

In the first part of the *Discourse*, then, Rousseau's avowed aim is to isolate the essential characteristics of the 'natural' man – i.e. to consider man 'just as he must have come from the hands of nature', stripped of 'all the supernatural gifts he may have received, and all the artificial faculties he can have acquired only by a long process'.[47] Rousseau assumes that the physical constitution of this 'natural' man is roughly the same as it is today;[48] he imagines such a man set down in the midst of a more or less realistic primeval forest; and he then proceeds to make a number of 'conjectures' about the behaviour of such a man in such a situation. These 'conjectures', it should be carefully noted, are by no means entirely chimerical: they are the product not only of a logical exercise in which the necessary consequences which follow from the postulated state are deduced, but also of quite searching empirical observations of the behaviour both of modern European man and (more importantly) of primitive peoples like the Hottentots and the Caribs – the latter of whom, as Rousseau notes, 'have as yet least of all deviated from the state of nature'.[49] In this state of 'pure nature', says Rousseau, man

in the *Discourse*, in the fragments expunged from or associated with the *Discourse*, or in the *Essay on the Origin of Languages*, to suggest that Rousseau ever wished to cast serious doubt on the biblical account of the historical origins of mankind, or to put forward any theory of his own as an alternative to it. In the *Discourse*, his account of the 'natural' man is not inconsistent with the biblical account of human origins, because it involves propositions of a different order. And in the *Essay*, as we shall see later, although the new theory of development which he there propounds *is* of the same order as the biblical theory, it is not inconsistent with it, since he starts *his* story only with the dispersion of mankind after the Flood. The fashionable interpretation reads far too much into the proximity of Rousseau's statement about 'laying all facts aside' to the comment on the biblical account which immediately precedes it. This comment (which is reproduced in note 44 above) was intended merely to give the *coup de grâce* to the writers whom Rousseau was accusing of having fathered on man in the state of nature various attributes which were in fact acquired by him in society. It has not even entered the heads of these writers, Rousseau says, 'to doubt whether the state of nature ever existed' – in spite of the clear evidence in Genesis that it had never in fact done so.

[47] *Discourse* (Everyman edn), p. 47.
[48] *Ibid.*, p. 47.
[49] *Ibid.*, p. 71. The footnotes to the *Discourse* (most of which, as I have already noted, are omitted from the Everyman edition) contain a great deal of factual information about savage peoples, largely gathered from the contemporary voyage literature.

will be found 'wandering up and down the forests, withou industry, without speech, and without home, an equal stran ger to war and to all ties, neither standing in need of h fellow-creatures nor having any desire to hurt them, an perhaps even not distinguishing them one from another'. But although his state is close to animality, he is not in fac an animal: he possesses certain innate qualities – notably fre will,[51] and 'perfectibility', or the 'faculty of self-improve ment'[52] – which the beasts do not possess at all. Nor is his stat necessarily an unhappy one: indeed, Rousseau goes out of h way on a number of occasions to emphasise the advantage of his situation relative to that in which modern 'civilised man finds himself.[53]

In summing up the first part of the *Discourse*, in order t prepare the way for the second part, Rousseau stresses tw points – first, that in this 'supposed primitive state'[54] th inequality of mankind 'is hardly felt, and . . . its influence i next to nothing'; and, second, that in such a state 'huma *perfectibility*, the social virtues, and the other faculties whic natural man potentially possessed, could never develop o themselves, but must require the fortuitous concurrence o many foreign causes that might never arise, and withou which he would have remained forever in his primitive con ditions'.[55] In the second part of the *Discourse*, then, it is thes 'fortuitous foreign causes' with which Rousseau mainly con cerns himself – 'the different accidents', as he puts it in memorable passage, 'which may have improved the huma understanding while depraving the species, and made ma wicked while making him sociable'.[56]

Rousseau's analysis of the state of 'pure nature' in the firs part of the *Discourse*, as we have seen, was 'conditional and hypothetical' in the sense that it was 'rather calculated t explain the nature of things, than to ascertain their actua

[50] *Ibid.*, p. 72. [51] *Ibid.*, p. 54. [52] *Ibid.*, pp. 54 and 74.
[53] Rousseau's emphasis on these advantages should not of course be con strued as indicating that in his opinion the state of 'pure nature' repre sented an ideal condition to which we should strive to return. The bes state for man, the state which according to Rousseau 'men were meant t remain in', was in fact a much more advanced state, similar to that i which 'the savages of America' were found. See below. p. 82.
[54] *Discourse*, p. 72. [55] *Ibid.*, p. 74. [56] *Ibid.*, p. 74.

origin'. His analysis in the second part of the *Discourse* of the various 'accidents' which may have led men away from this 'supposed primitive state', however, was clearly intended to have a closer correspondence with historical fact. The transition from the (supposed) 'state of nature' to the (actual) 'state of society', Rousseau says in effect, must be conceived to have taken place over historical time, and to have consisted of a 'slow succession of events and discoveries'[57] by which society was led through a number of 'intermediate situations'.[58] Now, 'when two facts are given as real', Rousseau argues, 'and have to be connected by a series of intermediate facts, which are unknown or supposed to be so', it is 'within the province of history . . . to supply such facts as may connect them'; and it is 'in the province of philosophy, when history is silent, to determine similar facts to serve the same end'.[59] In the present case, history *is* silent on certain points, or at any rate its voice is indistinct, so philosophy has to step in and try to fill the gap by making a choice, on probabilistic grounds, between a number of potential historical paths which mankind might in fact have taken. The making of this choice certainly involves 'conjectures', but, Rousseau argues, 'such conjectures become reasons when they are the most probable that can be drawn from the nature of things, and the only means of discovering the truth'.[60]

The particular conjectural–historical path chosen by Rousseau is so well known that a brief sketch of it will suffice here. 'Infant man', he assumes, was at first a gatherer, but he soon became obliged to enter into competition for the fruits of the earth with animals and with other men. Then, on the seashore and the banks of rivers, with the invention of the hook and line, he became a fisherman; and in the forests, with the invention of the bow and arrow, he became a hunter.[61] His superiority over the animals increased, and 'of those which could serve him or harm him' he became in time 'the master of some and the scourge of others'.[62] Gradually

---

[57] *Ibid.*, p. 76.   [58] *Ibid.*, p. 103.
[59] *Ibid.*, p. 75.   [60] *Ibid.*, p. 74.
[61] *Ibid.*, pp. 76–7.
[62] *Ibid.*, p. 77. The phrase 'of those which could serve him or harm him' has been omitted from the translation in the Everyman edition, presumably owing to an oversight.

he began on occasion to enter into one or another kind of 'loose association' with other individuals.[63] Then came 'the epoch of a first revolution', prepared for by the invention of stone implements and the art of making huts, which ended the wandering life, 'established and distinguished families', 'introduced a kind of property',[64] and brought man much closer to the 'last point of the state of nature'.[65] The period which supervened immediately after this 'first revolution', Rousseau argues, was 'the happiest and most stable of epochs' and 'altogether the very best man could experience; so that he can have departed from it only through some fatal accident, which, for the public good, should never have occurred'.[66] The example of savages, says Rousseau, 'most of whom have been found in this state, seems to prove that men were meant to remain in it, that it is the real youth of the world, and that all subsequent advances have been apparently so many steps towards the perfection of the individual but in reality towards the decrepitude of the species'.[67] The particular 'fatal accident' which took man out of this golden age and produced the second 'great revolution' in his condition was according to Rousseau the invention of 'metallurgy and agriculture', which introduced property in land and the division of labour, with all their disastrous consequences. 'Equality disappeared, property was introduced, work became indispensable, and vast forests became smiling fields which man had to water with the sweat of his brow, and where slavery and misery were soon seen to germinate and grow up with the crops.'[68]

It is magnificent, but it is not the four stages theory. There are of course certain important resemblances between the theory of development in the *Discourse* and the versions of the four stages theory put forward by (say) Turgot and Smith

[63] *Ibid.*, p. 78.   [64] *Ibid.*, p. 79.
[65] *Ibid.*, p. 76.   [66] *Ibid.*, pp. 82–3.
[67] *Ibid.*, p. 83. Cf. Rousseau's eulogy of 'the savages of America' in his earlier *Discourse on the Arts and Sciences*, where he refers to the Americans as 'those happy nations, who did not even know the name of many vices, which we find it difficult to suppress . . . whose simple and natural government Montaigne preferred, without hesitation, not only to the laws of Plato, but to the most perfect visions of government philosophy can ever suggest' (Everyman edn, p. 9, footnote 1).
[68] *Discourse*, p. 83.

out the differences are much more striking than the resemblances. Quite apart from the fact that Rousseau conceives
and defines both the 'first' and the 'last' stages differently
from Turgot and Smith, his account of the path taken by
mankind to get from one to the other is also different from
theirs in a number of crucial respects. It is obvious, for
example, that according to Rousseau's account mankind
'progresses' (in so far as it can be said to 'progress' at all)
only up to the invention of metallurgy and agriculture, and
definitely not beyond it. It is not quite so obvious, but equally
important, that Rousseau is much further from the concept of
an autonomous law-governed process of development than
Turgot and Smith. Admittedly he tries in the second part of
the *Discourse* to put the 'slow succession of events and discoveries' into what he calls 'the most natural order';[69]
admittedly, too, he sometimes speaks of certain events
'naturally' giving rise to others.[70] Much more often, however,
we find him talking in terms of 'different accidents', 'the
fortuitous concurrence of many foreign causes', and so on.
Nor, in the *Discourse*, are the successive 'stages' clearly and
consistently linked to different modes of subsistence: men
certainly start off on their path of development by becoming
hunters and fishers, but the 'first revolution' (which ushers
in permanent settlements) is not specifically associated with
the arrival of a new mode of subsistence, and the second
'great revolution' is associated with the invention of metallurgy as well as with that of agriculture.

If one really wants to read certain elements of the four
stages theory into Rousseau's account one can of course do
so – just as one can in the case of Lucretius's *De Rerum
Natura*, to which Rousseau's *Discourse* in fact bears an
interesting resemblance.[71] But there is one very important
element of the four stages theory which it would be virtually
impossible to read into it. The *Discourse* makes no reference
whatever to a pastoral stage. There is a vague statement at
one point about the capacity of animals to serve man;[72]

---

[69] *Ibid.*, p. 76.
[70] See, e.g. *ibid.*, pp. 77 and 84.
[71] Cf. A. O. Lovejoy and G. Boas, *Primitivism and Related Ideas in Antiquity* (Octagon Books, New York, 1965), pp. 240–2.
[72] See above, p. 81.

and an equally vague statement later on about lands *and*
cattle being the only real possessions men can have.[73] But
that is all. The idea that men might have passed through a
pastoral *stage* in their socio-economic development is completely absent from the *Discourse*. The definite impression
that one gets, in fact, is that men were still hunters and
fishers when agriculture began to be practised.[74]

If all we had were the *Discourse*, then, it would be difficult
to regard Rousseau as one of the pioneers of the four stages
theory in the 1750s. But fortunately (or unfortunately, perhaps, since it has brought a great number of problems in its
wake) we also have Rousseau's *Essay on the Origin of Languages*, which, although not published until three years after
his death,[75] may well have been substantially completed at
any rate by the early 1760s, and which does embody a version of the four stages theory proper.

In the *Discourse*, as we have seen, Rousseau's analysis of
the 'state of nature' was up to a point different in kind from
his analysis of the process of transition from the 'state of
nature' to the 'state of society': the former consisted of propositions which Rousseau insisted 'must not be considered
as historical truths', whereas the latter consisted of propositions which, although still in a certain sense 'conjectural',
were designed to have a closer correspondence with historical

[73] *Discourse*, p. 87.
[74] Cf. *ibid.*, pp. 80, 82, 83, and 84. H. Grange, in an interesting article on
the relation between the *Discourse* and the *Essay* (*Annales Historique
de la Révolution Française*, Vol. 39, 1967, pp. 291–307), remarks on
the fact that there is no reference to a pastoral stage in the *Discourse*
whereas in the *Essay* such a stage definitely comes into the picture and
considerable emphasis is laid upon it. But this difference, M. Grange
argues (p. 296), is in fact very superficial, because pasturage (like gathering, hunting, and fishing) can be practised without involving the establishment of relations of exchange, and therefore without inducing the
transition from the state of nature to the civil state. This may possibly be
true: but pasturage, surely, does involve the establishment of a new and
important form of *property*, and thus a new and important potential
source of inequality. There is another, much simpler, possible explanation
of the absence of a pastoral stage in the *Discourse* – namely, that Rousseau
at the time when he wrote this work had not yet begun to think in terms
of a pastoral stage in the development process.
[75] It first appeared in 1781, in a collection of Rousseau's *Traités sur la
Musique*. The edition of the *Essay* to which I shall refer in what follows
is the one published in 1970 by Guy Ducros, Bordeaux, and edited (very
competently) by Charles Porset.

truths. The first methodological difference one notices between the *Discourse* and the *Essay* is that in the relevant section of the latter – the 'long digression'[76] on the origin and development of society upon which Rousseau embarks in chapter IX[77] – the *whole* of the analysis (both of the starting-point and of the process of development from it) is clearly intended as a statement of historical fact. In the *Essay*, Rousseau is no longer concerned with evaluating the human institution which he is now studying (i.e. language), or with assessing the extent to which it is or is not 'natural' to mankind: all he is concerned to do is to trace out as accurately as possible its historical roots and the main paths of its development. Thus in the *Essay* there is no more talk about 'conjecture', or 'mere conditional and hypothetical reasonings', and much more emphasis on the problem of reconciling different sources of evidence.

The second methodological difference between the *Discourse* and the *Essay* relates to Rousseau's attitude towards the mode of subsistence. In the *Discourse*, as we have seen, the emphasis on the mode of subsistence was rather haphazard, and the successive 'stages' of development were not clearly and consistently linked to different modes of subsistence. In the *Essay*, by way of contrast, the mode of subsistence is explicitly given pride of place, and the linkage between the successive 'stages' and different modes of subsistence is very clear and consistent indeed. Not only this, but the *Essay* contains a generalised statement about the key role of the mode of subsistence (and of climate) which was quite advanced for its time and is in fact almost worthy of Smith or Turgot:

Thus, whether we are inquiring into the origin of the arts, or whether we are looking at manners in the earliest ages, we see that everything is fundamentally related [*tout se raporte dans son principe*] to the means of providing for subsistence; and so far as concerns those of these means which gather men together, they are determined by the climate and by the nature of the soil.[78]

[76] *Essay*, p. 89.   [77] *Ibid.*, pp. 91–127.
[78] *Ibid.*, p. 107. Cf. the similar statement in the fragment on the influence of climate which was apparently excluded from the *Discourse* (Pléiade edn of Rousseau's *Oeuvres Complètes*, Vol. III, p. 530).

Social science and the ignoble savage

In chapter IX of the *Essay*, Rousseau begins by giving us a picture of mankind in the 'first times', which he defines in a footnote as 'those of the dispersion of men, at whatever age of the human race one wishes to fix its period'.[79] Men in these times, says Rousseau, were scattered over the face of the earth: 'They had no society but that of the family, no laws but those of nature, no language but that of gesture and a few inarticulate sounds.[80] They were not bound by any idea of common brotherhood; and, having no arbiter but force, they believed themselves to be enemies of one another.'[81] At first sight we seem here to be once again in the state of 'pure nature' described in the first part of the *Discourse*, but we soon see that this is not in fact so. The men of whom Rousseau is talking at this particular point in the *Essay* are already settled in their huts, enjoying the 'golden age':

These times of barbarism were the golden age; not because men were united, but because they were separated. Each, it is said, considered himself the master of everything; that may be, but nobody knew about or desired anything but what was near at hand: his needs, far from bringing him nearer to his fellow-men, took him further away from them. Men, if you like, attacked one another when they met, but they met rarely. Everywhere there reigned the state of war, and the whole earth was at peace.[8]

The question of what these men had been like in the earlier period of the dispersion, before they became settled in their huts, is not dealt with until a little later in chapter IX.

In the meantime, Rousseau proceeds to give us a very important additional piece of information about these 'first men' – i.e. that they were 'hunters *or shepherds, and not husbandmen; the first form of property [biens] was flocks and herds, and not fields*'.[83] This is indeed news: in the *Discourse*, the 'first men' were exclusively hunters and remained so right up to the time of the second 'great revolution'; and

---

[79] *Essay*, p. 91, footnote 1. From what follows (particularly the reference to the 'first dispersion' on p. 97) it seems virtually certain that Rousseau was thinking of the dispersion of Noah's descendants after the Flood.

[80] This proposition is backed up by a footnote reference to the behaviour of 'the savages of America' (*Essay*, p. 91, footnote 2).

[81] *Ibid.*, p. 91.   [82] *Ibid.*, pp. 95–6.

[83] *Ibid.*, p. 97. (My italics.)

he 'first form of property' was not flocks and herds, but huts.
But Rousseau leaves aside for a moment the question of how
men came to be shepherds: the main point which he wishes
to emphasise at this juncture is simply that 'before property
in land was shared out, nobody dreamed of cultivating it'.[84]
In its capacity as a mode of subsistence, in other words, agriculture was a relatively late invention.

Now comes a crucial transition in the argument, which
enables Rousseau not only to get round to the two questions
he has broached but not yet solved (what men had been like
in the earlier period of the dispersion, and how they came to
be shepherds), but also to bring the biblical evidence into the
picture and to reconcile it with the secular evidence. You
will reply to what I have just said about the late invention
of agriculture, says Rousseau to his reader, by reminding me
that Cain was a husbandman and that Noah planted vine-
yards. The answer to this is that Cain, when he became a
fugitive, was forced to abandon agriculture, and that the
wandering life of Noah's descendants made them forget
about it too:

During the first dispersion of the human race, until the family
was settled [*arrêtée*] and man had a fixed habitation, there was
no more agriculture. Peoples who are not settled do not know
how to cultivate the land: such in times past were the nomads,
such were the Arabs living in their tents, the Scythians in their
waggons; such are still today the wandering Tartars, and the
savages of America.[85]

All the available evidence, both secular and sacred, Rousseau
argues, leads towards the same conclusion. It is true that we
already find agriculture on a large scale in the times of the
Patriarchs – but we have to remember that according to the
Scriptures ten very long-lived generations elapsed between
the 'first times' and the times of the Patriarchs. What were
men doing, then, during those ten generations?

Adam spoke, Noah spoke – all right. Adam had been taught by
God himself. In separating from one another, the children of Noah

4 *Ibid.*, p. 97.
5 *Ibid.*, pp. 97–8. The appearance here of the Arabs and Tartars, who had
not been mentioned at all in the *Discourse*, is worthy of note.

abandoned agriculture, and the common language perished wit
the first society . . .[86]

Scattered in the vast desert of the world, men fell back int
the stupid barbarism in which they would have been found i
they had sprung from the earth. If we follow this very natura
train of thought, it is easy to reconcile the authority of Scriptur
with the ancient records, and we are not reduced to describin
as fables those traditions which are as old as the peoples wh
have transmitted them to us.[87]

It now appears, then, that mankind at one stage in it
career did after all fall back into something rather like tha
state of 'pure nature' which was postulated (for different pur
poses) in the *Discourse*.[88] But Rousseau spends no more tim
on this in the *Essay*. He proceeds immediately to present hi
version of the four stages theory, in a passage which deserve
extended quotation:

In this state of brutishness it was necessary to live. The mos
active, the most able-bodied, those who were always going ahead
could live only on the fruits of the earth and by hunting: thu
they became hunters, violent and bloodthirsty; then, as time
passed, warriors, conquerors, and usurpers . . .

The greater number, less active and more peaceable, settled
down as soon as they could, gathered livestock together, tamed
them, and made them obedient to the will of man; in order to live
on them, they learned to look after them and to breed them, and
thus the pastoral way of life began.

Human industry increases with the needs that give birth to it
Of the three manners of life possible for man, namely hunting
the care of flocks and herds, and agriculture, the first trains the
body in strength, dexterity, and speed, and the mind in courage
and guile: it hardens men and makes them fierce. The country of
the hunters is not for very long that of the hunt. The game ha
to be pursued afar: hence horsemanship . . . The pastoral art
father of repose and the lazy passions, is the one which is the
most self-contained. It provides man, almost without any trouble,

---

[86] 'This would have happened', Rousseau proceeds, 'even if there had
never been a Tower of Babel.' There is a very distinct echo of Bernard
Lamy in this statement: see the 5th edition of the latter's *La Rhetorique,
ou L'Art de Parler* (Amsterdam, 1712), p. 82.

[87] *Essay*, p. 103.

[88] In the *Discourse*, the possibility that men might at some stage have 'fallen
back' into the state of pure nature had been virtually dismissed (cf.
Discourse, p. 45).

with his sustenance and his clothing; it even provides him with his dwelling . . . With regard to agriculture, which is slower to appear, it depends upon all the arts; it ushers in property, government, laws, and by degrees misery and crime . . .

To the foregoing division there correspond the three states of man considered in relation to society. The savage is a hunter, the barbarian is a shepherd, and the civilised man [*l'homme civil*] is a husbandman.[89]

Immediately after this account there follows what is obviously intended as a kind of succinct generalisation of it – the remark already quoted above to the effect that 'everything is fundamentally related to the means of providing for subsistence', etc.; and the remainder of chapter ix consists of an elaborate statement, *à la* Montesquieu, of the different ways in which the climate and the nature of the soil may influence (and as a matter of historical fact have actually influenced) those of these means which gather men together'.

All in all, this is quite an impressive performance, and in spite of the fact that Rousseau still discounts the possibility of 'progress' after the agricultural stage has supervened, it has a much stronger claim to be regarded as a version of the four stages theory than the relevant passages in the *Discourse*. As I have already noted above, the contact between analysis and historical fact is appreciably closer in the *Essay* than in the *Discourse*, and the emphasis on the mode of subsistence is far greater and much less alloyed by extraneous factors. It is true, of course, particularly if one is looking at the problem of the relation between the *Discourse* and the *Essay* purely in terms of the comparability of the 'chronologies' which they respectively embody, that the two documents can fairly readily be 'reconciled' with one another – at any rate up to a point.[90] But if we look at them from the point of view of the history of the four stages theory, they cannot quite so easily be 'reconciled'. In the *Essay*, the adoption of permanent settlements certainly takes its place as one

9 *Essay*, pp. 103–7. Cf. *ibid.*, p. 57; and cf. also the Pléiade edition of the *Oeuvres Complètes*, Vol. iii, p. 532. The influence of Montesquieu seems fairly apparent in some of these formulations.
0 The most illuminating exercise of this kind is that carried out by Michèle Duchet in the chapter on Rousseau in his *Anthropologie et Histoire au Siècle des Lumières* (Maspero, Paris, 1971).

of the important preconditions of the rise of agriculture as a
mode of subsistence, but it is no longer presented as a 'revolu
tion', whether the 'first' or any other; and so far as the
second 'great revolution' of the *Discourse* is concerned, thi
is described in the *Essay* exclusively in terms of the change
over to agriculture, without any specific mention of the in
vention of metallurgy. In the *Essay*, too, a pastoral stage
makes its appearance for the first time in Rousseau's work
Admittedly hunting and pasturage are presented, at least on
the face of it, as *alternative* stages: as men emerge from the
'state of brutishness' they are said to become *either* hunter
or shepherds. But there is a footnote in which Rousseau
seems at least to make a bow in the direction of the notion
that hunting and pasturage were successive rather than alter
native stages;[91] he specifically recognises that 'the first form
of property was flocks and herds, and not fields'; he states
clearly that the first compacts and the first quarrels among
men were associated with the ownership of this 'first' form of
property;[92] and he certainly leaves one with the impression
that at the time when the agricultural stage supervened the
majority of people were leading a pastoral rather than a
hunting way of life.[93]

The question of whether Rousseau should or should not be
regarded as one of the early pioneers of the four stages
theory therefore resolves itself into the question of when
exactly he wrote chapter IX of the *Essay*. This is a question
which will probably never be finally resolved.[94] My own feel
ing about it is that although the *Essay* may well have been
'to begin with' [*d'abord*] a 'fragment of the *Discourse on
Inequality*', as Rousseau himself seems to have described it,[95]
a fairly substantial amount of rewriting and elaboration of a

[91] The footnote appears on p. 105 of the *Essay*. It contains, incidentally, yet
another reference to the Americans.
[92] *Ibid.*, p. 117.
[93] A number of different passages in the *Essay* (particularly in the section on
pp. 107–17) strongly suggest this.
[94] The issues involved have been discussed by a large number of scholars,
including most notably Michèle Duchet (*op. cit.*, Part II, ch. 3, *passim*) and
Jacques Derrida (*De la Grammatologie*, Éditions de Minuit, Paris, 1967,
Part II, ch. 3, *passim*). There is a good summing-up by the editor in the
edition of the *Essay* to which I have been referring, pp. 7–24.
[95] *Essay*, p. 11.

number of sections probably took place at various stages between 1755 (when the *Discourse* appeared) and 1761–3 (when
the *Essay* had apparently reached something like its final
form). In particular, it seems to me very probable indeed that
much of chapter IX of the *Essay* was written some time after
the *Discourse*: on no other supposition does it seem possible
to explain (*inter alia*) the manifest absence of shepherds from
the *Discourse* and their equally manifest presence in the
Essay. Whether this development of Rousseau's thought was
original or derivative, whether it was the fruit of his own independent researches (perhaps inspired by a re-reading of
Montesquieu) or of the contemplation of other people's versions (whether written or oral) of the four stages theory, we
shall probably never know. And perhaps it does not really
matter. The interesting and important point is that as we go
from the *Discourse* to the *Essay* we see mirrored, as it were,
a movement which is observable over a period of time in the
social thought of the Enlightenment taken as a whole: a
movement from the simple idea that 'in the beginning all the
World was *America*' to the broader and more sophisticated
idea that while 'in the beginning' the world may indeed have
been America, it was not long before it became Arabia and
Tartary, and then Palestine.

By the end of the 1750s three more French thinkers – Quesnay, Helvétius, and Goguet – had made use of one or another
version of the four stages theory. So far as Quesnay is concerned, his expression of the theory in the 1750s seems to
have been exclusively an oral one, and the only evidence we
have about it is a letter from Mirabeau written (to Rousseau,
oddly enough) ten years after the occasion concerned – the
famous interview betwen Quesnay and Mirabeau at Ver-
sailles in 1757 at which Mirabeau was converted to Physiocracy. During this interview Quesnay reportedly explained to
Mirabeau

his system, or rather . . . that of nature; how the first men,
whether shepherds or huntsmen, etc., had lived on the spontaneous products of nature; how the population of nations which
have never engaged in cultivation always remains the same without any increase, and how they lead a nomadic existence in order

to plunder the successive products; how the business of cultivation has caused nations to become settled; how the increase in products can proceed only from their quality as wealth; their quality as wealth only from their exchange value; and their exchange value only from the consumption of these products . . .[96]

This is all no doubt extremely vague; and it is true that we cannot have a great deal of faith in Mirabeau's accuracy as a reporter. But I do not think that we would be reading too much into it if we regarded the statement just quoted as a first draft, so to speak, of the much more explicit and elaborate version of the four stages theory which Quesnay and Mirabeau included in their *Philosophie Rurale* in 1763.[97]

Helvétius's version of the theory appeared first in his *De l'Esprit* (1758).[98] This work is divided up into a number of 'discourses', and it is in the third of these that the four stages theory is introduced. In the first discourse, he has endeavoured to prove that '*physical sensibility* and *memory* are the productive causes of all our ideas; and that all our *false judgements* are the effect either of our *passions*, or of our ignorance'.[99] In the second discourse, his theme has been that 'in matters of *morality* as well as of *intellect* [*esprit*], it is *interest* alone which dictates all our *judgements*';[100] and he has illustrated this theme by referring to a number of apparently ridiculous and cruel customs which upon closer investigation are seen to have 'real or apparent utility' to the societies concerned, given the particular conditions of life obtaining in them.[101] In the third discourse, the conclusion towards which he is arguing is that 'all men . . . have in them the *physical power* to raise themselves up to the *highest ideas*; and that the *differences in intellect* which we observe among them depend on the *different circumstances* in which they find

[96] R. L. Meek, *The Economics of Physiocracy* (Allen and Unwin, London, 1962), p. 18.
[97] Translated in *ibid.*, 57–64; and see below, pp. 132–3.
[98] The edition of *De l'Esprit* which I have used was published in Paris in 1758, and is described as a 'nouvelle édition, revue et corrigée sur un exemplaire non châtré de la premiere édition'.
[99] *Op. cit.*, Vol. i, p. vii.
[100] *Ibid.*, Vol. i, p. viii.
[101] *Ibid.*, Vol. i, pp. 131–4. One of the customs to which he refers here is the killing of old people in savage nations before the tribe goes off on a hunting expedition.

themselves placed, and the *different education* which they receive'.[102] It is in the course of an argument directed towards this general conclusion, in an important chapter on the origin of the passions, that the four stages theory suddenly makes its appearance.

'All that is, and all that will be', says Helvétius, 'is only a necessary development.' Men are put on earth 'under the guardianship of pleasure and pain', and their first task is to satisfy their needs. At first they will be savage people living in the forests, getting their subsistence by hunting and gathering.[103] Then, as population increases, the following sequence of events will occur:

After having, in part, destroyed the animals, when the peoples can no longer live by their hunting, the dearth of food will teach them the art of raising flocks and herds. These flocks and herds will supply their needs, and the hunting peoples will be changed into pastoral peoples. After some centuries, when the latter have increased enormously, and a given area of land cannot provide for the subsistence of a greater number of inhabitants without being made fertile through human labour, then the pastoral peoples will disappear and give place to agricultural peoples. The necessities of hunger, by revealing the art of agriculture to them, will soon afterwards teach them the art of measuring and dividing up land. When this division has been made, each man's ownership must be secured: thence arises a host of sciences and laws. Since different pieces of land, by reason of differences in their nature and their cultivation, yield different fruits, men will make exchanges with one another; they will appreciate the advantage that would be afforded by agreeing on a general means of exchange [*un échange général*] to represent all commodities; and they will choose for this purpose certain shells or certain metals. When societies have reached this point of perfection, all equality between men will be shattered . . .[104]

Here, then, is a succinct and relatively unambiguous statement of the four stages theory, with a single unifying principle (the pressure of population) embodied in it in order to account for progress through the first three stages. Helvétius does not make any further specific use of this theory in *De*

---

[102] *Ibid.*, Vol. II, pp. x–xi.
[103] *Ibid.*, Vol. II, pp. 2–3.
[104] *Ibid.*, Vol. II, p. 4.

l'Esprit, but in his later work *De l'Homme,* as we shall see later,[105] it plays a rather more important part.

Goguet's version of the theory is contained in the first volume of his remarkable work *De l'Origine des Loix, des Arts, et des Sciences; et de leurs Progrès chez les Anciens Peuples,* which appeared in the same year (1758) as Helvétius's *De l'Esprit.*[106] After the Flood and the confusion of tongues, and 'the dispersion of families which that event occasioned',[107] says Goguet (much in the manner of Turgot and Rousseau), the majority of people 'soon fell into a profound ignorance' and 'almost the whole earth was plunged into an extreme barbarism'.[108] Men were then essentially gatherers,[109] and 'led a life little different from that of the animals'.[110] But eventually families were re-united, political societies were established, the arts were born, and progress began – although it proceeded at different rates among different peoples:

Subsistence is the first and most important object with which people will concern themselves in newly-developing societies; but the means of acquiring it will have been more or less perfected according to the climate and the genius of the different peoples. In some countries, they will have begun by perfecting the art of hunting and fishing. Hunting above all, in the case of the majority of the peoples of antiquity, was the principal occupation of the first men. They devoted themselves to it as much through the need for subsistence as through the necessity of defending their lives against the attacks of ferocious beasts. There are still today a great many nations in both continents which are occupied only in hunting and fishing.

But industrious peoples were not slow in observing that among this huge number of animals spread out over the surface of the earth there were species which of their own accord gathered together and lived in a community. It was also perceived that these species were naturally less wild than the others. They

---

[105] Below, pp. 133–5.
[106] The edition of this work which I have used is stated on the title page to have been published at The Hague in 1758.
[107] *Op. cit.,* Vol. I, p. v; and see also p. xiv.
[108] *Ibid.,* Vol. I, p. 7. Cf. Turgot, in R. L. Meek, *Turgot on Progress, Sociology and Economics,* p. 42; and Rousseau, *Essay,* p. 103.
[109] *Ibid.,* Vol. I, pp. 10, 157, and 160.
[110] *Ibid.,* Vol. I, p. 8.

sought means to tame them, to shut them up in enclosures, and to cause them to multiply so that they might always have a certain quantity at their disposition. The majority of peoples in the first centuries, and for a long time afterwards, drew their subsistence only from flocks and herds. We know several powerful and very extensive nations which still practise the same manner of life. Their flocks and herds provide for all their needs. Finally men applied themselves to an examination of the different products of nature, and to finding ways of turning them to account.

The land offers a great number of plants and fruits, which even in the absence of cultivation provide men with pleasant and substantial food. They began by picking out the best species, and above all those which would keep for a long time after having been gathered: they were minded to lay in stocks of them. Then they learned the art of making them grow, and even of raising their quantity and quality by cultivation. It is to this discovery that we owe that prodigious number of arts and sciences which we enjoy today. So long as peoples knew no means of subsistence other than hunting, fishing, and tending their flocks and herds, they did not make any great progress in the arts. This way of life obliged them continually to change their place of abode, and, moreover, it did not compel them to make use of all the resources of which human industry is capable. The nations which do not practise any agriculture have only a very indifferent knowledge of the arts and sciences. But the cultivation of the land has obliged the peoples who devote themselves to it to settle in one area, and to invent a great number of arts which they need in order to succeed in it.[111]

And these 'arts' produced by agriculture, Goguet emphasises in a number of places, have in their turn 'produced commerce', and commerce has in due course 'multiplied and diversified the respective individual interests of different members of society'.[112]

In Goguet's book, the four stages theory is not just a passing notion: its ethos in fact pervades the greater part of the first volume. It is true that since Goguet's main emphasis is on the stimulus given to the arts by the introduction of agriculture, he tends in some places to group the pre-agricultural stages together.[113] The important point, however, is

[111] *Ibid.*, Vol. I, pp. 174–7.
[112] *Ibid.*, Vol. I, p. 64; and see also p. 69 and pp. 570ff.
[113] See, e.g. *ibid.*, Vol. I, pp. 34 and 36.

that the idea of successive developmental stages based on different modes of subsistence is used as one of the basic organising principles in the first main part of his account. It is important to note, too, that in Goguet's view the developmental process involves more or less continuous progress: he has no time for those who 'attribute chimerical virtues to the first centuries'.[114] And it is also important to note that he evidently does not consider that the use of the four stages theory involves anything in the way of 'conjecture' – at any rate in the pejorative sense of that word. One of his chief aims, in fact, in tracing the progress of laws, arts, and sciences among the ancient peoples, is, as he puts it, 'to give as little as possible to conjecture' and whenever humanly possible to follow 'history and the order of the facts'.[115] On those occasions, he says, when I have found myself almost destitute of facts and historical records, particularly in relation to the early ages,

I have referred to what the writers, both ancient and modern, have to tell us about the manners of savage peoples. My belief is that the behaviour of these nations can provide us with very sure and certain knowledge about the condition in which their first tribes found themselves, immediately after the confusion of tongues and the dispersion of families. One can derive from these reports, both ancient and modern, points of comparison which are capable of removing many doubts which would otherwise perhaps remain concerning certain extraordinary facts of which I have thought it proper to make use. The reports on America in particular have been of very great use to me in this connection. We can form an opinion about conditions in the old world shortly after the Flood, from those which still existed in the greater part of the new world at the time when it was discovered. In comparing what the first travellers tell us about America with the information which antiquity has handed down to us concerning the manner of life of all the peoples of our continent in the times that were regarded as the first ages of the world, we perceive a most striking conformity and a most pronounced relationship. Thus it is in order to back up the testimony of the writers of antiquity, and to bring home the possibility and even the reality of certain facts which they recount, that I have frequently brought together the reports of modern travellers and the histori-

[114] *Ibid.*, Vol. I, p. 743.   [115] *Ibid.*, Vol. I, p. xxviii; and see also pp. i–ii.

cal narratives of the writers of antiquity, and deliberately intermingled their accounts. These different outlines, when brought
together and compared, mutually support one another, and serve
as a basis for everything I have believed myself able to put
forward concerning the march of the human mind in its discoveries and its progress.[116]

For its time, this methodological statement was quite out-
standing. No one before Goguet had so clearly and carefully
defined the nature of the assistance which it was then believed that reports on primitive peoples – in particular the
Americans – might provide in the construction of socio-
economic histories of mankind's development.

Although no less than five French thinkers would thus
appear to have employed the four stages theory in one way
or another during the 1750s, one should not too hastily conclude that the theory must therefore have been part of every
French writer's stock-in-trade by the end of the decade. Voltaire and Diderot, for example, show few signs of having
been affected by the theory, either in the 1750s or later. And
it is an interesting fact, too, that there is remarkably little
trace of the theory in the *Encyclopedia*.[117] It is true that
M. René Hubert, whose authority in this field cannot lightly
be questioned, thought himself able to detect the presence in
the *Encyclopedia* of a stadial theory of development bearing
a close resemblance to our four stages theory.[118] This was
indeed a brilliant piece of detection on M. Hubert's part –
but perhaps it was just a shade too brilliant. In no individual
contribution to the *Encyclopedia* (not excluding those of
Turgot, Rousseau, and Quesnay) can any statement of the
four stages theory as such in fact be found: its existence has
to be deduced by putting together a large number of separate articles on such subjects as hunting, fishing, corn, cook-
ing, Scythians, Tartars, Hottentots, Eskimos, Iroquois, etc.

[116] *Ibid.*, Vol. I, pp. xxx–xxxii. Goguet's documentation throughout the book
is in fact very thorough and covers a vast range of authorities.
[117] The first seven volumes of the original *Encyclopedia* appeared at various
dates in the 1750s. In 1759, after the appearance of the seventh volume,
the publication of the work was prohibited (as it had also been on an
earlier occasion, in 1752), and the remaining ten volumes of text did not
appear until 1765, when they were all issued simultaneously.
[118] René Hubert, *Les Sciences Sociales dans l'Encyclopédie* (Paris, 1923),
pp. 289–93; and see also ch. IV, *passim*, and pp. 114–16.

And the composite picture which one then obtains is to say the least a little blurred. For example, one certainly gets the impression from articles such as 'Sauvages (Géog. Mod.)', 'Eskimaux', and 'Iroquois' that the peoples concerned live primarily by hunting and fishing; but the mode of subsistence of such peoples is often not given any special emphasis, and sometimes (e.g. in the article 'Hottentots') not even clearly stated. Again, if we read articles such as 'Scythes' and 'Tartares' we will certainly find mention of the fact that most of these peoples are shepherds and do not cultivate any land; but once again their mode of subsistence is not always emphasised, and in the case of other peoples (e.g. Bedouins) it is not even mentioned. From articles such as 'Blé', 'Agriculture', 'Vénerie', and 'Chasse', again, we may perhaps infer that in the opinion of the authors agriculture was a later and in some sense higher mode of subsistence than hunting and pasturage: but this is never stated at all clearly, and alternative inferences from what is said are perfectly possible.[119] Nor can one find in the *Encyclopedia* any very clear notion of a commercial stage in the development of society, although it is true that there are some quite interesting hints in the article 'Commerce' of the way in which industry and trade are generated by agriculture.[120]

In this connection it must of course be remembered that of the five French thinkers whom we have considered in this chapter, only two – Helvétius and Goguet – actually published their contributions in the 1750s, and that in the case of Helvétius the theory was used in only one chapter of a long book. Quesnay's contribution, if it was in fact made in the 1750s, was purely oral; Turgot's statement of the theory, although almost certainly written in the 1750s, was not published until many years later; and Rousseau's statement may not have been written in the 1750s at all. And these five, so far as I have been able to ascertain, are the only ones who could *possibly* qualify as pioneers. There was a sense, no doubt, in which the theory could be said to have been 'in the air' in France at this time. But it was not so obviously 'in the air' that it required no talent to observe it and pluck it out.

[119] It is interesting to note that in 'Chasse' it is argued that hunting probably came *after* pasturage.　　　[120] Cf. Hubert, *op. cit.*, pp. 292 and 300.

4

The Scottish pioneers of the 1750s

When we move the locale of our investigation into the early
origins of the four stages theory from France to Scotland, we
are immediately confronted with a set of rather similar problems concerning the dating of key contributions and the
extent to which the work of one thinker was derived from
that of another. In the case of Scotland, the basic question
relates to the role of Adam Smith in the emergence and development of the theory. The point here is that although the
first *published* versions of the theory in Scotland were those
of Sir John Dalrymple (1757) and Lord Kames (1758), a good
case can be made out for regarding Smith, rather than either
Dalrymple or Kames, as the originator of the theory. It is
true that there is no clear reference to the four stages theory
in any of Smith's *published* work until *The Wealth of Nations*
(1776). We now know for certain, however, that Smith used
the theory extensively in his lectures on Jurisprudence at
Glasgow University in the 1762–3 session; it seems *probable*
that he was already using a version of it when he started
delivering his full Jurisprudence course to the Moral Philosophy class at Glasgow in 1752–3; and it seems at least *possible* that he used a version of it in a course of lectures which
he gave in Edinburgh in 1750–1. Before we enter this field of
doubt and danger, however, let us consider briefly the contributions of Dalrymple and Kames – both of whom, it
should be noted at once, were members of Smith's circle.[1]

To Dalrymple belongs the honour, if such it be, of producing the earliest published version of the four stages
theory – or at any rate the earliest published version that I

---

[1] Some of Dalrymple's connections with Smith are noted by W. R. Scott in
his *Adam Smith as Student and Professor* (Glasgow, 1937), p. 81, and by
John Rae in his *Life of Adam Smith* (London, 1895), pp. 40 and 75. On
Kames's connections with Smith, see A. F. Tytler, *Memoirs of Kames* (2nd
edn, Edinburgh, 1814), Vol. I, pp. 266–71.

have so far been able to find. It occurs in his *Essay Toward. a General History of Feudal Property in Great Britain* (1757) – a book in which an attempt was made by the author, con sciously following in the steps of Montesquieu,[3] 'to unite philosophy and history with jurisprudence, and to write ever upon a subject of law like to a scholar and a gentleman'.[4] Hi: version of the theory is to be found at the beginning o chapter III, which is entitled 'History of the Alienation o. Land-property'. In order to trace the progress of this 'curiou and interesting' subject, says Dalrymple, 'the progress o society must be traced'[5] – a task which is carried out in the following passage:

The first state of society is that of hunters and fishers; among such a people the idea of property will be confined to a few, and but very few moveables; and subjects which are immoveable, will be esteemed to be common. In accounts given of many American tribes we read, that one or two of the tribe will wander five or six hundred miles from his usual place of abode, plucking the fruit, destroying the game, and catching the fish throughout the fields and rivers adjoining to all the tribes which he passes, with out any idea of such a property in the members of them, as makes him guilty of infringing the rights of others, when he does so.

The next state of society begins, when the inconveniences and dangers of such a life, lead men to the discovery of pasturage During this period, as soon as a flock have brouzed upon one spot of ground, their proprietors will remove them to another; and the place they have quitted will fall to the next who pleases to take possession of it: For this reason such shepherds will have no notion of property in immoveables, nor of right of possession longer than the act of possession lasts. The words of Abraham to Lot are: 'Is not the whole land before thee? separate thyself, I pray thee, from me. If thou wilt take the left hand, then will I go to the right; or if thou depart to the right hand, then will I go to the left'. And we are told that the reason of this separation, was, the quantity of flocks, and herds, and tents, which each of

---

2 The edition of *Feudal Property* which I have used, and from which the quotations in the text are taken, is 'the second edition corrected and enlarged' which appeared in London in 1758. The quoted statements are substantially the same in the 1st edition of 1757.
3 See Dalrymple's references to Montesquieu in his dedication and preface (*Feudal Property*, pp. iv and ix).
4 *Ibid.*, p. ix.   5 *Ibid.*, p. 75.

hem had, and which the land was unable to support; lord Stairs wisely observes, that the parts of the earth which the patriarchs njoyed, are termed in the scripture, no more than their *posses-ions.*

A third state of society is produced, when men become so umerous, that the flesh and milk of their cattle is insufficient for heir subsistance, and when their more extended intercourse with each other, has made them strike out new arts of life, and particu-arly the art of agriculture. This art leading men to bestow thought nd labour upon land, increases their connection with a single portion of it; this connection long continued, produces an affection; nd this affection long continued, together with the other, pro-luces the notion of property in land . . .[6]

Dalrymple's version of the four stages theory, it will be noted, is oriented towards the problem of property, and stands fairly and squarely within the Grotius–Pufendorf–Locke tradition.[7] The basic idea is that in the hunting and fishing stage there is virtually no notion of property in things at all (except in a very small number of movables); that in the pastoral stage the notion of property is extended to a much larger number of movables (notably 'flocks, and herds, and tents'), but not as yet to immovables; and that it is only in the agricultural stage that the notion of property in land is generated. Like most of the later versions of the theory, Dalrymple's version embodies a principle (or rather, in his case, two separate principles) purporting to explain the transition from one 'state of society' to the next. Like most of the later versions, too, Dalrymple's adduces American society as an illustration of the first stage and patriarchal society as an illustration of the second. It is true that the passage quoted constitutes a three stages rather than a four stages theory, and that Dalrymple nowhere specifically delineates 'commerce' as the fourth stage. But as the sequel shows, he is at any rate fully seized of the importance of the 'degree of commerce' in a country,[8] seeing clearly that 'people living in towns . . . are in a more improved state of society than people living in the country',[9] and even in one place using

[6] *Ibid.*, pp. 75–6.   [7] Cf. above, pp. 13ff.
[8] *Feudal Property*, p. 103.   [9] *Ibid.*, p. 83.

the different 'degrees of commerce' in England and Scotland (in conjunction with the influential idea that 'power follows property') to explain the different degrees of power possessed by the Commons in these two countries.[10]

It is very noticeable, however, that Dalrymple, having stated the four (or three) stages theory quite unambiguously in the passage quoted above, makes very little specific use of it in what follows. It is true that he draws a number of comparisons between conditions in 'simple' or 'uncivilized' nations and those in 'polished' nations,[11] and that he frequently speaks in terms of the 'progress of society' through 'stages' of various kinds.[12] Only rarely, however, does he expressly (or even impliedly) relate these 'stages' to different modes of subsistence. The impression one is left with is that Dalrymple regarded the four stages theory as something whose use lay mainly, if not exclusively, in illuminating the problem of changes in the state of property. The idea that it could be made into a great generalising principle capable of illuminating a whole host of developmental problems, was still to come.

A not inconsiderable step in the direction of this idea was made by Kames in two works of his which appeared in 1758 – the second edition of his *Essays on the Principles of Morality and Natural Religion*[13] (the first edition of which had been published in 1751), and his well-known book *Historical Law-Tracts*.[14] In the *Essays*, it is true, the theory does not play a very important role. It is introduced only in chapter vii, entitled 'Of Justice and Injustice', in which Kames deals critically with Hume's views on the relations between justice and property; and although it is stated clearly enough, and in a rather wider context than it had been in Dalrymple's book the year before, its connection with the main burden of

---

[10] *Ibid.*, p. 272. Cf. p. 121, where Dalrymple speaks of a certain assertion seeming strange of 'so commercial a nation as the English'.

[11] See, e.g. *ibid.*, pp. 190–2, 253–4, and 258–9.

[12] See, e.g. *ibid.*, pp. 124, 126, and 223ff.

[13] *Essays on the Principles of Morality and Natural Religion* (2nd edn, London, 1758).

[14] *Historical Law-Tracts* (Edinburgh, 1758).

he argument is a little tenuous.[15] In the *Historical Law-Tracts*, however, the use of the theory is more pervasive – and also more interesting.

The theory appears initially in the form of a lengthy footnote in the first 'tract' in the book, dealing with the history of the criminal law, where it is used with some ingenuity to explain the 'early perfection of the criminal law in Egypt'.[16] The relevant passage is by no means unimpressive, and deserves extended quotation:

Hunting and fishing, in order for sustenance, were the original occupations of man. The shepherd life succeeded; and the next stage was that of agriculture. These progressive changes, in the order now mentioned, may be traced in all nations, so far as we have any remains of their original history. The life of a fisher or hunter is averse to society, except among the members of single families. The shepherd life promotes larger societies, if that can be called a society, which hath scarce any other than a local connection. But the true spirit of society, which consists in mutual benefits, and in making the industry of individuals profitable to others as well as to themselves, was not known till agriculture was invented. Agriculture requires the aid of many other arts. The carpenter, the blacksmith, the mason, and other artificers, contribute to it. This circumstance connects individuals in an intimate society of mutual support, which again compacts them within a narrow space. Now, in the first state of man, *viz.* that of hunting and fishing, there obviously is no place for government, except that which is exercised by the heads of families over children and domesticks. The shepherd life, in which societies are formed, by the conjunction of families for mutual defence, requires some sort of government; slight indeed in proportion to the slightness of the mutual connection. But it was agriculture which first produced a regular system of government. The intimate union among a multitude of individuals, occasioned by agriculture, discovered a number of social duties, formerly unknown. These behoved to be ascertained by laws, the observance of which must be enforced by punishment. Such operations cannot be carried on, otherwise than by lodging power in one or more persons, to direct the resolutions, and apply the force of the whole society. In short, it may be laid down as an universal

[15] The relevant passage appears on pp. 77–8 of the 2nd edition of the *Essays*.
[16] *Historical Law-Tracts*, Vol. I, p. 77, footnote.

maxim, that in every society, the advances of government toward perfection, are strictly proportioned to the advances of the society towards intimacy of union.

When we apply these reflections to the present subject, we find that the condition of the land of Egypt makes husbandry of absolute necessity; because in that country, without husbandry there are no means of subsistence. All the soil, except what is yearly covered with the river when it overflows, being a barren sand unfit for habitation, the people are confined to the low grounds adjacent to the river. The sandy grounds produce little or no grass; and however fit for pasture the low grounds may be during the bulk of the year, the inhabitants, without agriculture would be destitute of all means to preserve their cattle alive during the inundation. The Egyptians must therefore, from the beginning, have depended upon husbandry for their subsistence and the soil, by the yearly inundations, being rendered extremely fertile, the great plenty of provisions produced by the slightest culture, could not fail to multiply the people exceedingly. But this people lived in a still more compact state, than is necessary for the prosecution of husbandry in other countries; because their cultivated lands were narrow in proportion to their fertility. Individuals, thus collected within very narrow bounds, could not subsist a moment without a regular government. The necessity after every inundation, of adjusting marches by geometry naturally productive of disputes, must alone have early taught the inhabitants of this wonderful country, the necessity of due submission to legal authority. Joining all these circumstances, we may assuredly conclude, that, in Egypt, government was coeval with the peopling of the country; and this, perhaps, is the single instance of the kind. Government, therefore, must have long subsisted among the Egyptians in an advanced state; and for that reason it ceases to be a wonder, that their laws were brought to perfection more early than those of any other people.[17]

The next appearance of the theory in *Historical Law-Tracts* is in the second essay, dealing with the history of promises and covenants. Here the hunting, pastoral, and agricultural stages are reviewed only very briefly, and Kames concentrates on describing how 'the invention of agriculture produced to the industrious a superfluity, with which foreign necessaries were purchased'; how 'commerce' was then extended and a special class of merchants arose; and how

[17] *Ibid.*, Vol. I, pp. 77–80, footnote.

these developments increased the authority of promises and covenants.[18] Its final appearance[19] is in the third essay, dealing with the history of property, where it plays a very prominent part indeed, becoming in effect a kind of analytical framework within which a large portion of the argument is set. As an example of Kames's approach, two paragraphs from a key section of this essay may be quoted:

In the two first stages of the social life, while men were hunters or shepherds, there scarce could be any notion of land-property. Men being strangers to agriculture, and also to the art of building, if it was not of huts, which could be raised or demolished in a moment, had no fixed habitations, but wandred about in hords or clans, in order to find pasture for their cattle.[20] In this vagrant life men had scarce any connection with land more than with air or water. A field of grass might be considered as belonging to a hord or clan, while they were in possession . . . but the moment they removed to another quarter, there no longer subsisted any connection betwixt them and the field that was deserted. It lay open to new-comers, who had the same right as if it had not been formerly occupied. Hence I conclude, that while men led the life of shepherds, there was no relation formed betwixt them and land, in any manner so distinct as to obtain the name of Property.[21]

Agriculture, which makes the third stage of the social life, produced the relation of land-property. A man who has bestowed labour in preparing a field for the plough, and who has improved this field by artful culture, forms in his mind a very intimate connection with it. He contracts, by degrees, a singular affection for a spot, which, in a manner, is the workmanship of his own hands. He chuses to live there, and there to deposit his bones. It is an object which fills his mind, and is never out of thought at home or abroad. After a summer's expedition, or perhaps years of a foreign war, he returns with avidity to his own house, and to his own field, there to pass his time in ease and plenty. By such trials the relation of property being gradually evolved, is disjoined from possession; and to this disjunction, the lively perception of

18 The key passage will be found in *ibid.*, Vol. I, pp. 92–3.
19 Apart from two rather faint echoes in the sixth and seventh essays (see *ibid.*, Vol. I, pp. 297–8 and 313).
20 There is a footnote reference at this point to Herodotus's account of the Scythians.
21 There is a footnote reference at this point to 'the description given by Thucydides of the original state of Greece'.

property with respect to an object so considerable, mainly contributes.[22]

In the second of these two paragraphs there is a distinct – and rather suspicious – echo of Dalrymple;[23] but Kames's use of the four stages theory in these contributions of his in 1758 goes appreciably beyond Dalrymple's. Kames employs the theory to illuminate the history not only of property but also of government, criminal law, contract, and indeed (up to a point) of society as a whole; and there is no doubt that in this respect his version of the theory was more advanced than any other version actually *published* in the 1750s.

The operative word here is of course 'published'. Kames was a prolific writer but not, on the whole, a conspicuously creative one; and in none of his pre-1758 works have I been able to find any more than the vaguest hints of the four stages theory – even in contexts where one might reasonably have expected to find it (e.g. in discussions of property).[24] It is a particularly striking fact that although a quite unambiguous version of the theory appears in the second (1758) edition of Kames's *Essays on the Principles of Morality and Natural Religion*, there is virtually no trace of it in the first (1751) edition of this work.[25] If, then, Kames's use of the theory, and his realisation of its potentialities, date only from the mid-1750s or thereabouts, the question of whether

---

22 *Historical Law-Tracts*, Vol. I, pp. 144–6. Cf. also pp. 126–8 and 139–40.
23 Cf. the passage from Dalrymple quoted above, p. 101.
24 See, for instance, Kames's *Essays upon Several Subjects concerning British Antiquities* (Edinburgh, 1747), pp. 127–9, where the extension of the idea of property is discussed in more or less complete abstraction from the mode of subsistence. In the appendix to this work, however, there is a reference to man in his 'original state' – feeding, apparently, on acorns and water and living in 'scattered Habitations' – and to the fact that 'the Culture of Corn laid the Foundation of a more extensive Intercourse' (p. 194).
25 The only hint of anything like it is in the following two sentences (*Essays*, 1st edn, Edinburgh, 1751, p. 107): 'And accordingly we find, in perusing the history of mankind, as far back as we have any traces of it, that there never has been, among any people or tribe, such a thing as possession of goods in common. For, even before agriculture was invented, when men lived upon the natural fruits of the earth, tho' the plenty of pasture made separate possessions unnecessary, yet individuals had their own cattle, and enjoyed the produce of their cattle separately.' The only purpose of these statements, in their context, is to support Kames's theory that men have always been 'endued with the sense or feeling of property'.

he borrowed it from Smith is bound to arise. As I have already said, we know for certain that in his Jurisprudence course at Glasgow University, *at any rate in the 1762–3 session*,[26] Smith was employing a highly sophisticated version of the four stages theory, and using it to illuminate a wide range of problems relating to the history of law and government. What the question now at issue really comes down to, then, is simply whether Smith had also been employing the theory for these purposes in (or before) the mid-1750s, and, if so, whether details of his analysis were likely to have come to the notice of Kames. The answer to both these questions seems to me very probably to be 'yes'. It must be emphasised again, however, that we are here in a sphere of considerable uncertainty, in which all we can really do is to decide upon the direction in which the accumulated probabilities lead.

Smith was elected to the Chair of Logic at Glasgow University in January 1751, but did not start lecturing there until the beginning of the next academic session, in October 1751. The lectures which he gave during the 1751–2 session, in his capacity as Professor of Logic, were described as follows by John Millar:[27]

[26] It is to the 1762–3 session that the new set of student's notes of Smith's Glasgow lectures on Jurisprudence, which was discovered a few years ago in Aberdeen, specifically relates. These notes are being edited by Professor P. Stein, Professor D. Raphael, and myself, for publication in Glasgow University's forthcoming bicentennial edition of Smith's *Works and Correspondence*.

[27] In a communication to Dugald Stewart, on the occasion of the preparation by the latter of a *Biographical Memoir* of Smith which was read at the Royal Society of Edinburgh on 21 January and 18 March 1793. The quotations from this *Memoir* in the text are taken from the Kelley reprint of 1966, which in its turn was taken from Vol. x of Stewart's *Collected Works* (Edinburgh, 1858). Millar appears to have attended Smith's lectures as a student, very soon after Smith's arrival at Glasgow. 'It was also during Mr. Millar's studies at Glasgow', wrote John Craig, 'that he formed an acquaintance and friendship with Dr. Adam Smith. He had attended the Logic and Moral Philosophy Classes before Dr. Smith was appointed to these Chairs; but, having come to the University for instruction, not merely to go through a common routine, he eagerly seized the opportunity of hearing Lectures which excited, and fully gratified, the public expectation. His intelligence and ardour soon attracted Dr. Smith's notice, and at this time was laid the foundation of that mutual esteem, which, during the few years they were afterwards Professors in the same University, produced lasting intimacy and friendship. It is probable that

Social science and the ignoble savage

In the Professorship of Logic, to which Mr. Smith was appointed on his first introduction into this University, he soon saw the necessity of departing widely from the plan that had been followed by his predecessors, and of directing the attention of his pupils to studies of a more interesting and useful nature than the Logic and Metaphysics of the schools. Accordingly, after exhibiting a general view of the powers of the mind, and explaining so much of the ancient logic as was requisite, to gratify curiosity with respect to an artificial method of reasoning, which had once occupied the universal attention of the learned, he dedicated all the rest of his time to the delivery of a system of Rhetoric and Belles-lettres.[28]

But it is important (for reasons which will shortly appear) to note that during his first session at Glasgow Smith lectured not only to the Logic class but also to the Moral Philosophy class. When Smith came to Glasgow the then Professor of Moral Philosophy, Thomas Craigie, was ill, and before the session began it was arranged that the work of his class should be shared out among 'several masters', of whom Smith had agreed to be one.[29] In a letter to Professor William Cullen dated 3 September 1751 Smith wrote as follows: 'I shall, with great pleasure, do what I can to relieve him [Professor Craigie] of the burden of his class. You mention natural jurisprudence and politics as the parts of his lectures which it would be most agreeable for me to take upon me to teach. I shall very willingly undertake both.'[30]

In November 1751 Craigie died, and in April 1752 Smith was translated from his Chair of Logic to the now-vacant

Mr. Millar's attention was first directed to that particular line of research, in which he afterwards became so eminent, by Dr. Smith's Lectures and conversation; and it was with much pleasure, that he afterwards seized every opportunity of acknowledging his obligations to the instructions he at this time enjoyed' (*Account of the Life and Writings of John Millar, Esq.* by John Craig, prefixed to the 4th edn of Millar's *The Origin of the Distinction of Ranks*, Edinburgh, 1806, pp. iv–v).

[28] *Biographical Memoir*, p. 11.
[29] John Rae, *op. cit.*, pp. 42–4; and W. R. Scott, *op. cit.*, p. 140.
[30] John Rae, *op. cit.*, p. 44. Rae states (p. 43) that Cullen suggested those particular subjects 'as being the most likely to suit Smith's convenience and save him labour, inasmuch as he had lectured on them already' – i.e. at Edinburgh. It may well be true that Smith had already lectured on these subjects at Edinburgh, and that Cullen suggested them to Smith for this reason, but the evidence about this is by no means as clear-cut as Rae seems to have assumed. Cf. below, pp. 110ff.

The Scottish pioneers of the 1750s

Chair of Moral Philosophy. John Millar's description of Smith's Moral Philosophy course is as follows:

His course of lectures on this subject [Moral Philosophy] was divided into four parts. The first contained Natural Theology; in which he considered the proofs of the being and attributes of God, and those principles of the human mind upon which religion is founded. The second comprehended Ethics, strictly so called, and consisted chiefly of the doctrines which he afterwards published in his *Theory of Moral Sentiments*. In the third part, he treated at more length of that branch of Morality which relates to *Justice*, and which, being susceptible of precise and accurate rules, is for that reason capable of a full and particular explanation.

Upon this subject he followed the plan that seems to be suggested by Montesquieu; endeavouring to trace the gradual progress of jurisprudence, both public and private, from the rudest to the most refined ages, and to point out the effects of those arts which contribute to subsistence, and to the accumulation of property, in producing correspondent improvements or alterations in law and government. This important branch of his labours he also intended to give to the public; but this intention, which is mentioned in the conclusion of *The Theory of Moral Sentiments*, he did not live to fulfil.

In the last part of his lectures, he examined those political regulations which are founded, not upon the principle of *justice*, but that of *expediency*, and which are calculated to increase the riches, the power, and the prosperity of a State. Under this view, he considered the political institutions relating to commerce, to finances, to ecclesiastical and military establishments. What he delivered on these subjects contained the substance of the work he afterwards published under the title of *An Inquiry into the Nature and Causes of the Wealth of Nations*.[31]

Now this description, by and large, almost certainly relates to the course of lectures as Smith gave it during his earliest years in the Chair of Moral Philosophy, which was apparently when Millar himself attended them.[32] After the publication of *The Theory of Moral Sentiments* in 1759, it seems that the plan of Smith's lectures 'underwent a considerable

---

[31] *Biographical Memoir*, p. 12. The italics in the first sentence of the second paragraph are mine.

[32] See R. L. Meek, 'Smith, Turgot, and the "Four Stages" Theory' (*History of Political Economy*, Vol. 3, no. 1, Spring 1971), p. 17.

change',[33] with much less attention being devoted to Ethics and much more to Jurisprudence and Political Economy. But the interesting thing is that the first sentence of the second paragraph of Millar's above-quoted account, which apparently relates to – and no doubt accurately describes – the 'Jurisprudence' section of Smith's course *in its early form*, also accurately describes the relevant section of Smith's course *in 1762–3*. In that year, as we know from the new set of student's notes to which extensive reference will be made later in this chapter, Smith certainly endeavoured to 'trace the gradual progress of jurisprudence' and to point out 'the effects of those arts which contribute to subsistence . . . in producing correspondent improvements or alterations in law and government'. And in that year, too, the main analytical framework within which these 'effects' were considered was the four stages theory. It seems very likely, then, that Smith's use of the four stages theory, or at any rate of something closely resembling it, may be dated back at least as far as his early years in the Chair of Moral Philosophy at Glasgow.

May it perhaps be dated back even further – to the mysterious lectures which Smith gave in Edinburgh from 1748 until his departure for Glasgow in 1751? There seems little doubt that these Edinburgh lectures were in the main on the subject of Rhetoric and Belles Lettres, but there is some evidence that at any rate during the last year of his period of residence in Edinburgh Smith also lectured on Jurisprudence. We do not need to rely here on the slightly dubious evidence of John Callender of Craigforth, to the effect that Smith 'went to Edinburgh about 1750 and privately taught the Civil Law to Students of Jurisprudence':[34] we may instead rely on evidence provided – albeit indirectly – by Smith himself. Dugald Stewart tells us that in 1755 Smith drew up, and 'presented . . . to a society of which he was then a member', a paper giving 'a pretty long enumeration . . . of certain leading principles, both political and literary, to which he was anxious to establish his exclusive right, in order to prevent the possibility of some rival

---

[33] *Biographical Memoir*, p. 42.
[34] Edinburgh University MSS, La. ɪɪ, 451(2).

claims which he thought he had reason to apprehend'.[35] From this paper, which he says was actually in his possession, Stewart quotes (apparently verbatim) the following statement by Smith:

A great part of the opinions enumerated in this paper, is treated of at length in some lectures which I have still by me, and which were written in the hand of a clerk who left my service six years ago [i.e. presumably, in 1749]. They have all of them been the constant subjects of my lectures since I first taught Mr. Craigie's class, the first winter I spent in Glasgow, down to this day, without any considerable variation. They had all of them been the subjects of lectures which I read at Edinburgh the winter before I left it, and I can adduce innumerable witnesses, both from that place and from this, who will ascertain them sufficiently to be mine.[36]

The important thing to remember here is that the subjects upon which Smith lectured to 'Mr. Craigie's class' in the first winter he spent in Glasgow (i.e. 1751–2) were 'natural jurisprudence' and 'politics'.[37] What Smith is saying, then, in the statement quoted by Stewart, is that a large number of the 'leading principles' of one or both of these two subjects which he was putting forward in his Moral Philosophy lectures at Glasgow in 1755, and which he feared that some person or persons unknown were about to plagiarise, had all also been used by him ('without any considerable variation') as early as the winter of 1751–2 at Glasgow and even as far back as the winter of 1750–1 at Edinburgh.

Did this long list of 'leading principles', drawn up by Smith in 1755, include a version of the four stages theory? For reasons which I have sufficiently rehearsed elsewhere,[38] I would myself think it most unlikely that it did not do so. Certainly, at any rate, if we assume that Smith by 1755 had in fact arrived at the main principles of the theory of socio-economic development which we know for certain that he

---

[35] *Biographical Memoir*, p. 67.
[36] *Ibid.*, p. 68.   [37] Above, p. 108.
[38] 'Smith, Turgot, and the "Four Stages" Theory', pp. 20–3. Having now carried out the comparison mentioned in the footnote on p. 23 of this article, I no longer think it probable that the 'Division of Labour' and 'Land and Water Carriage' fragments are ascribable to the Edinburgh period. Apart from this, I think that my arguments still stand.

was putting forward in his lectures only seven years later, he might at the earlier date very reasonably have feared plagiarisation of these principles. Studies in the general field of the 'history of civil society' were at that time being given a considerable impetus in France by the work of Rousseau, as Smith himself pointed out in the *Edinburgh Review* in the same crucial year 1755;[39] and, nearer home and perhaps more importantly, men like Robertson and Kames were also showing signs of a growing interest in the early origins and gradual progress of society.[40] Even to one not possessed of Smith's rather suspicious and volatile temperament, it might well have appeared advisable round about 1755 to stake a claim to originality in respect of an idea which seemed as novel and significant as the four stages theory. And if Smith *was* putting forward a version of the four stages theory in the mid-1750s – in his Moral Philosophy lectures, in his contributions at the meetings of the various societies to which he belonged, and in private conversation – it is very likely that news of this would soon have come, whether directly or indirectly, to the ears of men like Dalrymple and Kames.[41]

All this, it may be said, is very largely conjecture. And it has to be admitted that there is as yet no absolutely unequivocal evidence that Smith had in fact used the four stages theory in his Jurisprudence lectures before Dalrymple and Kames published their versions of it in 1757 and 1758 respec-

---

[39] See *The Early Writings of Adam Smith* (Kelley reprint, ed. J. R. Lindgren, 1967), pp. 23ff.

[40] See 'Smith, Turgot, and the "Four Stages" Theory', pp. 20–2. In connection with Robertson, it is interesting – though hardly conclusive – to note that according to Alexander Carlyle he was 'so much addicted to the translation of other people's thoughts, that he sometimes appeared tedious to his best friends' (*Autobiography of Alexander Carlyle*, 2nd edn, 1840, p. 285). Cf. *ibid.*, pp. 170–1, where Carlyle makes the same point again, and also p. 287.

[41] Cf. *Biographical Memoir*, p. 11, where Millar is reported as saying: 'From the permission given to students of taking notes, many observations and opinions contained in these lectures have either been detailed in separate dissertations, or engrossed in general collections, which have since been given to the public.' The reference here is to Smith's lectures on Rhetoric and Belles Lettres; but the same would apply *a fortiori* to his Jurisprudence lectures. Cf. also *Biographical Memoir*, p. 67, where Stewart speaks of the dangers of plagiarisation to which Smith was 'peculiarly liable' owing to 'his situation as a Professor, added to his unreserved communications in private companies'.

tively. Nor, in those of Smith's writings ascribable to the period up to 1760 (his contributions to the 1755 issue of the *Edinburgh Review*,[42] his *Theory of Moral Sentiments*,[43] his essay on *The First Formation of Languages*,[44] and most (but not all) of the pieces published posthumously under the title *Essays on Philosophical Subjects*)[45] is there any clear and direct reference to the four stages theory as such. But there is in these earlier writings quite unmistakable evidence of a 'train of thinking' very similar to that which underlay the four stages theory; there is an appreciable number of references, often in significant contexts, to the American Indians; and there is evidence of a considerable interest in Rousseau's *Discourse on Inequality*. Let us take a brief glance at these aspects of Smith's earlier work, then, before we turn to the details of his Jurisprudence lectures.

Dugald Stewart, in the invaluable *Biographical Memoir* of Smith from which we have already quoted so extensively, draws special attention to Smith's omnipresent interest in what he (Stewart) calls '*Theoretical* or *Conjectural History*'. In the want of direct evidence about early societies, writes Stewart in a well-known passage,[46] 'we are under a necessity of supplying the place of fact by conjecture; and when we are unable to ascertain how men have actually conducted themselves upon particular occasions, of considering in what manner they are likely to have proceeded, from the principles of their nature, and the circumstances of their external situation'.[47] In this respect, Stewart argues, there is a close analogy between the enquiries in Smith's essay on *The First Formation of Languages* and those in 'a variety of his other

[42] *Early Writings of Adam Smith*, pp. 5–28.
[43] The 1st edition of *The Theory of Moral Sentiments* was published in 1759.
[44] This essay was not published until 1767, when it appeared at the end of the 3rd edition of *The Theory of Moral Sentiments*, but all the indications are that it was in fact written before 1760.
[45] *Early Writings of Adam Smith*, pp. 29–223. It seems very likely that the three essays placed under the general head of 'The Principles which Lead and Direct Philosophical Enquiries' (those on 'The History of Astronomy', 'The History of the Ancient Physics', and 'The History of the Ancient Logics and Metaphysics') were written at a relatively early date. The dating of the remaining essays which were included in the posthumous volume is more doubtful: cf. W. R. Scott, *op. cit.*, pp. 52, footnote, 59–61, 283, and 312.
[46] Cf. below, p. 232.　　　　　　　[47] *Biographical Memoir*, pp. 33–4.

disquisitions'[48] – notably *The Wealth of Nations* and his lectures on Jurisprudence.[49] In all these enquiries the basic
assumption was that men would always react in the same way
to the same 'external situation', since 'the principles of their
nature' were always essentially the same; and it was precisely
this assumption, or 'train of thinking', which made it *possible*,
in the want of direct evidence, to 'supply the place of fact by
conjecture'. I shall argue below[50] that Stewart pushes this
'analogy' too far: the role of 'conjecture' was in fact much
more significant in Smith's essay on *The First Formation of
Languages* than it was in *The Wealth of Nations* and his
lectures on Jurisprudence. Nevertheless, it is true that the
basic assumption, or 'train of thinking', was more or less the
same throughout; and, as Stewart very perceptively saw, it
was indeed its ubiquity which more than anything else gave
unity to Smith's thought as a whole.

In the essay on *The First Formation of Languages*, Smith
starts by asking how 'two savages, who had never been
taught to speak, but had been bred up remote from the
societies of men', *would* begin to form a language, what
names they *would* naturally bestow on new objects, and so
on.[51] In his essay on 'The History of Astronomy', again, in
order to elucidate the ideas of mankind in 'the first ages of
society', he postulates the existence of 'a savage, whose subsistence is precarious', and tries to reconstruct the way in
which a savage in that situation *would* regard natural phenomena.[52] It is clear that it would not have been sensible to
ask these questions, or possible to give plausible answers to
them, in the absence of the basic assumption just referred
to. And in *The Theory of Moral Sentiments* the same 'train of
thinking' is applied to the general problem of the origin
of the 'characters' and 'manners' of different nations: 'The
different situations of different ages and countries are apt,
in the same manner, to give different characters to the
generality of those who live in them . . .'[53] 'In general, the

[48] *Ibid.*, p. 37.   [49] *Ibid.*, p. 36.   [50] See below, pp. 234ff.
[51] *Early Writings of Adam Smith*, pp. 225ff.
[52] *Ibid.*, pp. 47ff. Cf. also p. 117.
[53] *Theory of Moral Sentiments* (6th edn, 1790), p. 236. The wording of this
passage, and of the others quoted and referred to in this paragraph and

style of manners which takes place in any nation, may commonly, upon the whole, be said to be that which is most suitable to its situation.'[54] Clearly there is an important and interesting sense in which the particular 'train of thinking' which underlies these statements also underlay the four stages theory; and the fact that Smith throughout his life apparently came near to being obsessed with it – not only in his writing, it seems, but even in his conversation[55] – can perhaps be taken as another indication that his promulgation of the four stages theory was likely to have been early rather than late, and original rather than derived.

Smith's use of this 'train of thinking' in his pre-1760 writings was associated with a number of significant references to the actual practices of contemporary savage peoples,[56] and in particular to those of the Americans.[57] In several places in *The Theory of Moral Sentiments*, for example, the Americans play an important role in the argument. In the chapter on the influence of 'custom and fashion' on moral sentiments, for instance, where the two passages just quoted occur, Smith makes an elaborate comparison between the characters and manners of 'civilized nations' on the one hand and 'savages and barbarians' on the other, using 'the savages in North America' as his main example of the latter, and showing (in accordance with his general principle) how the differences arise from differences in their situation.[58]

In his well-known 'Letter to the Authors of the Edinburgh Review' (1755), Smith's interest in savage peoples, and his concern with the problem of the development of society from savagery to civilisation, are made manifest in the long and fascinating section on Rousseau's *Discourse on Inequality* with which the 'Letter' concludes.[59] This section starts with an interesting comparison between Rousseau's system and that of Mandeville, and proceeds to a discussion of Rousseau's

---

the next, are substantially the same in the 6th edition of 1790 and the 1st edition of 1759.
[54] *Theory of Moral Sentiments* (6th edn), p. 242.
[55] *Biographical Memoir*, pp. 36–7.
[56] E.g. *Early Writings of Adam Smith*, pp. 48–9 and 246–7.
[57] E.g. *ibid.*, pp. 148 and 150–1.
[58] *Theory of Moral Sentiments*, pp. 230–44. Cf. also pp. 229, 331, and 337.
[59] *Early Writings of Adam Smith*, pp. 23–8.

evaluation of 'the savage life' – a subject, Smith says, of which 'no author ever proposed to treat . . . who did not excite the public curiosity'. Rousseau, he continues, 'intending to paint the savage life as the happiest of any, presents only the indolent side of it to view'.[60] In order to give 'a specimen of his [Rousseau's] eloquence', Smith translates three long passages from the *Discourse* – all of them, interestingly enough, being taken from the second part of that work, in which Rousseau deals with what Smith describes as 'the first beginnings and gradual progress of society'.[61] It seems fairly clear that Smith chose these particular passages not solely because of their eloquence, but also because they made points or raised problems in which Smith himself was interested. It should be noted, however, that while Smith on several occasions praised Rousseau's eloquence,[62] he also described the *Discourse* as 'a work which consists almost entirely of rhetoric and description';[63] and in another place he characterised Rousseau as an author 'more capable of feeling strongly than analising accurately'.[64] No doubt Smith felt that the analysis of the 'gradual progress of society' which he himself had by now worked out was much more 'accurate' than Rousseau's.

Let us now turn, then, to this analysis of the progress of society, in the form in which, according to the student's report, Smith expounded it in his lectures on Jurisprudence to his Moral Philosophy class at Glasgow in the 1762–3 session.[65] The four stages theory is brought into the picture very shortly after Smith embarks upon the substantive part of his course, at the point where he begins dealing with the problem of the origin of property rights. The first of the

[60] *Ibid.*, p. 25. [61] *Ibid.*, pp. 25–8.
[62] *Ibid.*, pp. 25, 162, and 227.
[63] *Ibid.*, p. 25. [64] *Ibid.*, p. 162.
[65] The set of student's notes from which the quotations that follow are taken is bound in six separate volumes. The recto pages in each volume have been numbered by the editors 1, 2, 3, 4, etc., right through to the end of the volume, and these are the page numbers used in the references to the passages quoted below. The passages are reproduced more or less as the student wrote them, but punctuation and capitalisation have up to a point been rationalised, and occasional amendments made to style and spelling, in the interests of readability.

ive causes 'from whence property may have its occasion', mith says, is *occupation*,[66] but before we start considering his or any of the other causes in detail 'it will be proper to observe that the regulations concerning them must vary considerably according to the state or age society is in at that ime. There are four distinct states which mankind pass hro:– 1st, the Age of Hunters; 2[dly], the Age of Shepherds; 3[dly], the Age of Agriculture; and 4[thly], the Age of Commerce.'[67] Smith then proceeds to discuss the nature of these our successive stages, with particular reference to the process vhereby society moves from one stage to the next. His account is of considerable importance, and requires quotation *in extenso*:

f we should suppose 10 or 12 persons of different sexes settled n an uninhabited island, the first method they would fall upon or their sustenance would be to support themselves by the wild 'ruits and wild animals which the country afforded. Their sole pusiness would be hunting the wild beasts or catching the fishes. The pulling of a wild fruit can hardly be called an imployment. The only thing amongst them which deserved the appellation of a business would be the chase. This is the age of hunters. In process of time, as their numbers multiplied, they would find the chase too precarious for their support. They would be necessitated to contrive some other method whereby to support themselves. At first perhaps they would try to lay up at one time when they had been successful what would support them for a considerable time. But this could go no great length. – The contrivance they would most naturally think of would be to tame some of those wild animals they caught, and by affording them better food than what they could get elsewhere they would enduce them to continue about their land themselves and multiply their kind. Hence would arise the age of shepherds. They would more probably begin first by multiplying animals than vegetables, as less skill and observation would be required. Nothing more than to know what food suited them. We find accordingly that in almost all countries the age of shepherds preceded that of agriculture. The Tartars and Arabians subsist almost entirely by their flocks and herds. The Arabs have a little agriculture, but the Tartars none at all. The whole of the savage nations which subsist by flocks have no notion of cultivating the ground. The only instance that has the appearance of an objection to this rule is the state of the

[66] *1762–3 Notes*, Vol. I, p. 25.   [67] *Ibid.*, Vol. I, pp. 26–7.

117

North American Indians. They, tho they have no conception of flocks and herds, have nevertheless some notion of agriculture. Their women plant a few stalks of Indian corn at the back of their huts. But this can hardly be called agriculture. This corn does not make any considerable part of their food; it serves only as a seasoning or something to give a relish to their common food; the flesh of those animalls they have caught in the chase. – Flocks and herds therefore are the first resource men would take themselves to when they found difficulty in subsisting by the chase.

But when a society becomes numerous they would find a difficulty in supporting themselves by herds and flocks. Then they would naturally turn themselves to the cultivation of land and the raising of such plants and trees as produced nourishment fit for them. They would observe that those seeds which fell on the dry bare soil or on the rocks seldom came to any thing, but that those which entered the soil generally produced a plant and bore seed similar to that which was sown. These observations they would extend to the different plants and trees they found produced agreable and nourishing food. And by this means they would gradually advance in to the Age of Agriculture. As society was farther improved, the severall arts, which at first would be exercised by each individual as far as was necessary for his welfare, would be seperated; some persons would cultivate one and others others, as they severally inclined. They would exchange with one an other what they produced more than was necessary for their support, and get in exchange for them the commodities they stood in need of and did not produce themselves. This exchange of commodities extends in time not only betwixt the individualls of the same society but betwixt those of different nations. Thus we send to France our cloths, iron work and other trinkets and get in exchange their wines. To Spain and Portugall we send our superfluous corn and bring from thence the Spainish and Portuguese wines. Thus at last the Age of Commerce arises. When therefore a country is stored with all the flocks and herds it can support, the land cultivated so as to produce all the grain and other commodities necessary for our subsistence it can be brought to bear, or at least as much as supports the inhabitants when the superfluous products whether of nature or art are exported and other necessary ones brought in exchange, such a society has done all in its power towards its ease and convenience.[68]

[68] *Ibid.*, Vol. i, pp. 27–32.

118

The Scottish pioneers of the 1750s

Having established the elements of his four stages theory in this way, Smith proceeds to use it in order to explain the changes in 'laws and regulations with regard to property' which occur as society develops. Since this exercise sets the pattern for many others of the same kind which Smith engages in at later points in the course, it will once again be useful to reproduce it in full:

It is easy to see that in these severall ages of society, the laws and regulations with regard to property must be very different. – In Tartary, where as we said the support of the inhabitants consists in herds and flocks, *theft* is punished with immediate death; in North America, again, where the age of hunters subsists, theft is not much regarded. As there is almost no property amongst them, the only injury that can be done is the depriving them of their game. Few laws or regulations will be requisite in such an age of society, and these will not extend to any great length, or be very rigorous in the punishments annexed to any infringements of property. Theft as we said is not much regarded amongst a people in this age or state of society; there are but few opportunities of committing it, and these too can not hurt the injured person in a considerable degree. – But when flocks and herds come to be reared, property then becomes of a very considerable extent; there are many opportunities of injuring one another and such injuries are extremely pernicious to the sufferer. In this state many more laws and regulations must take place; theft and robbery being easily committed, will of consequence be punished with the utmost rigour. In the age of agriculture, they are not perhaps so much exposed to theft and open robbery, but then there are many ways added in which property may be interupted as the subjects of it are considerably extended. The laws therefore tho perhaps not so rigorous will be of a far greater number than amongst a nation of shepherds. In the age of comerce, as the subjects of property are greatly increased the laws must be proportionally multiplied. The more improved any society is and the greater length the severall means of supporting the inhabitants are carried, the greater will be the number of their laws and regulations necessary to maintain justice, and prevent infringements of the right of property.[69]

Very soon after this, the four stages theory is introduced once again in order to help answer a new question – 'how

9 *Ibid.*, Vol. i, pp. 32–5.

long and in what circumstances property continues and at
what time it is supposed to be at an end'.[70] At first, says Smith
– i.e. in the hunting stage – 'property was conceived to end
as well as to begin with possession'.[71] But when the age of
shepherds arrived, 'property would necessarily be extended
a great deal farther';[72] and 'a still greater [extension] followed
on the introduction of agriculture'.[73] This theme is developed
at some length, with illustrations taken from the experience
of various uncultivated peoples – including, of course, the
Americans.[74] A little later, when Smith comes on to accession
(the second of the five possible sources of property rights)
the same kind of procedure is adopted. 'In the age of
hunters', says Smith, 'there was no room for accession, all
property at that time consisting in the animalls they had
caught.'[75] In the age of shepherds, again, 'accession could
hardly extend to any thing farther than the milk and young
of the animalls';[76] but the opportunities of accession 'multiply
to a number almost infinite when agriculture and private
property in land is introduced'.[77] And when dealing with
succession (another of the five sources), Smith draws attention to the fact that in the age of hunters 'there could be no
room for succession as there was no property': succession in
fact began in the age of shepherds, as a consequence of the
great extension of property which took place in that age.[78] I
do not wish to give the impression that Smith's lectures on
property were *dominated* by the four stages theory: there is
a great deal of material (particularly in the sections on succession and voluntary transference) to which the theory is
much less relevant and where it is not even mentioned. But
from the extensive use which *is* made of it, not only in this
part of the course but in later parts as well, there can be
little doubt that Smith regarded it as an organising principle
of considerable power and importance.

When he has exhausted the subject of 'real rights', Smith
proceeds to consider 'personal rights', which take their origin

[70] *Ibid.*, Vol. I, p. 40.　　　　[71] *Ibid.*, Vol. I, p. 41.
[72] *Ibid.*, Vol. I, p. 44.　　　　[73] *Ibid.*, Vol. I, pp. 46–7.
[74] See, e.g. Vol. I, pp. 46–7 (verso), where an anecdote taken from Charlevoix
is related at some length.
[75] *Ibid.*, Vol. I, p. 63 (verso).　　　　[76] *Ibid.*, Vol. I, p. 64.
[77] *Ibid.*, Vol. I, pp. 65–6.　　　　[78] *Ibid.*, Vol. I, p. 91 (verso).

om some kind of obligation arising either from contract,
uasi-contract, or injury.[79] There is nothing about the four
ages theory in the short section on quasi-contract, but there
re some interesting echoes of it in the two sections dealing
espectively with contract and injury. In the contract sec-
on, one of Smith's main concerns is to trace the history of
ontractual obligations from 'the first periods of society',
hen 'contracts were noways binding' (owing, in part, to
he small value of the subjects which in an early period
ould be the objects of contract'),[80] to the period of 'the
xtension of commerce',[81] when 'all contracts which were
ecessary for the carrying on of business' came to be regarded
s sustaining action.[82] In the injury section, again, he
mphasises several times 'the weakness of government in . . .
arly periods of society, which made it very delicate of inter-
eddling with the affairs of individualls'[83] – a point which
e illustrates by referring to the accounts by Charlevoix and
afitau of the customs of 'the Iroquois and severall other of
e savage nations of North America';[84] and he makes it
lear, in the following passage, that the extent to which
overnment is strong enough to 'intermeddle' depends upon
e extent to which society has advanced beyond the age of
unters:

mong the northern nations which broke into Europe in the
eginning of the 5th century, society was a step farther advanced
an amongst the Americans at this day. They are still in the
ate of hunters, the most rude and barbarous of any, whereas the
thers were arrived at the state of shepherds, and had even some
ttle agriculture. The step betwixt these two is of all others the
reatest in the progression of society, for by it the notion of pro-
erty is extended beyond possession, to which it is in the former
ate confined. When this is once established, it is a matter of no
reat difficulty to extend this from one subject to another, from
erds and flocks to the land itself.– They had therefore got a
ood way before the Americans; and government, which grows
p with society, had of consequence acquired greater strength.

Ibid., Vol. II, pp. 41–2.
Ibid., Vol. II, p. 47.   [81] *Ibid.*, Vol. II, p. 53.
Ibid., Vol. II, p. 69.   [83] *Ibid.*, Vol. II, p. 96.
Ibid., Vol. II, p. 96. The student actually writes 'Pére Charlevoix and de
la Fulage', but it seems fairly clear that Lafitau was meant.

We find accordingly that it intermeddled more with thos
affairs . . .[85]

There is virtually nothing about the four stages theory i
the fairly extensive sections which follow on the rights whic
'belong to a man as a member of a family'; but the theor
comes fully into its own again in the ensuing sections on th
rights which belong to him as 'a member of a society'.[86] Hei
Smith is of course concerned primarily with *government* – it
nature, its origin, and its progress from the first ages c
society up to the present day. In his account of the earl
progress of government, the framework of reference throug
out is the four stages theory, which is used to an extent an
with a degree of sophistication unknown in any of the pro
vious literature. It would be impossible to summarise Smith
argument without vulgarising it: the following five passage
are selected for quotation merely in order to give somethin
of the flavour of his account:

In the age of hunters there can be very little government of an
sort, but what there is will be of the democraticall kind. A natio
of this sort consists of a number of independent families, n
otherwise connected than as they live together in the same tow
or village and speak the same language. With regard to th
judicial power, this in these nations as far as it extends is po
sessed by the community as one body. The affairs of privat
families, as long as they concern only the members of one famil
are left to the determination of the members of that famil
Disputes betwixt others can in this state but rarely occur, but
they do, and are of such a nature as would be apt to disturb th
community, the whole community then interferes to make up th
difference . . . The design of their intermeddling is to preserv
the public quiet and the safety of the individualls; they therefor
endeavour to bring about a reconcilement betwixt the parties
variance. This is the case amongst the savage nations of Americ
as we are informed by Father Charlevoix and Monsieur Laffita
who give us the most distinct account of the manners of thos
nations . . .[87]

The age of shepherds is that where government properly firs
commences. And it is at this time too that men become in an
considerable degree dependent on others. The appropriation c

[85] *Ibid.*, Vol. ii, pp. 97–8. Cf. p. 152.
[86] *Ibid.*, Vol. iii, p. 1.   [87] *Ibid.*, Vol. iv, pp. 4–5.

locks and herds renders subsistence by hunting very uncertain
and precarious. Those animalls which are most adapted for the
use of man, as oxen, sheep, horses, camels, etc., which are also
the most numerous, are no longer common but are the property
of certain individualls. The distinctions of rich and poor then
arise. Those who have not any possessions in flocks and herds can
find no way of maintaining themselves but by procuring it from
the rich. The rich therefore, as they maintain and support those
of the poorer sort out of the large possessions which they have
in herds and flocks, require their service and dependance . . .
The patriarchs we see were all a sort of independent princes who
had their dependents and followers attending them, being maintain'd by the produce of the flocks and herds which were committed to their care . . .[88]

In the age of the hunters a few temporary exertions of the
authority of the community will be sufficient for the few occasions of dispute which can occur. Property, the grand fund of all
dispute, is not then known . . . But here when in the manner
above mentioned some have great wealth and others nothing, it
is necessary that the arm of authority should be continually
stretched forth, and permanent laws or regulations made which
may ascertain the property of the rich from the inroads of the
poor, who would otherwise continually make incroachments upon
it, and settle in what the infringement of this property consists
and in what cases they will be liable to punishment. Laws and
government may be considered in this and indeed in every case
as a combination of the rich to oppress the poor, and preserve
to themselves the inequality of the goods which would otherwise
be soon destroyed by the attacks of the poor, who if not hindered
by the government would soon reduce the others to an equality
with themselves by open violence . . . Settled laws therefore, or
agreements concerning property, will soon be made after the
commencement of the age of shepherds . . .[89]

In the age of hunters it is impossible for a very great number
to live together. As game is their only support they would soon
exhaust all that was within their reach. Thirty or forty families
would be the most that could live together, that is, about 140 or
150 persons. These might live by the chase in the country about
them. They would also naturally form themselves into these
villages, agreeing to live near together for their mutuall security.
In the same manner tho they could not conveniently enlarge their
village, yet severall sets or tribes of this sort would agree to

[88] *Ibid.*, Vol. IV, pp. 7–9.   [89] *Ibid.*, Vol. IV, pp. 22–3.

settle their villages as near as they could conveniently, that they might be at hand to give one another assistance and protection against the common enemy . . . In the age of shepherds these societies or villages may be somewhat larger than in that of hunters. But still they can not be very large, as the country about would soon be eat up by their flocks and herds. So that the ground for 4 or 5 miles about will not be able to maintain the flocks of above 1000 people, and we never find that the villages amount to a greater number in any country of shepherds. These may in like manner combine together under their different heads to support one another against the attacks of others. We see the Grecian nations were in this manner led on by Agamemnon. – There is however one great difference betwixt men in the one state and in the other. The hunters can not form any very great schemes, nor can their expeditions be very formidable. It is impossible that 200 hunters could live together for a fortnight . . . A scalping party seldom consists of above ten or twelve. So that there can be no great danger from such a nation . . . The case is the same with respect to shepherds as long as we suppose them stationary; but if we suppose them moving from one place to another, 4 or 5 miles every day, we can set no bounds to the number which might enter into such an expedition. If then one clan of Tartars (for instance) should, setting out on an expedition, defeat another, they would necessarily become possessed of every thing which before belonged to the vanquished . . . So that tho a country possessed by shepherds is never extremely populous yet immense armies may be collected together which would be an even match for any of its neighbours . . .[90]

In the last lecture I endeavoured to shew in what manner those governments which, originally Tartarian ones or under chiefs in the same manner as the Tartars, came from thence to settle in towns and become republican in many parts of Greece, and the same was the case in Italy, Gaul, etc. We may easily conceive that a people of this sort, settled in a country where they lived in pretty great ease and security and in a soil capable of yielding them good returns for cultivation, would not only improve the earth but also make considerable advances in the severall arts and sciences and manufactures, providing they had an opportunity of exporting their sumptuous produce and fruits of their labour. Both these circumstances are absolutely necessary to bring about this improvement in the arts of life amongst a people in this state. The soil must be improveable, otherwise there can be

[90] *Ibid.*, Vol. iv, pp. 36–40.

nothing from whence they might draw that which they should work up and improve. That must be the foundation of their labour and industry. It is no less necessary that they should have an easy method of transporting their sumptuous produce into foreign countries and neighbouring states. When they have an opportunity of this, then they will exert their utmost industry in their severall businesses; but if their be no such opportunity of commerce, and consequently no opportunity of increasing their wealth by industry in any considerable degree, there is little likelyhood that they should ever cultivate arts to any great degree, or produce more sumptuous produce than will be consumed within the country itself; and this will never be wrought up to such perfection as when there are greater spurs to industry. Tartary and Araby labour under both these difficulties. For in the first place their soil is very poor and such as will hardly admit of culture of any sort . . . Neither have they any opportunity of commerce, if it should happen that they should make any advances in arts and sciences . . . In these countries therefore little or no advances can be expected, nor have any yet been made. But in Greece all the circumstances necessary for the improvement of the arts concurred. The severall parts were seperated from each other by mountains and other barriers, no less than Arabia, but is [*sic*] far more adapted to culture. They would therefore have many inducements to cultivate the arts and make improvements in society. The lands would be divided and well improved and the country would acquire considerable wealth.[91]

These quotations will, I hope, give some indication of the 'train of thinking' which Smith pursues in his survey of the early progress of government in these notable sections of his lectures. What comes out very clearly here is not only Smith's ingenious and all-pervasive use of the four stages theory as such, but also his conscious acceptance of the more general 'environmental' or 'materialist' approach which underlay that theory. His use of the theory as such, of course, gradually lessens as he comes closer to modern times, where his analysis is mainly concerned with the governmental system (and, in the next part of the course, the economic system) of countries like Britain, which in Smith's time were obviously in the 'commercial' stage of their development. But the

[91] *Ibid.*, Vol. IV, pp. 60–3.

'economic' part begins with an impressive argument designed to show that 'in a certain view of things all the arts, the sciences, law and government, wisdom and even virtue itself tend all to this one thing, the providing meat, drink, rayment, and lodging for men . . .'[92] and echoes of the theory as such are to be heard from time to time even in the sections which immediately follow.[93] And near the end of the course, when Smith comes on to deal with such subjects as 'the causes of the slow progress of opulence', 'taxes or revenue', 'the influence of commerce on manners', and 'arms', it frequently reappears (in whole or in part) in something very like its original form.[94] The four stages theory and the more general notions underlying it were in fact used so frequently in Smith's lectures in the early 1760s, and with such a degree of confidence and maturity, that it is very hard to believe that he had not been putting them forward in his lectures, in one form or another, *before* 1757 and 1758, when Dalrymple and Kames respectively published their versions of the theory. All the evidence suggests that it was in fact Smith who was the leader, and Dalrymple and Kames who were the followers.

If Dalrymple and Kames got the theory from Smith, then, rather than vice versa, where did Smith get it from? There was a sense, as I have indicated above,[95] in which the emergence of the theory was a kind of by-product of the contemporary historical and anthropological studies which were every intellectual's meat and drink at this time: the theory owed its origin not so much to the discovery of any new facts by its progenitors as to the imposition by them of a new pattern, a new set of emphases, on the body of facts revealed in these contemporary studies. The question of where Smith

[92] *Ibid.*, Vol. vi, p. 20.
[93] E.g. *ibid.*, Vol. vi, pp. 103–4.
[94] Since the 1762–3 notes stop short a little over half-way through the 'economic' section of Smith's lectures, one is obliged here to rely on the other set of student's notes published by Edwin Cannan in 1896 under the title *Lectures on Justice, Police, Revenue and Arms*. It appears very probable that this set of notes relates to the lectures delivered in the 1763–4 session. The material in the 1762–3 notes corresponds roughly to that in the Cannan notes up to but not beyond p. 208 of the published edition of the latter. References to the different modes of subsistence which are distinguished in the four stages theory will be found on pp. 208, 222ff., 237, 253ff., and 260 of the Cannan edition.
[95] Pp. 65–6.

(and Turgot) got the theory from, then, comes down to the question of the influences leading them to look at the known facts in this new kind of way. So far as the purely literary influences are concerned, the answer is I think fairly straightforward. If we recall the three 'streams of thought' described in Chapter 1 above,[96] we can say that Smith was mainly influenced by the first of these (the Grotius–Pufendorf–Locke stream) and Turgot by the second and third (the Bossuet and Fontenelle streams); but that in addition, and perhaps even more important, there were certain common influences operating on both men – notably Montesquieu's *The Spirit of Laws*.

But to say this is not really to say very much. One has still to explain why Smith and Turgot were predisposed to be influenced by particular authors, and by particular passages in their works, rather than by other authors and other passages. It is no answer – or at any rate only part of the answer – to say that their attitude was derived from the Lockean theory of knowledge, since it is precisely the question of the particular interpretation which they placed on this theory which is at issue. It is true, of course, that when Lockean sensationalism is combined with moral relativism and an 'interest'-oriented utilitarianism, as in the case of Helvétius, a strong emphasis on the mode of subsistence becomes almost inevitable. But the main part of the answer must surely be sought elsewhere. My own feeling is that thinking of the type we are considering, which lays primary emphasis on the development of economic techniques and socio-economic relationships, is likely to be a function, first, of the rapidity of contemporary economic advance, and, second, of the facility with which a contrast can be observed between areas which are economically advancing and areas which are still in 'lower' stages of development. In the 1750s and 60s, in cities like Glasgow and in areas such as the more advanced provinces in the north of France, the whole social life of the communities concerned was being rapidly and visibly transformed, and it was fairly obvious that this was happening as a result of profound changes taking place in economic techniques and basic socio-economic relationships. And the new

[96] Pp. 12ff.

forms of economic organisation which were emerging could be fairly easily compared and contrasted with the older forms of organisation which still existed, say, in the Scottish Highlands, or in the remainder of France – or among the Indian tribes in America. If changes in the mode of subsistence were playing such an important and 'progressive' role in the development of contemporary society, it seemed a fair bet that they must also have done so in that of past society.

My main concern in this book, however, is not so much with causes as general, deep-seated, and speculative as these, but rather with the way in which the four stages theory was influenced by contemporary notions of savagery, particularly among the Americans. No one who reads the work of the French and Scottish pioneers of the 1750s can fail to notice that all of them without exception were very familiar with the contemporary studies of the Americans; that most of them had evidently pondered deeply upon their significance; and that some were almost obsessed by them. As I have already mentioned above,[97] the studies of the Americans provided the new social scientists with a plausible working hypothesis about the basic characteristics of the 'first' or 'earliest' stage of socio-economic development. But once again the question of predisposition comes into the picture. Why, exactly, did they accept this hypothesis with such manifest enthusiasm? The evidence from similarities, after all, even in the relatively sophisticated form which it assumed in Lafitau's book, was hardly overwhelming (particularly when the constraint of the time-scale of Genesis was removed); and it would have been quite possible to take the line (as some writers indeed did) that the Americans had degenerated from some 'higher' state, or, alternatively, that American-type societies had in fact coexisted with societies of other types in the 'first' or 'earliest' ages. There seems to have been a predisposition, among the majority of the pioneers, in favour of the proposition that 'in the beginning all the World was *America*', and it is this predisposition which cries out for some kind of explanation.

There were, I think, two basic reasons for it. In the first place, those who believed that there was an innate tendency

97 Pp. 66–7.

for society to advance through higher and higher stages towards some kind of 'perfection' might well be disposed, in order to demonstrate the great power of this innate tendency, to postulate a starting-point as far removed from contemporary society as possible. And the ignoble savages of America, as Robertson pointed out, provided one of the very few remaining examples of 'the rudest form in which we can conceive [man] to subsist.'[98] It is no accident, I believe, that the majority of our pioneers were in one sense or another 'perfectibilists'. This statement must immediately be qualified, of course: even Turgot, the great exponent of perfectibilist doctrine, thought that the savages could score at least *some* points over contemporary Europeans; and Adam Smith, the great believer in the power of the invisible hand, was extremely critical of certain disturbing aspects and tendencies of European society. But by and large what I have just said is true. Among the pioneers the only real exception is Rousseau,[99] who, precisely because he did *not* think that contemporary European society represented an advance over earlier forms, made the Americans noble rather than ignoble, and postulated that 'progress', so far from beginning with their type of society, in fact ended with it. And this, surely, is the kind of exception that proves the rule.

In the second place, men like Turgot and Smith were apt to ascribe the superiority of contemporary European society (in so far as they did in fact recognise its superiority) to the existence of certain important socio-economic institutions and phenomena which then as now were often coming under attack – notably inequality, property rights, and the accumulation of capital. In order to demonstrate the inherent utility of these things, what better than to make the developmental process start with an American-type society in which none of them existed, and in which the people (it could be said) *therefore* lived at a very low material and cultural level? One could then very effectively correlate the gradual progress of society towards 'perfection' with the gradual emergence and growth of the institutions and phenomena in question. I am not

[98] Above, p. 67.
[99] Helvétius may also perhaps be regarded as an exception, although not such a 'real' one as Rousseau.

saying, of course, that the four stages theory was a wicked capitalist plot. All I am saying is that if there was in fact a predisposition among some of the pioneers to accept the notion that the 'first' stage was an American-type society, this may have been in part a product of what has come to be known as the 'bourgeois optimism' of the eighteenth century.

5

The ignoble savage and 'the history of rude nations'

The pioneers of the 1750s, whose work we have been considering in the last two chapters, did not have to wait very long for followers. Nor did these followers appear only in France and Scotland: already in 1760, for example, von Justi was telling his German readers that 'history, as well as the nature of the thing and the growth of human understanding – these teach us that all peoples changed from hunters and fishermen to shepherds, from shepherds to tillers of the soil, and finally from tillers to scholars, artists, and merchants'.[1] But it was in fact very largely in France and Scotland that the four stages theory underwent its most spectacular development in the ensuing decades, and it is upon certain aspects of its history in these two countries that I shall concentrate in the remainder of this book. In the present chapter I shall be concerned in particular with the contribution of a number of important French and Scottish followers who, in the period between 1760 and 1780, used one or another version of the four stages theory to illuminate what Adam Ferguson called 'the history of rude nations'.[2]

I do not wish, however, to give the impression that the pioneers themselves ceased to make any further germane contributions after 1760. This was indeed true enough of Dalrymple, and perhaps of Rousseau – and also of Goguet, who died in 1758. But all the others continued to develop the ideas which they had put forward in the 1750s. Of Smith

---

[1] J. H. G. von Justi, *Die Natur und das Wesen der Staaten* (Berlin, 1760), p. 8. Von Justi, like his predecessors, adduces the Americans as an example of a people who are still to be found in the original hunting and fishing stage.

[2] 'Of the History of Rude Nations' was the title which Ferguson gave to Part II of his *Essay on the History of Civil Society*, the 1st edition of which appeared in 1767. This work is discussed below, pp. 150–5.

and Turgot I shall speak again in the next chapter, with particular reference to the way in which they helped to effect a kind of transition from the four stages theory to classical political economy.[3] So far as Kames is concerned, his post-1760 work on 'the history of rude nations' is of some interest in itself, and will be considered separately at a later point in the present chapter.[4] Of the two remaining pioneers, Quesnay and Helvétius, I shall say a word or two now.

Quesnay's most important contribution to the development of the four stages theory was made in chapter 8 of his *Philosophie Rurale*, written in collaboration with Mirabeau and published in 1763.[5] The relevant section of the chapter begins with a masterly statement of the general idea underlying the four stages theory – the idea that the overall shape and behaviour of society depend upon its mode of subsistence. This statement, which bears an interesting resemblance to a certain passage in Smith's Jurisprudence lectures to which reference has been made above,[6] is followed by a striking account of the progress of society through its main socio-historical stages of development. After the initial gathering stage, three different 'modes of life', derived from three different 'kinds of subsistence',[7] are distinguished – hunting, pastoral, and agricultural; and the section ends with an account of the so-called 'commercial societies' which, it is claimed, are bound eventually to be set up alongside agricultural societies. It is true that Quesnay and Mirabeau do not state clearly that hunting, pastoral, and agricultural societies are likely to succeed one another *in this order*. It is also true that, in accordance with the Physiocratic paradigm, 'commercial societies' are envisaged as developing not *out of* agricultural societies but rather *alongside* them.[8] However, the overall emphasis on the determining character of the mode of subsistence is what really matters; and it was certainly within a broad 'materialist' framework very similar to that laid down in the *Philosophie Rurale* that the economic and philosophical

---

[3] Below, pp. 219ff.   [4] Below, pp. 155ff.

[5] A translation of the relevant section of the chapter will be found in R. L. Meek (ed.), *Precursors of Adam Smith, 1750–1775* (Dent, London, 1973), pp. 104–13.

[6] Above, p. 126.   [7] R. L. Meek, *op, cit.*, pp. 108–9.

[8] Cf. *ibid.*, p. 104.

ideas of the Physiocratic school were subsequently set. By the time Du Pont came to prepare his *Table Raisonnée des Principes de l'Economie Politique* in 1773, as we shall see later,[9] there was no doubt in his mind about the validity and importance of this kind of approach – or, for that matter, about the order in which the different 'modes of life' normally succeeded one another.

So far as Helvétius is concerned, in his seminal work *De l'Homme*, which was published posthumously in 1773,[10] the four stages theory is met with more frequently than in *De l'Esprit*, and the basic idea underlying it is presented in a forceful and original manner. The most effective statement of the theory itself is to be found near the end of the book, where it is set out in question-and-answer form and placed in the context of a more general anthropological theory:[11]

Q. What is man?

A. An animal, it is said, rational, but undoubtedly sentient, weak, and adapted to reproduce himself.

Q. In his capacity as a sentient being, what must man do?

A. Shun pain, seek pleasure ...

Q. In his capacity as a weak animal, what must he also do?

A. Unite together with other men, whether to defend himself against animals which are stronger than he is, or to assure himself of a subsistence for which the beasts contend with him, or finally to catch those which serve him as food. From this arise all the agreements relative to hunting and fishing.

Q. In his capacity as an animal adapted to reproduce himself, what happens to man?

A. The means of subsistence diminish as his species multiplies.

Q. What must he therefore do?

A. When the lakes and forests are emptied of fish and game, he must seek new means of providing for his sustenance.

Q. What are these means?

[9] Below, pp. 182–4.
[10] The edition of *De l'Homme* from which I have worked, and to which the page references below relate, is dated 1773 and stated to be published in London.
[11] On the 'anthropology' of Helvétius, see the interesting account in Michèle Duchet, *Anthropologie et Histoire au Siècle des Lumières* (Maspero, Paris, 1971), pp. 377–406.

Social science and the ignoble savage

A. They come down to two. When the inhabitants are still few in number, they raise live-stock, and the peoples are then shepherds. When the inhabitants have increased very greatly, and are obliged to seek the means of providing for their sustenance in a smaller area of ground, they work the land, and the peoples are then husbandmen.[12]

In more abbreviated and less picturesque form, other formulations of the theory are to be found at various strategic points earlier in the book.[13] More important, however, is the noteworthy statement of the basic idea underlying the theory which occurs in the course of Helvétius's discussion of 'the unequal perfection of the senses'.[14] One of the main points which he is making in this part of his book is that the influence of climate on man's intelligence (at any rate after a certain point in his history) is virtually negligible. If this were *not* so, Helvétius argues, we would expect to find some country or countries, blessed by a specially favourable climate, whose inhabitants had shown a marked and constant superiority over those of other countries. But, says Helvétius,

a climate which has generated such a people is still unknown. History does not show in any of them a constant superiority of spirit over the others: it proves on the contrary that from Delhi to Petersburg all peoples have been successively foolish and enlightened; that in the same situations all nations, as Mr. Robertson notes,[15] have the same laws and the same spirit, and that it is for this reason that we find again among the Americans the manners of the ancient Germans.[16]

Here is made manifest a most interesting and important confluence of two different currents of thought. On the one

[12] *De l'Homme*, Vol. II, pp. 350–1.
[13] See, e.g. Vol. I, pp. 111–12, p. 135 (footnote *a*), and p. 311 (note 24); also Vol. II, p. 17.
[14] *De l'Homme*, Vol. I, section II, ch. XII, pp. 128–36.
[15] Duchet (*op. cit.*, pp. 384–5, footnote 38) says that Helvétius is here referring to a passage in Robertson's *History of America*. Since the latter book did not appear until 1777, five years after *De l'Homme*, Duchet is obliged to suggest that Helvétius must have seen it prior to its publication. In actual fact, the passage referred to by Helvétius was almost certainly from Robertson's *History of the Reign of the Emperor Charles V*, which appeared in 1769. See below, p. 139.
[16] *De l'Homme*, Vol. I, p. 130, footnote *a*. The word which for want of a better single English equivalent I have twice translated here as 'spirit' is of course *esprit*.

hand, those thinkers who were becoming concerned with the problem of the nature and causes of the development of society were finding that they could get little help from Montesquieu's theory of the influence of climate. The difficulty was, of course, that climate (at any rate in the narrow sense of the word) was something which, although it might differ greatly from one country to another, remained more or less changeless over time. Yet nations with favourable climates, as Helvétius noted, had not displayed any marked and constant superiority over the others; and the patterns of socio-economic change in countries with quite different climates had often been surprisingly similar.[17] If one could not look to climate for an explanation of changes and differences in the manners of nations, then, what *could* one look to? A plausible answer to this question seemed to be provided by another current of thought, which, as we have already seen,[18] emerged as a kind of by-product of the old controversies about the origin of the Americans. The observed similarities between the Americans and, say, the ancient Germans, it began to be argued, were not (as had previously been thought) evidence of the genetic descent of the former from the latter: they were in fact evidence of nothing more than that the two peoples were both in the same 'situation' – i.e. speaking very broadly, that they both got their living in the same way. Here, then, in embryo was a ready-made answer to the question which had been raised as a result of the critique of Montesquieu's theory of the influence of climate: changes and differences in the manners of nations were due to changes and differences in their mode of subsistence. It was an answer, as we have just seen, that Helvétius eagerly seized upon.

---

[17] Helvétius was quite prepared to admit that differences in temperature and climate might *indirectly* occasion differences in the manners and pursuits of different peoples. 'It may well be', he wrote, 'that savages who are hunters in countries of forests become shepherds in countries of pastures. But it is no less true that in all the different countries people will always perceive the same relations between objects. In addition, from the moment when nomadic peoples have united into nations, when the marshes have been drained and the forests felled, differences in climate have had no appreciable influence whatever on their spirit' (*De l'Homme*, Vol. I, p. 135, footnote *a*). [18] Above, pp. 64–5.

Social science and the ignoble savage

William Robertson, whom Helvétius refers to in this connection and to whose work we must now turn, was one of the first – at any rate in print – to draw this conclusion specifically from the controversies about the origin of the Americans, and to argue the point out at length. The first occasion on which he did so was in one of the notes appended to the preliminary volume of his *History of the Reign of the Emperor Charles V* (1769); but his awareness of some of the issues involved was displayed as early as 1755, in his sermon on 'The Situation of the World at the Time of Christ's Appearance' and in an account which he wrote in the same year for the *Edinburgh Review* of a book on North America by William Douglass.

Robertson's 1755 sermon was designed to show that Christianity was introduced into the world at the precise time 'when the world stood most in need of such a revelation, and was best prepared for receiving it'.[19] The political, moral, religious, and domestic state of the world, Robertson argues, were all as propitious at that time as they possibly could have been. What this sermon reveals, more than anything else, is the influence of the 'providential' view of history. Robertson's account of the way in which God works is in fact very similar to Bossuet's.[20] 'The Supreme Being', says Robertson, 'conducteth all his operations by general laws'; the motion by which his works 'advance towards their finished and complete state' is 'gradual and progressive';[21] and he 'seldom effects by supernatural means, any thing which could have been accomplished by such as are natural'.[22] Given these assumptions, the way is laid open for a historian to look for 'circumstances in the situation of the world'[23] which contributed towards the success of Christianity – and, more generally, towards the making of what Robertson here calls 'the civil history of mankind'.[24] And there are a number of other hints in the sermon of what was later to come, the most interesting, perhaps, being a statement to the effect that in

19 *The Works of William Robertson* (Edinburgh, 1840), Vol. i, p. lxxviii.
20 Cf. above, pp. 23–6.
21 *Works*, Vol. i, p. lxxviii.
22 *Ibid.*, Vol. i, p. lxxix.
23 *Ibid.*, Vol. i, p. lxxxv.
24 *Ibid.*, Vol. i, p. lxxvii.

the Highlands and Islands of Scotland 'society still appears in its rudest and most imperfect form'.[25]

In William Douglass's book on North America,[26] which Robertson reviewed in the *Edinburgh Review* later in 1755,[27] it was suggested that society appeared in its rudest and most imperfect form not in the Highlands and Islands of Scotland, but in America:

America may with much Propriety be called the youngest Brother and meanest of Mankind; no Civil Government, no Religion, no Letters; the *French* call them *Les Hommes des Bois*, or Men-Brutes of the Forrest: They do not cultivate the Earth by planting or grazing: Excepting a very inconsiderable Quantity of *Mays* or *Indian Corn*, and of *Kidney-Beans* (in *New England* they are called *Indian Beans*) which some of their *Squaas* or Women plant; they do not provide for To-Morrow, their Hunting is their necessary Subsistence not Diversion; when they have good Luck in Hunting, they eat and sleep until all is consumed and then go a Hunting again.[28]

This statement, and a number of others like it,[29] mark Douglass's book out as one of some importance in its own right. It is also of importance because Smith had it in his library and quoted from it twice in *The Wealth of Nations*.[30] And Robertson's remarks upon it in the *Edinburgh Review* are important too. He singles out for citation Douglass's statement that America may be called 'the youngest Brother and meanest of Mankind', together with the accompanying description of the Americans' primitive mode of subsistence

---

[25] *Ibid.*, Vol. I, p. lxxxv. See also Robertson's interesting comments on commerce (p. lxxix), the progress of luxury (p. lxxxii), and domestic slavery (p. lxxxiv).

[26] *A Summary, Historical and Political, of the first Planting, Progressive Improvements, and present State of the* British *Settlements in* NORTH-AMERICA, by W. D., M. D. [William Douglass]. The first part of this work appeared in Boston in 1747, the second in 1749, and the third in 1750. It was a 2-volume reprint of the whole work, appearing in London in 1755, which afforded the occasion for Robertson's review in the *Edinburgh Review*. The page references below are to the first part which appeared in Boston in 1747, and which is best described as Vol. I, Part I.

[27] *The Edinburgh Review for the Year 1755* (2nd edn, 1818), pp. 97–105.

[28] Douglass, *op. cit.*, Vol. I, Part I (Boston, 1747), pp. 153–4.

[29] See, for example, *ibid.*, pp. 155 and 173.

[30] See James Bonar, *A Catalogue of the Library of Adam Smith* (2nd edn, London, 1932), p. 59.

and a number of other comments of Douglass's which make the Americans out to be very ignoble savages indeed. The most significant of Robertson's remarks, however, occurs in a footnote where he compares a particular practice of the Americans (as reported by Douglass) with a similar practice of the Malayans (as reported by Montesquieu). 'Similar causes', says Robertson in introducing this comparison, 'always produce similar effects'.[31]

In Robertson's *History of Scotland* (1759) there is nothing which is of direct relevance to the four stages theory. Nor, at first sight, does there appear to be very much of relevance to it in his *History of the Reign of the Emperor Charles V* (1769), the first volume of which (in the three-volume edition of 1769) consisted of a disquisition on *The Progress of Society in Europe*. One peruses the latter with some sense of anticipation, in view of John Callander's reported statement that Smith used to say to him that Robertson had borrowed 'the first vol. of his histy. of Cha. V' from his (i.e. Smith's) Glasgow lectures on Jurisprudence.[32] So far as the actual text of *The Progress of Society in Europe* is concerned, the links with Smith's Jurisprudence lectures seem too tenuous to justify this charge of plagiarism (if in fact it was ever made); and there is not a great deal in it that is really relevant to the four stages theory.[33] When we turn to the so-called 'Proofs and Illustrations' appearing at the end of the volume, however, we find one lengthy note which is indeed of considerable relevance and importance.[34] It begins with an attempt by Robertson to collect together and arrange in an orderly way the main statements made by Caesar and Tacitus about the institutions and customs of the ancient Germans, commencing

[31] *The Edinburgh Review for the Year 1755*, p. 104, footnote.
[32] The reference here is to the account given (at second hand) by John Callander of Craigforth (Edinburgh University MSS, La. ɪɪ, 451(2)).
[33] See, however, the reference to barbarous nations subsisting 'entirely by hunting or pasturage' (*Works*, Vol. ɪ, p. 8). See also *ibid.*, p. 11, where Robertson notes that the 'amazing uniformity' in the feudal laws which were established in European countries 'hath induced some authors to believe that all these nations . . . were originally the same people'. But argues Robertson, the uniformity 'may be ascribed, with greater probability, to the similar state of society and of manners to which they were accustomed in their native countries, and to the similar situation in which they found themselves on taking possession of their new domains'.
[34] *Works*, Vol. ɪ, pp. 370–2.

with those relating to their mode of subsistence and concluding with those relating to their treatment of crime.
Robertson then goes on to remark that 'there is still one race
of men nearly in the same political situation' with that of
the Germans 'when they first settled in their new conquests;
I mean the various tribes and nations of savages in North
America'. The question arises, therefore, as to 'whether this
similarity in their political state has occasioned any resemblance between their character and manners.'[35] In order to
deal with this question Robertson extracts from Charlevoix
a number of facts about the 'character and manners' of the
Americans, and arranges them under the same headings as
those he has just used in the case of the ancient Germans
(with the mode of subsistence at the beginning and the treatment of crime at the end). The result of this comparative
exercise, according to Robertson, is to show that there *is* in
fact a resemblance, and indeed a very close one, between the
'character and manners' of the two peoples. From this
Robertson draws the following significant conclusion:

The resemblance holds in many other particulars. It is sufficient
for my purpose to have pointed out the similarity of those great
features which distinguish and characterise both people. Bochart,
and other philologists of the last century, who, with more erudi-
tion than science, endeavoured to trace the migrations of various
nations, and who were apt, upon the slightest appearance of
resemblance, to find an affinity between nations far removed from
each other, and to conclude that they were descended from the
same ancestors, would hardly have failed, in viewing such an
amazing similarity, to pronounce with confidence, 'That the
Germans and Americans must be the same people.' But a philosopher will satisfy himself with observing, 'That the characters of
nations depend on the state of society in which they live, and on
the political institutions established among them; and that the
human mind, whenever it is placed in the same situation, will, in
ages the most distant, and in countries the most remote, assume
the same form, and be distinguished by the same manners.'[36]

And in the final paragraph of the note, which immediately

[35] *Ibid.*, Vol. i, p. 371.
[36] *Ibid.*, Vol. i, p. 372. It was this passage, almost certainly, to which
Helvétius was referring in the comments from *De l'Homme* which I have
quoted on p. 134, above.

follows this, Robertson comes very close, in effect, to defining 'state of society' as 'mode of subsistence':

I have pushed the comparison between the Germans and Americans no farther than was necessary for the illustration of my subject. I do not pretend that the state of society in the two countries was perfectly similar in every respect. Many of the German tribes were more civilized than the Americans. Some of them were not unacquainted with agriculture; almost all of them had flocks of tame cattle, and depended upon them for the chief part of their subsistence. Most of the American tribes subsist by hunting, and are in a ruder and more simple state than the ancient Germans. The resemblance, however, between their condition is greater, perhaps, than any that history affords an opportunity of observing between any two races of uncivilized people, and this has produced a surprising similarity of manners.[37]

The leading ideas expressed in the remarkable passages just quoted were further developed in Robertson's *History of America* (1777). In Book IV of this work Robertson discusses the 'manners and policy' of America's 'most uncivilized inhabitants', and in Book VII he reviews the 'institutions and manners of the Mexicans and Peruvians'.[38] The main framework of reference throughout these two books is the notion that 'in every inquiry concerning the operations of men when united together in society, the first object of attention should be their mode of subsistence. According as that varies, their laws and policy must be different'.[39] And here once again, in even more striking language than that used earlier in the note to which I have just drawn attention, Robertson explains that it is to this basic notion, rather than to any fanciful theories about genetic descent, that the evidence concerning the 'similitude' between the Americans and one or another ancient people of the Old World should properly lead us:

[37] *Ibid.*, Vol. I, p. 372. Cf. also *ibid.*, p. 369.
[38] *Ibid.*, Vol. II, pp. viii–ix.
[39] *Ibid.*, Vol. II, p. 104. 'The institutions', Robertson continues, 'suited to the ideas and exigencies of tribes, which subsist chiefly by fishing or hunting, and which have as yet acquired but an imperfect conception of any species of property, will be much more simple than those which must take place when the earth is cultivated with regular industry; and a right of property, not only in its productions, but in the soil itself, is completely ascertained.'

'The history of rude nations'

Nothing can be more frivolous or uncertain than the attempts to discover the original of the Americans, merely by tracing the resemblance between their manners and those of any particular people in the ancient continent. If we suppose two tribes, though placed in the most remote regions of the globe, to live in a climate nearly of the same temperature, to be in the same state of society, and to resemble each other in the degree of their improvement, they must feel the same wants and exert the same endeavours to supply them. The same objects will allure, the same passions will animate them, and the same ideas and sentiments will arise in their minds. The character and occupations of the hunter in America must be little different from those of an Asiatic, who depends for subsistence on the chase. A tribe of savages on the banks of the Danube must nearly resemble one upon the plains washed by the Missisippi. Instead then of presuming from this similarity, that there is any affinity between them, we should only conclude, that the disposition and manners of men are formed by their situation, and arise from the state of society in which they live. The moment that begins to vary, the character of a people must change. In proportion as it advances in improvement, their manners refine, their powers and talents are called forth. In every part of the earth, the progress of man hath been nearly the same; and we can trace him in his career from the rude simplicity of savage life, until he attains the industry, the arts, and the elegance of polished society. There is nothing wonderful, then, in the similitude between the Americans and the barbarous nations of our continent. Had Lafitau, Garcia, and many other authors attended to this, they would not have perplexed a subject, which they pretend to illustrate, by their fruitless endeavours to establish an affinity between various races of people, in the old and new continents, upon no other evidence than such a resemblance in their manners as necessarily arises from the similarity of their condition.[40]

The general idea lying behind the four stages theory is revealed to us here, very clearly indeed, as one of the unintended by-products of the origins literature. But the studies of the Americans, as Robertson also makes very clear, were responsible for much more than this. Once the manners of the Americans began to attract the attention of 'philosophers',[41] as distinct from conquerors and missionaries, he

[40] *Ibid.*, Vol. II, pp. 85–6.
[41] 'Almost two centuries elapsed after the discovery of America', says

says, it was discovered that 'the contemplation of the condition and character of the Americans, in their original state, tended to complete our knowledge of the human species; might enable us to fill up a considerable chasm in the history of its progress; and lead to speculations no less curious than important'.[42] The point here, as Robertson explains, is the following:

In order to complete the history of the human mind, and attain to a perfect knowledge of its nature and operations, we must contemplate man in all those various situations wherein he has been placed. We must follow him in his progress through the different stages of society, as he gradually advances from the infant state of civil life towards its maturity and decline . . . The philosophers and historians of ancient Greece and Rome, our guides in this as well as every other disquisition, had only a limited view of this subject, as they had hardly any opportunity of surveying man in his rudest and most early state. In all those regions of the earth with which they were well acquainted, civil society had made considerable advances, and nations had finished a good part of their career before they began to observe them. The Scythians and Germans, the rudest people of whom any ancient author has transmitted to us an authentic account, possessed flocks and herds, had acquired property of various kinds, and, when compared with mankind in their primitive state, may be reckoned to have attained to a great degree of civilization.

But the discovery of the New World enlarged the sphere of contemplation, and presented nations to our view, in stages of their progress, much less advanced than those wherein they have been observed in our continent. In America, man appears under the rudest form in which we can conceive him to subsist. We behold communities just beginning to unite, and may examine the sentiments and actions of human beings in the infancy of social life, while they feel but imperfectly the force of its ties, and have scarcely relinquished their native liberty. That state of primeval simplicity, which was known in our continent only by the fanciful description of poets, really existed in the other.[43]

But the trouble is, Robertson proceeds, that the modern 'philosophers', in their analysis of this living model of 'the

Robertson, 'before the manners of its inhabitants attracted, in any considerable degree, the attention of philosophers' (*ibid.*, Vol. II, p. 92).
[42] *Ibid.*, Vol. II, p. 92.   [43] *Ibid.*, Vol. II, p. 90.

infancy of social life', have all too often begun 'to erect systems, when they should have been searching for facts on which to establish their foundations'.[44] Robertson instances the work of Buffon, de Pauw, and Rousseau as examples of this kind of illegitimate system-building, and then embarks upon what he claims to be a non-conjectural, fact-based account of the bodily constitution of the Americans, the qualities of their minds, their domestic state, their political state and institutions, their system of war and public security, and their arts. We need not follow Robertson through the intricate details of his account, important though much of it no doubt is as a landmark in the development of cultural anthropology.[45] What interests us here is the way in which certain basic elements of the four stages theory are used as a guide to the discussion. It is true that Robertson nowhere (so far as I am aware) speaks of 'commerce' as a separate stage of development; and it is also true that he was by no means an unwavering apostle of the doctrine of progress.[46] But again and again in the *History of America* it is stated or implied (for example) that peoples who live mainly by hunting and fishing – as the majority of the Americans outside Mexico and Peru are said to do – are the least civilised of all;[47] that from this primitive mode of subsistence of the Americans 'the form and genius of their political institutions' may be deduced;[48] that 'the acquisition of dominion over the animal creation' is one of the 'steps of capital importance' in the progress of nations,[49] and the fact that the Americans

[44] *Ibid.*, Vol. II, p. 92.

[45] See M. Harris, *The Rise of Anthropological Theory* (Routledge, London, 1969), pp. 33–4.

[46] Robertson often speaks of the 'advance' or 'progress' of mankind without any qualification. On the other hand, we have already quoted a passage in which he talks about man advancing 'from the infant state of civil life towards its maturity and decline' (above, p. 142); and there are other instances of his application of the 'human life' analogy to the development of society (see, e.g. *Works*, Vol. II, p. 99).

[47] *Works*, Vol. II, pp. 104–5.

[48] *Ibid.*, Vol. II, p. 107. The four 'deductions' of this kind which Robertson proceeds to make in the following pages are that the Americans are 'divided into small independent communities'; that they are 'in a great measure, strangers to the idea of property'; that they 'retain a high sense of equality and independence'; and that among them 'government can assume little authority' (*ibid.*, Vol. II, pp. 107–9).

[49] *Ibid.*, Vol. II, p. 219.

have not taken this step is 'the most notable distinction between the inhabitants of the Ancient and New Worlds';[50] that although 'the life of a hunter gradually leads man to a state more advanced'[51] – i.e. to agriculture – the progress which most of the American nations (apart from Peru)[52] have made along this road is very slight;[53] and that the degree to which individual nations are civilised is closely linked with the extent to which they do in fact mix agriculture with their hunting and fishing.[54]

It is important to add that Robertson's use of the four stages theory was by no means dogmatic or mechanical: his intention throughout was to use it, not as a substitute for the facts, but rather as an organisational framework within which the facts could usefully be set. He would not have subscribed to the notion that society naturally and necessarily proceeded from hunting to pasturage and then from pasturage to agriculture, being impelled on this course by unavoidable endogenous causes. He certainly believed that there was an innate tendency for hunting societies to move towards agriculture, but he did not believe that there was only one possible road from the first of these modes of subsistence to the second. Nor did he believe that the mode of subsistence was always the most important determining factor, as his interesting analyses of the effects of climate,[55] and of the special influence exerted by religion in Peru,[56] clearly demonstrate. Nevertheless, Robertson succeeded in defining the role of the mode of subsistence very clearly and strikingly; his use of the concepts of hunting, pastoral, and agricultural societies was firmly within the broad tradition of the four stages theory; and he was more conscious than any of his fellow-Scots of the manner in which the emergence of this theory was linked with the contemporary debates about the origin of the Americans. It remains only to be added that

---

[50] *Ibid.*, Vol. II, pp. 106–7. Both the reindeer and the bison are tameable, Robertson claims, and yet in America they have not been tamed. In another place, however, Robertson noted the success of the Peruvians in taming llamas (*ibid.*, Vol. II, p. 219).

[51] *Ibid.*, Vol. II, p. 105.   [52] *Ibid.*, Vol. II, p. 234.

[53] *Ibid.*, Vol. II, pp. 101, 105, and 227.

[54] *Ibid.*, Vol. II, pp. 109, 11, and 221.

[55] See, e.g. *ibid.*, Vol. II, pp. 132–3.   [56] *Ibid.*, Vol. II, pp. 231ff.

while Robertson deliberately tried to steer a course somewhere between the two extremes of the kind of glorification
of the Americans in which Rousseau was wont to indulge
and the kind of denigration of them which had been encouraged in particular by the work of Buffon and de Pauw, the
general impression he left was that the latter approach was
far closer to the truth than the former. America, from Robertson's account, appeared by and large as an extremely
unpleasant country where

> The sedge is wither'd from the lake,
> And no birds sing[57]

and the Americans, however much their character and constitution might be the fault of their state of society rather
than of themselves, appeared much more as ignoble than as
noble savages.[58]

Let us now turn to the famous book by Cornelius de Pauw,
entitled *Recherches Philosophiques sur les Américains* (1768–
1769), which created something of a sensation in its day and
from which Robertson may well have derived some of the
ideas of which we have just been speaking.[59] There is a great
deal of the curious and the bizarre in de Pauw's book – canni-
bals, albinos, giants, and hermaphrodites figure prominently
in its pages, together with detailed descriptions of picturesque practices like circumcision and infibulation – but it is
best known for its sustained stress on the ignobility of the
Americans, which is blamed largely upon the inhospitable
climate of the country. Here, however, we shall be concerned
mainly with two other features of the book which have been
less frequently noted – its elaboration of an interesting version of the four stages theory, and its use of the basic idea

[57] Dr H. E. Briggs, in an article in *Publications of the Modern Language
Association of America*, Vol. 59, 1944, pp. 184–99, has claimed that
Keats's withered sedge and songless birds may well in fact owe their
origin to his reading of Robertson's *History of America*, with its rather
stark picture of the American scene.
[58] See, e.g. note 52 in the 'Notes and Illustrations' appended to the
History of America (*Works*, Vol. II, pp. 337–9). Cf. R. H. Pearce, *The
Savages of America* (revised edn, Johns Hopkins, Baltimore, 1965),
pp. 86–8.
[59] Cornelius de Pauw, *Recherches Philosophiques sur les Américains*
(Berlin, 1768 (Vol. I) and 1769 (Vol. II)).

lying behind the theory (much in the manner of Robertson
to dispose of the old notion that similarities are proof of
genetic descent.

De Pauw's statement of the four stages theory occurs in
the course of an extended discussion of the reasons why the
Americans, after the very long period for which it must be
assumed that they have lived in their country, are still to be
found in a savage or semi-savage state. When we go as far
back in history as we can, says de Pauw, we see the majority
of peoples 'raising themselves successively from brutishness'
– containing within themselves, as they do, the 'germ of
perfectibility'.[60] And it is agriculture, says de Pauw, which
has 'led men by the hand, step by step' from the uncivilised
to the civilised state: 'property and all the arts are . . . born
in the womb of agriculture'.[61] Thus we may rank the different
kinds of savages whom we find in the world in accordance
with their greater or lesser distance from the state of 'moral
perfection' towards which agriculture enables mankind to
progress. De Pauw's ranking, based on a kind of hierarchy of
five different modes of subsistence, is as follows:

The cultivators constitute the first category, because their subsistence is the least precarious and their way of life the least tur-
bulent and the least uneasy: they have the time to invent and
perfect their instruments; they have the leisure to think and
reflect.

The nomads follow next, but they differ from the first in that
they are obliged to go in search of pasture-land and to accom-
pany their flocks and herds; they are never settled . . . The
Tartars, the Arabs, the Moors, and the Lapps are those of the
nomads with whom we are most familiar: their manners may be
regarded as the true model of the life of pastoral peoples or
shepherds; intermediate between the savage condition and the
civil state, it is almost equidistant from these two points.

There are the nations which we have called rhizophagous: we
mean by this those which live in the forests on roots and fruits
which accrue without any cultivation. Their manners depend
greatly on the products and the quality of the land: those which
have coconut palms and cabbage-trees are better off and less
savage than those which see nothing rising above their huts but
the branches of beeches and the tops of oaks . . .

[60] *Op. cit.*, Vol. I, p. 98.   [61] *Ibid.*, Vol. I, p. 99.

The fishing peoples form the fourth class: their mode of existence does not differ appreciably from that of the shepherds or nomads, except that the latter have in their tame flocks and herds an assured means of support, whereas the fishers have to look as much to chance as to their skill for their physical necessaries . . . Those of these peoples with whom we are most familiar are the Greenlanders and the Eskimos.

Finally, the hunters constitute the last category, and are the most savage of all: wandering, and unsure of what is in store for them from one day to the next, they are bound to fear the reunion and multiplication of their fellow-creatures as the greatest of evils . . . A savage hunter [is] . . . never at peace with men or with animals; his instincts are wild and his manners barbarous; and the more his mind is occupied with ways of providing for his subsistence, the less does he reflect on the possibility of becoming civilised.[62]

So far as the last three of these modes of subsistence are concerned, it is not of course implied in de Pauw's account that men normally start out as hunters, and then in the course of time become successively fishers and gatherers. Hunting, fishing, and gathering are presented as *alternative* ways of life, any of which may characterise 'the savage condition' in the infancy of society.[63] Which of these three modes of subsistence will in fact be adopted by any given savage nation, it is suggested, will depend mainly upon climatic and geographical conditions, but also to some extent upon the physical constitution of the people. The Americans, de Pauw argues, live in a very harsh environment, and their physical constitution may well have been enfeebled as a result of some tremendous natural catastrophe, of more recent date than the biblical Flood. For these and other reasons, the Americans have not only been hindered from moving forward from the savage state, but many of them have also persisted in that way of life which is furthest removed from 'moral perfection' – i.e. they still remain hunters.

The first two modes of subsistence in de Pauw's list, however, are *not* simply alternatives: they are also fairly clearly

---

[62] *Ibid.*, Vol. I, pp. 99–101.
[63] For instance, de Pauw gives the Greenlanders and Eskimos as examples of peoples who 'have never perhaps issued from infancy and the original state' (*op. cit.*, Vol. I, p. 98). Yet as we know from the passage just quoted in the text, the Greenlanders and Eskimos are 'fishing peoples'.

meant to represent developmental *stages* through which nations are likely to pass if and when they manage to leave the 'savage condition' – which they will the more easily be able to do the higher their chosen mode of subsistence stands on de Pauw's list. The innate tendency is for a nation to move towards agriculture, but if it possesses domesticable animals it may well pass through the 'intermediate' pastoral stage on the way, as the Tartars, Arabs, Moors, and Lapps were doing,[64] and as the Tunguses of Siberia were beginning to do.[65] It was a sure sign of the immense backwardness of the Americans that (*pace* Montesquieu)[66] there were twenty provinces in the New World where the people were unacquainted with maize for every one province where they actually made use of it,[67] *and* that in spite of the availability of animals such as caribou, moose, and bison the Americans had made no progress whatever in domesticating them.[68]

Passing now to the second interesting feature of de Pauw's book, we find him saying of the Americans, near the end of the discussion I have just described, that

those who have studied their manners, especially those of the northern peoples, are astonished to find that they are, so to speak, the same as those of the ancient Scythians, and from this apparent similarity they deduce lines of filiation, and the descent of one of these peoples from the other; but since the manners of the Scythians were simply the true expressions of the savage life, it was natural to observe such a similarity between the mode of existence of all the savages in the world, once they have gathered into bands.[69]

And a little later in the book de Pauw returns to this 'great principle', as he calls it, to show that the existence of certain similarities between the Canadians and the Tunguses of Siberia does *not* prove that the former are genetically descended from the latter: all it proves is that both peoples are savages living by hunting and fishing in the same kind of environment:

---

[64] *Ibid.*, Vol. I, p. 100.   [65] *Ibid.*, Vol. I, p. 143.
[66] *The Spirit of Laws*, Book XVIII, section 9.
[67] De Pauw, *op. cit.*, Vol. I, p. 110.
[68] *Ibid.*, Vol. I, p. 111.   [69] *Ibid.*, Vol. I, p. 113.

I return here to that great principle of which I have already made use, and say that it is not only natural but also necessary that there should be, as between savages located in such similar climates, as many resemblances as there possibly are between the Tunguses and the Canadians. Equally barbarous, equally living by hunting and fishing in countries which are cold, infertile, and covered with forests, what disproportion between them would one expect? Where people feel the same needs, where the means of satisfying them are the same, where the atmospheric influences are so similar, can the manners be contradictory, and can the ideas vary?[70]

If one adheres to this truth, de Pauw goes on, 'all will be explained, all difficulties will be smoothed away. The Tunguses live in huts; the Americans also do so; but this is not astonishing, since they are savages. Both live dispersed in small families, as befits hunters . . .'[71] And a number of additional illustrations of the working of the 'great principle' are given: if both the Tunguses and the Canadians adore the skins of animals, for example, this once again is surely a very natural thing for peoples who are hunters to do.[72] And de Pauw concludes this part of his discussion by pointing out that there are certain differences between the Tunguses and the Canadians which are more important than these resemblances. In particular, the Siberians have begun to mix some pasturage with their hunting, and this has already had the effect of allowing them to confine their hunting expeditions to a smaller area, thus reducing the possibility of bloody conflicts with their neighbours.[73]

In de Pauw's subsequent work he tried to cash in on the success of his book on the Americans: *Recherches Philosophiques sur les Egyptiens et les Chinois* appeared in 1774, and *Recherches Philosophiques sur les Grecs* in 1787–8. There is little trace of the 'great principle' in the first of these; but in the second a general environmentalist bias is more evident, and in a number of places he evidently takes the importance of the mode of subsistence more or less for granted.[74] But nowhere in either of these later books is there

[70] *Ibid.*, Vol. I, p. 139.
[71] *Ibid.*, Vol. I, p. 139.
[72] *Ibid.*, Vol. I, pp. 142–3.
[73] *Ibid.*, Vol. I, pp. 143–4.
[74] *Recherches Philosophiques sur les Grecs*, Vol. I, (Berlin, 1787), pp. 43, 140–1, and 267. Cf. also *ibid.*, Vol. II, (Berlin, 1788), pp. 132 and 238.

anything of comparable interest to the discussions which have described above. In de Pauw's case, as in that of man other contemporary writers, the current controversies abou the Americans brought out the best, as well as the worst, i him.

Adam Ferguson's *Essay on the History of Civil Society*, th first edition of which appeared in 1767[75] – about the sam time as Robertson's *Charles V* and de Pauw's book on th Americans – is undoubtedly one of the most notable work of the epoch. Original, subtle, and provocatively complex, i is nowadays rightly regarded as one of the first importan exercises in the field which modern sociologists have marke out as their own. In our discussion of it here, we shall con centrate mainly on Part II – 'Of the History of Rude Nations – which has helped to give the title to our present chapter Let us note first, however, Ferguson's sophisticated statemen of the law of unintended consequences, which occurs i another part of the book:

Mankind, in following the present sense of their minds, in striving to remove inconveniencies, or to gain apparent and contiguou advantages, arrive at ends which even their imagination coul not anticipate; and pass on, like other animals, in the tract of thei nature, without perceiving its end . . .

Every step and every movement of the multitude, even in wha are termed enlightened ages, are made with equal blindness to th future; and nations stumble upon establishments, which ar indeed the result of human action, but not the execution of an human design.[76]

This statement, particularly when read in its context, is easil the most advanced formulation of the law of unintende consequences in the whole of the half-century we are con sidering. The basic idea of the law was almost always *implie* in the work of the new social scientists, of course, but no on else at this time actually *expressed* it with anything like th clarity and force of Ferguson.

[75] The edition of the *Essay* which I have used, and to which the pag references below relate, is stated on the title page to be the 6th edition published in London in 1793.
[76] *Essay*, pp. 204–5.

'The history of rude nations'

Part II of the *Essay* begins with a long methodological discussion of the validity or otherwise of the information about 'the history of rude nations' which is derived from antiquity. The history of mankind, says Ferguson,

from every quarter brings an intimation that human affairs have had a beginning. Nations, distinguished by the possession of arts, and the felicity of their political establishments, have been derived from a feeble original, and still preserve in their story the indications of a slow and gradual progress, by which this distinction was gained.[77]

Where, however, are we to obtain the detailed factual information which we need about 'the original character of mankind'? All too frequently, says Ferguson, we are tempted to 'rest the whole on conjecture . . . and to imagine, that a mere negation of all our virtues is a sufficient description of man in his original state'. But this is an idle exercise: somehow or other, if we are to get anywhere at all, we must 'build on the facts which are preserved for our use'.[78] One difficulty here is that the 'domestic antiquities' of nations are for the most part 'the mere conjectures or the fictions of subsequent ages', and must therefore be interpreted with great caution.[79] From the Greek and Roman historians, however, we can get a great deal of reliable information about 'the tribes from whom we descend', although even here there is the danger of misinterpreting the 'general terms' of which writers like Caesar and Tacitus made use.[80] And, in addition, just as Thucydides understood 'that it was in the customs of barbarous nations he was to study the more ancient manners of Greece', so we today should likewise understand that it is in the present condition of Arab clans and American tribes that we may 'behold, as in a mirrour, the features of our own progenitors'.[81]

At first sight, Ferguson appears to be saying here no more than that 'in the beginning all the World was *America*'. But what he is in fact saying is something rather more cautious, specific, and important than this. From the study of peoples like the Arabs and the Americans, he states, 'we are to draw

[77] *Ibid.*, p. 123. [78] *Ibid.*, p. 125. [79] *Ibid.*, p. 127.
[80] *Ibid.*, pp. 130–3. [81] *Ibid.*, p. 133.

our conclusions with respect to the influence of situations, in which we have reason to believe that our fathers were placed'.[82] The idea here, quite clearly, is that if we want to know what our fathers were like, we should first look at the historical and geographical facts and try to ascertain what mode of subsistence they followed and what kind of environment they inhabited. We may then behold their features 'as in a mirrour', if we so wish, by studying the present condition of *clans or tribes following the same mode of subsistence and living in the same kind of environment*. For, asks Ferguson, 'what should distinguish a German or a Briton, in the habits of his mind or his body, in his manners or apprehensions, from an American, who, like him, with his bow and his dart, is left to traverse the forest; and in a like severe or variable climate, is obliged to subsist by the chace?'[83] Here the 'great principle' which de Pauw and Robertson use in order to dispose of the notion that similarities imply genetic descent is in effect transformed by Ferguson into a tool of anthropological research.

Part II of the *Essay* now continues with a section entitled 'Of Rude Nations prior to the Establishment of Property', the purpose of which is 'to form some general conception of our species in its rude state'. Of barbarous and savage nations, Ferguson begins by saying,

some intrust their subsistence chiefly to hunting, fishing, or the natural produce of the soil. They have little attention to property, and scarcely any beginnings of subordination or government. Others, having possessed themselves of herds,[84] and depending for their provision on pasture, know what it is to be poor and rich. They know the relations of patron and client, of servant and master, and by the measures of fortune determine their station. This distinction must create a material difference of character, and may furnish two separate heads, under which to consider the history of mankind in their rudest state; that of the savage, who is not yet acquainted with property; and that of the barbarian, to whom it is, although not ascertained by laws, a principal object of care and desire.[85]

[82] *Ibid.*, pp. 133–4.
[83] *Ibid.*, p. 134.
[84] The 6th edition has 'herbs', which is clearly an error.
[85] *Essay*, pp. 135–6.

This approach represents an interesting amalgam of three elements: Montesquieu's identification of savages with hunters and barbarians with herdsmen;[86] the dynamisation of these categories which is characteristic of the four stages theory; and the concern with changes in property which derives from the Grotius–Pufendorf–Locke tradition. In the remainder of this section of the *Essay*, the peoples of America are accepted by Ferguson as a model of the savage or hunting stage,[87] and their characteristics are carefully studied on the basis of the accounts of the usual authorities – notably Charlevoix and Lafitau. Particular attention is paid to the fewness of 'subjects of property' among these peoples,[88] and to the consequential absence of 'distinctions of rank or condition'[89] and 'any settled form of government'.[90]

In the third and final section of Part II, entitled 'Of Rude Nations under the Impressions of Property and Interest', Ferguson suggests that the impulse to socio-economic improvement is provided primarily by private property, which already exists – if only in very few subjects – even in savage societies. Mankind, 'under the impressions of property and interest', gradually 'acquire industry', accumulate wealth, and become 'secured in the possession of what they fairly obtain';[91] and as an unintended consequence of this the mode of subsistence changes:

A hoard, collected from the simple productions of nature, or a herd of cattle, are, in every rude nation, the first species of wealth. The circumstances of the soil, and the climate, determine whether the inhabitant shall apply himself chiefly to agriculture or pasture; whether he shall fix his residence, or be moving continually about with all his possessions.[92]

Ferguson now proceeds to give some concrete historical examples:

[86] *The Spirit of Laws*, Book XVIII, section 11.
[87] 'Where savage nations, as in most parts of America, mix with the practice of hunting some species of rude agriculture', writes Ferguson, 'they still follow, with respect to the soil and the fruits of the earth, the analogy of their principal object' (*Essay*, p. 137).
[88] *Ibid.*, p. 137.   [89] *Ibid.*, p. 139.
[90] *Ibid.*, p. 143.   [91] *Ibid.*, p. 161.
[92] *Ibid.*, pp. 161–2.

In the west of Europe; in America, from south to north, with a few exceptions; in the torrid zone, and every where within the warmer climates; mankind have generally applied themselves to some species of agriculture, and have been disposed to settlement. In the north and middle region of Asia, they depended entirely on their herds, and were perpetually shifting their ground in search of new pasture. The arts which pertain to settlement have been practised, and variously cultivated, by the inhabitants of Europe. Those which are consistent with perpetual migration, have, from the earliest accounts of history, remained nearly the same with the Scythian or Tartar.[93]

And later in the book he explains how, in those societies which are able to move beyond the barbarian state, 'the enjoyment of peace . . . and the prospect of being able to exchange one commodity for another, turns, by degrees, the hunter and the warrior into a tradesman and a merchant'.[94] The end-product of the developmental process, in other words, is very often that 'polished and commercial' state in which most of the countries of Europe find themselves.[95]

Ferguson's version of the four stages theory is highly idiosyncratic, and rather more flexible and rich in content than these brief quotations may perhaps have suggested.[96] One of the interesting things about it is that it is used not only as the framework of a theory of socio-economic development, but also as the basis of an *evaluation* both of the savage state and of the modern commercial state. In Ferguson's view, savage society has certain obvious vices, but it also has certain actual and potential virtues. The potential virtues can be realised only when the savage state has been left behind, which happens mainly as a result of 'the impressions of property and interest' and of the eventual extension of the division of labour. By these means, 'polished and commercial' nations have gained – or at any rate appear to have gained – 'the ends that were pursued by the savage in his forest,

[93] *Ibid.*, p. 162.
[94] *Ibid.*, p. 302.
[95] Section III of Part IV of the *Essay* is entitled 'Of the Manners of Polished and Commercial Nations'.
[96] Cf. the short summary of the theory which appears in Ferguson's *Institutes of Moral Philosophy* (Edinburgh, 1769), pp. 28–9, and also the rather curious version in his later book *Principles of Moral and Political Science* (Edinburgh, 1792), Vol. I, pp. 58–9.

knowledge, order, and wealth'.[97] But the fly in the ointment here, of course, is that the two main engines of improvement, private property and the division of labour, inevitably usher in certain evils of their own. Thus even if we admit that man is susceptible of improvement, and has in himself a principle of progression, and a desire of perfection',[98] and even if we reject the idea that 'the images of youth, and of old age' can be applied to nations,[99] perpetual progress and improvement cannot simply be taken for granted. On the contrary, it is always necessary to study carefully 'the sources of internal decay, and the ruinous corruptions to which nations are liable, in the supposed condition of accomplished civility',[100] and to take all necessary steps to root out these evils. But they *can* be rooted out. Ferguson's last word to the readers of his *Essay* is that 'no nation ever suffered internal decay but from the vice of its members':[101] it is only the *voluntary* neglects and corruptions'[102] of mankind which can bring about 'relaxations in the national spirit'.[103] Thus Ferguson, in spite of his serious and profound critique of the evils and vices of 'commercial nations', is certainly no primitivist. The price of real and continued progress in commercial societies is merely eternal vigilance; and the savage, if not positively ignoble, is by no means as noble as men like Rousseau suggest. As Professor Pearce puts it, Ferguson's *Essay* demonstrated 'that men in becoming civilized had gained much more than they had lost; and that civilization, the act of civilizing, for all of its destruction of primitive virtues, put something higher and greater in their place'.[104]

If we turn now to Lord Kames's *Sketches of the History of Man* (1774),[105] let it not be merely as comic relief. Kames, with his readiness to pontificate on every subject under the sun, his ubiquitous polygeneticism, and his conspicuous failure to deal adequately with certain problems relating to

---

97 *Essay*, p. 307.   98 *Ibid.*, p. 13.   99 *Ibid.*, p. 349.
100 *Ibid.*, p. 350.   101 *Ibid.*, p. 467.   102 *Ibid.*, p. 374. (My italics.)
103 Section III of Part V of the *Essay* is entitled 'Of Relaxations in the National Spirit incident to Polished Nations'.
104 R. H. Pearce, *op. cit.*, p. 85.
105 The edition of the *Sketches* which I have used, and to which the page references below relate, is stated on the title page to be 'a new edition, in three volumes', published in Edinburgh in 1807.

Social science and the ignoble savage

the Americans, is easy enough to make sport of. But he ha
some very solid achievements to his credit, not least in th
field of the four stages theory. We have already seen tha
his exercises in this field in 1758 were by no means lackin
in ingenuity;[106] and in his *Sketches of the History of Man,*
work of his old age, the theory is developed further and
applied, on the whole, in an interesting and fruitful way. I
is true that there is a strong element of dogmatism in hi
application of the theory, which shows itself particularl
when he comes to deal with the Americans. But there ar
important successes to be weighed against this failure; and
even the failure, as we shall see, is quite an instructive one

The *Sketches* begins with a 'Preliminary Discourse' i
which, rather unpromisingly (and unnecessarily), Kames pos
tulates that God, when he scattered men abroad after th
Tower of Babel episode, at the same time miraculousl
equipped them with bodily constitutions which were fitted
for the different climates they were to inhabit.[107] In their new
environments, deprived of society, men reverted to savagery
'From that state of degeneracy', Kames says, 'they have
been emerging gradually'; and his main aim in the *Sketches*
as he puts it, is 'to trace out that progress towards maturity
in different nations'.[108] What follows is divided into three
long books: i. Progress of Men independent of Society; ii
Progress of Man in Society; and iii. Progress of Sciences. The
four stages theory is outlined at the beginning of Book i, and
is then used throughout Books i and ii as a kind of unifying
device.

'In temperate climes', says Kames, 'men fed originally on
fruits that grow without culture, and on the flesh of land
animals.' All savages whose food depends on the chase have
'an appetite for hunting' – a state of affairs which Kames
cannot resist describing as 'an illustrious instance of provi
dential care'.[109] So far as fishing is concerned, 'savages pro
bably did not attempt to draw food from the sea or from
rivers, till land-animals became scarce'.[110] Then, eventually
mankind moved on to the next stage:

[106] Above, pp. 102ff.
[108] *Ibid.*, Vol. i, p. 65.
[110] *Ibid.*, Vol. i, p. 69.

[107] *Sketches*, Vol. i, pp. 60–1.
[109] *Ibid.*, Vol. i, pp. 67–8.

Plenty of food procured by hunting and fishing, promotes population: but as consumption of food increases with population, wild animals, sorely persecuted, become not only more rare, but more shy. Men, thus pinched for food, are excited to try other means for supplying their wants. A fawn, a kid, or a lamb, taken alive and tamed for amusement, suggested probably flocks and herds, and introduced the shepherd-state. Changes are not perfected but by slow degrees: hunting and fishing continue for a long time favourite occupations; and the few animals that are domesticated, serve as a common stock to be distributed among individuals, according to their wants. But as the idle and indolent, though the least deserving, are thus the greatest consumers of the common stock, an improvement crept in, that every family should rear a stock for themselves. Men by that means being taught to rely on their own industry, displayed the hoarding principle, which multiplied flocks and herds exceedingly. And thus the shepherd-state was perfected, plenty of food being supplied at home, without ranging the woods or the waters. Hunting and fishing, being no longer necessary for food, became an amusement merely, and a gratification of the original appetite for hunting.[111]

The shepherd-state, Kames proceeds, is 'friendly to population', and sooner or later hunger once again takes a hand in leading men to the next socio-economic stage, that of agriculture:

Men by plenty of food multiply apace; and, in process of time, neighbouring tribes, straitened in their pasture, go to war for extension of territory, or migrate to land not yet occupied. Necessity, the mother of invention, suggested agriculture. When corn growing spontaneously was rendered scarce by consumption, it was an obvious thought to propagate it by art . . . As the land was possessed in common, the seed of course was sown in common; and the product was stored in a common repository, to be parcelled out among individuals in want, as the common stock of animals had been formerly. We have for our authority Diodorus Siculus, that the Celtiberians divided their land annually among individuals, to be laboured for the use of the public; and that the product was stored up, and distributed from time to time among the necessitous. A lasting division of the land among the members of the state, securing to each man the product of his own skill and

111 *Ibid.*, Vol. I, pp. 71–2.

Social science and the ignoble savage

labour, was a great spur to industry, and multiplied food exceedingly. Population made a rapid progress, and government became an art; for agriculture and commerce cannot flourish without salutary laws.[112]

The coming of 'commerce', and the nature of its various virtues and vices, are described at length by Kames in subsequent chapters.

After his description of the transition to agriculture, Kames embarks upon a new development. The progress through these socio-economic stages, he says, has 'in all temperate climates of the Old World, been precisely uniform', but in 'the extremes of cold and hot climates' it has been different in two respects. The first difference lies in the particular mode of subsistence with which the savages start:

In very cold regions, which produce little vegetable food for man the hunter-state was originally essential. In temperate regions, as observed above, men subsisted partly on vegetable food, which is more or less plentiful in proportion to the heat of the climate. In the torrid zone, natural fruits are produced in such plenty and perfection, as to be more than sufficient for a moderate population; and, in case of extraordinary population, the transition to husbandry is easy.[113]

The second difference lies in the fact that it is only in temperate regions that the process of development, as it were, goes all the way. In very cold regions which are 'unfit for corn', the process 'stops short' at the pastoral stage: 'Thus the Tartars, like the Laplanders, are chained to the shepherd-state, and can never advance to be husbandmen.'[114] And in very hot regions, at any rate in the absence of 'extraordinary population', the developmental process never really gets going at all: the inhabitants of the torrid zone 'at present subsist on vegetable food; and probably did so from the beginning'.[115] This is all no doubt rather schematic, but it does represent a serious attempt to bring the influence of climate into the developmental picture, and, by so doing, to make the four stages theory conform rather more closely with the observed facts.

[112] Ibid., Vol. I, pp. 73–4.
[114] Ibid., Vol. I, pp. 79–81.
[113] Ibid., Vol. I, p. 78.
[115] Ibid., Vol. I, p. 81.

158

In the remainder of Book I of the *Sketches* Kames re-
peatedly uses the four stages theory to illuminate his discussions of a number of important topics – the growth of
population,[116] for example, and the progress of property,[117]
manners,[118] and luxury.[119] And in Book II he uses it in connection with such problems as the origin of national societies,[120] the growth of patriotism,[121] and 'the origin and
progress of American nations'.[122] It is in relation to this last
problem that his treatment is, to say the least, rather less
than satisfactory. He starts off on the wrong foot by arguing
that the Americans cannot possibly be 'descended from any
people of the old world', and by postulating yet another
separate creation' to account for their existence.[123] But his
real troubles commence when he begins to consider the fact
that the North American tribes, 'instead of advancing, like
other nations, toward the maturity of society and government . . . continue to this hour in their original state of hunting and fishing'.[124] It is not the want of 'animals capable to
be domesticated' that has prevented them moving forward
from the hunting stage to the pastoral stage: the bison are
there for the taming.[125] What then can explain their lack of
progress? To answer this, Kames refers back to the built-in
mechanism which in his version of the four stages theory is
assumed to generate the movement from one stage to the
next: 'Want of food, occasioned by rapid population, brought
on the shepherd-state in the old world. That cause has not
hitherto existed in North America: the inhabitants, few in
number, remain hunters and fishers, because that state
affords them a competency of food.'[126] But this of course
immediately raises the further question – 'By what adverse
fate are so rich countries so ill peopled?'[127] Here Kames has
recourse to the then-familiar notion, fostered by Buffon, that
the American males 'are feeble in their organs of generation
. . [and] have no ardour for the female sex'.[128]

16 *Ibid.*, Vol. I, p. 84.
17 *Ibid.*, Vol. I, pp. 92–3.   118 *Ibid.*, Vol. I, pp. 278–80.
19 *Ibid.*, Vol. I, p. 492.   120 *Ibid.*, Vol. II, pp. 41–2.
121 *Ibid.*, Vol. II, p. 128.   122 *Ibid.*, Vol. II, pp. 352ff.
23 *Ibid.*, Vol. II, p. 360.   124 *Ibid.*, Vol. II, p. 361.
125 *Ibid.*, Vol. II, pp. 361–2.   126 *Ibid.*, Vol. II, p. 362.
127 *Ibid.*, Vol. II, p. 363.   128 *Ibid.*, Vol. II, p. 364.

But worse is yet to come. Kames, as an honest observer, i
obliged to note that whereas in the temperate regions of the
Old World all nations have passed through the pastoral stage
before arriving at agriculture and commerce, the North
Americans have 'advanced to some degree of agriculture
without passing through the shepherd-state at all. Admit
tedly 'husbandry . . . is among those people still in it:
infancy',[129] but it does exist and cannot be ignored. Kames i
completely baffled by this: all he can say is that 'the fact . .
is singular, of a people using corn before tame cattle: there
must be a cause, which on better acquaintance with tha:
people will probably be discovered'.[130]

In addition to this vexing problem there are of course
others. Why, for example, have the Mexicans and Peruvian.
made 'great advances towards the perfection of society'
whereas the northern tribes are still largely hunters and
fishers? And why are the Mexicans and Peruvians, who live
in the torrid zone, so 'highly polished in the arts of society
and government', whereas in the Old World the inhabitant:
of the torrid zone are 'for the most part little better than
savages'?[131] What Kames should have realised at this point
was that his formulation of the four stages theory had been
too rigid, and that he had been trying to apply it in too
mechanical a fashion. He did not realise this, however: all
he felt able to say, in the face of such problems, was this
'America is full of political wonders . . . We are not suffi
ciently acquainted with the natural history of America, no
with that of its people, to attempt an explanation of these
wonders.'[132] This is laughable enough, perhaps; but having
laughed at it, let us note that Kames, to his credit, at leas
did not try to distort the facts to fit the theory. Having
observed and recorded the discrepancy between fact and
theory, he was honest enough to admit his inability to explain
it, and brave enough to move on.

With John Millar, the last of the historians of civil society
whose work I propose to consider in any detail in the pre
sent chapter, the four stages theory and the basic 'materialist

129 *Ibid.*, Vol. II, p. 369.   130 *Ibid.*, Vol. II, p. 371.
131 *Ibid.*, Vol. II, p. 371.   132 *Ibid.*, Vol. II, p. 371.

ideas and techniques associated with it become central and pervasive to a quite unprecedented degree. In Millar's books and lectures, it is hardly too much to say, the new social science of the Enlightenment comes of age. For one thing, the range of topics with which it deals is appreciably increased: although Millar's main emphasis is still on the development of systems of law and government, he is also concerned to explain the changes which occur (for example) in the condition of women, in father–child and master–servant relationships, in manners and morals, and in literature, art, and science, as society develops. No one before Millar had ever used a materialist conception of history – for, in his hands, that is what it in effect became – so ably and consistently to illuminate the development of such a wide range of social phenomena.

For another thing, in Millar's case the array of source-material employed is wider, and his disposition of it is more skilful and stimulating, than in the case of most of his contemporaries. No longer is there any special emphasis on the Americans: the works of Lafitau and Charlevoix are still frequently cited, but these works now take their place quite naturally alongside the accounts given by many other authorities, both ancient and modern, of many other peoples. And side by side with the classical and modern histories and the whole range of voyage literature, we find numerous quotations from the Old Testament (now used in a quite unembarrassed way as a source of anthropological data), from ancient poets like Homer and modern poets like Pope, and from Macpherson's Ossian. Clearly with Millar we have reached the stage, whose coming was foreshadowed above, at which the earlier studies of the similarities between the Americans and the ancients have led to, and have up to a point been absorbed in, wider comparative studies of relatively primitive peoples (both past and present) in which differences as well as similarities are stressed.[133]

Millar's great achievement was to transform the four stages theory and the more general ideas associated with it into a true *philosophy of history*, of the kind which Voltaire wrote about but never himself wrote. And not only did Millar

[133] Above, pp. 65–6.

Social science and the ignoble savage

apply this philosophy of history more expertly than anyone else at that time, but he also *formulated* it more explicitly, and more carefully, than anyone else. He was fully aware of the fact that the method he was using was a comparatively new one,[134] and that no one had yet succeeded in explaining in general terms exactly what the use of this method implied. In the introduction to his *Origin of Ranks*[135] Millar tried to do just this, the essence of his explanation being contained in the following passage, which is too important to be quoted otherwise than in full:

In searching for the causes of those peculiar systems of law and government which have appeared in the world, we must undoubtedly resort, first of all, to the differences of situation, which have suggested different views and motives of action to the inhabitants of particular countries. Of this kind, are the fertility or barrenness of the soil, the nature of its productions, the species of labour requisite for procuring subsistence, the number of individuals collected together in one community, their proficiency in arts, the advantages which they enjoy for entering into mutual transactions, and for maintaining an intimate correspondence. The variety that frequently occurs in these, and such other particulars, must have a prodigious influence upon the great body of a people; as, by giving a peculiar direction to their inclinations and pursuits, it must be productive of correspondent habits, dispositions, and ways of thinking.

[134] See, e.g. Millar's *Historical View of the English Government* (3rd (posthumous) edn, London, 1803), Vol. IV, pp. 284–5, where he describes how 'the attempts to delineate systems of jurisprudence . . . opened at length a new source of speculation, by suggesting an enquiry into the circumstances which have occasioned various and opposite imperfections in the law of different countries . . .' In this enquiry, as he goes on to make clear, it was 'more especially' the contributions of Montesquieu, Kames, and Smith which directed the attention of 'speculative lawyers' to the examination of 'the first formation and subsequent advancement of civil society', etc.

[135] *The Origin of Ranks* was first published in 1771, the full title of this first edition being *Observations Concerning the Distinction of Ranks in Society*. A 2nd edition, not greatly changed, followed in 1773, and a 3rd ('corrected and enlarged') edition in 1779. The title of the 3rd edition was changed to *The Origin of the Distinction of Ranks*, and substantial textual alterations were made – not least to the introduction, which was completely rewritten and greatly enlarged. The edition which I have used, and to which the page references below relate, is the 4th (posthumous) edition of 1806, which is substantially the same in content as the 3rd apart from the addition of a biography of Millar by John Craig.

'The history of rude nations'

When we survey the present state of the globe, we find that, in many parts of it, the inhabitants are so destitute of culture, as to appear little above the condition of brute animals; and even when we peruse the remote history of polished nations, we have seldom any difficulty in tracing them to a state of the same rudeness and barbarism. There is, however, in man a disposition and capacity for improving his condition, by the exertion of which, he is carried on from one degree of advancement to another; and the similarity of his wants, as well as of the faculties by which those wants are supplied, has every where produced a remarkable uniformity in the several steps of his progression. A nation of savages, who feel the want of almost every thing requisite for the support of life, must have their attention directed to a small number of objects, to the acquisition of food and clothing, or the procuring shelter from the inclemencies of the weather; and their ideas and feelings, in conformity to their situation, must, of course, be narrow and contracted. Their first efforts are naturally calculated to increase the means of subsistence, by catching or ensnaring wild animals, or by gathering the spontaneous fruits of the earth; and the experience, acquired in the exercise of these employments, is apt, successively, to point out the methods of taming and rearing cattle, and of cultivating the ground. According as men have been successful in these great improvements, and find less difficulty in the attainment of bare necessaries, their prospects are gradually enlarged, their appetites and desires are more and more awakened and called forth in pursuit of the several conveniencies of life; and the various branches of manufacture, together with commerce, its inseparable attendant, and with science and literature, the natural offspring of ease and affluence, are introduced, and brought to maturity. By such gradual advances in rendering their situation more comfortable, the most important alterations are produced in the state and condition of a people: their numbers are increased; the connections of society are extended; and men, being less oppressed with their own wants, are more at liberty to cultivate the feelings of humanity: property, the great source of distinction among individuals, is established; and the various rights of mankind, arising from their multiplied connections, are recognised and protected: the laws of a country are thereby rendered numerous; and a more complex form of government becomes necessary, for distributing justice, and for preventing the disorders which proceed from the jarring interests and passions of a large and opulent community. It is evident, at the same time, that these, and such other effects of improvement, which have so great a tendency to

163

vary the state of mankind, and their manner of life, will be pro
ductive of suitable variations in their taste and sentiments, and in
their general system of behaviour.

There is thus, in human society, a natural progress from ignor
ance to knowledge, and from rude to civilized manners, the
several stages of which are usually accompanied with peculiar
laws and customs.[136]

This, then, was Millar's formulation of the great master
principle which he believed would enable him to penetrate
as he himself put it (much in the manner of Marx), 'beneath
that common surface of events which occupies the details of
the vulgar historian'.[137] But, he insisted, the principle must
on no account be interpreted mechanistically. As he went on
to make clear, immediately following the last statement
quoted above,

various accidental causes, indeed, have contributed to accelerate
or to retard this advancement in different countries. It has even
happened that nations, being placed in such unfavourable cir
cumstances as to render them long stationary at a particular
period, have been so habituated to the peculiar manners of
that age, as to retain a strong tincture of those peculiarities
through every subsequent revolution. This appears to have
occasioned some of the chief varieties which take place in the
maxims and customs of nations equally civilized.[138]

In addition, Millar believed, it was necessary to define very
carefully the relation between the master-principle and cer
tain other views of historical causation such as the climatic
theory of Montesquieu and the 'great man' theory. So far as
the climatic theory was concerned, Millar agreed that 'among
the several circumstances which may affect the gradual im
provements of society, the difference of climate is one of the
most remarkable'. There were undoubtedly certain differ
ences in 'dispositions and talents' which did spring, albeit
indirectly, from extremes of heat and cold.[139] But the notion
that climatic differences 'have a more immediate influence
upon the character and conduct of nations, by operating

---

[136] *Origin of Ranks*, pp. 2–4.
[137] *Historical View of the English Government*, Vol. IV, p. 101.
[138] *Origin of Ranks*, pp. 4–5.
[139] *Ibid.*, pp. 8–9.

insensibly upon the human body, and by effecting correspondent alterations in the temper',[140] was according to Millar illfounded and misleading. It could not possibly provide an adequate explanation of 'the character of different nations', as was sufficiently shown by the fact that nations with the same climate often had entirely different manners and institutions, and that the same nation often had different manners and institutions at different periods in its history.[141] And the 'great man' theory was also open to attack, on the grounds that 'the greater part of the political system of any country [is] derived from the combined influence of the whole people' – although Millar was quite prepared to admit, subject to certain qualifications, that 'a variety of peculiar institutions will sometimes take their origin from the casual interposition of particular persons'.[142]

So all-pervasive is Millar's use of this master-principle that when we begin looking for a typical example of its application for purposes of quotation we find ourselves faced with an *embarras de richesse*. We could select almost any part of the first section of his lectures on Government, where the four stages theory appears as the guiding principle throughout;[143] almost any of the chapters in his *Origin of Ranks*; a

---

[140] *Ibid.*, p. 9.   [141] *Ibid.*, p. 11.   [142] *Ibid.*, p. 5.

[143] There are several sets of students' notes of Millar's lectures on Government in Glasgow University Library. One of these sets is described in an attached autograph note by the Duke of Hamilton as 'the original lectures of James [*sic*] Millar given to me by his son'. It is by no means certain, however, that this was in fact the actual set of notes from which Millar himself lectured, and a number of mysteries regarding its origin, and its relation to the other sets of notes which are extant, still remain to be cleared up. There does seem little doubt, however, that this set of notes gives an accurate indication of the topics with which Millar dealt in his lectures and of his general approach to them. It may therefore be worthwhile to quote verbatim the short section of the notes in which, under the heading 'State of Government among *Savages*', the four stages theory is introduced and explained:

'Having examined the general principles of Government, we shall consider in what manner these have been combined, so as to produce different forms of Government in different Ages.

The first object of mankind is to produce subsistence. To obtain the necessaries, the comforts, the conveniencies of life. Their next aim is to defend their persons and their acquisitions against the attacks of one another.

It is evident, therefore, that the more inconsiderable the possessions of any people, their political regulations will be the more simple. And

large number of passages in the early chapters of his *Historical View of the English Government*;[144] and almost any of the remarkable dissertations published posthumously as Volume IV of the third (1803) edition of the *Historical View.* At a venture, let us take his suggestive account in the *Origin of Ranks* of 'the rank and condition of women in different ages'.[145] However wrong some of the main conclusions which he reached on this subject may now appear in retrospect, his treatment illustrates very well the basic methodology which imbued all his work.

In the rudest period of society, Millar begins, the state of mankind is extremely unfavourable to the passions which unite the sexes:

A savage who earns his food by hunting and fishing, or by gathering the spontaneous fruits of the earth, is incapable of attaining any considerable refinement in his pleasures. He finds so much difficulty, and is exposed to so many hardships in procuring mere necessaries, that he has no leisure or encouragement to aim at the luxuries and conveniencies of life. His wants are few, in propor-

the more opulent a nation becomes its government ought to be the more complicated.

Property is at the same time the principal source of authority, so that the opulence of a people, not only makes them stand in need of much regulation, but enables them to establish it.

By tracing the progress of wealth we may thus expect to discover the progress of Government. I shall take notice of *4 great stages* in the acquisition of property.

1. Hunters and Fishers, or mere Savages.
    – Indians of America.
    – Some inhabitants of northern and eastern parts of Tartary.
    – Of the Terra Australis.
    – Of southern coast of Africa.
2. Shepherds.
    – Greater part of Tartars. Arabs.
    – Nations on southern coast of Africa.
    – Ancient Germans.
3. Husbandmen.
    – Several tribes on the southern coast of Africa.
    – In East Indies.
    – Towns and villages in ancient Greece and Italy.
    – Gothic nations after their settlement in the Roman Empire.
4. Commercial people.
    – All polished nations.'

[144] I am thinking in particular of Book I, chapters II, III, and IV.
[145] This is the title of chapter I of *The Origin of Ranks* – a very extensive chapter which occupies 95 pages of the 1806 edition.

tion to the narrowness of his circumstances. With him, the great object is to be able to satisfy his hunger, and, after the utmost exertions of labour and activity, to enjoy the relief of idleness and repose. He has no time for cultivating a correspondence with the other sex, nor for attending to those enjoyments which result from it; and his desires being neither cherished by affluence, nor inflamed by indulgence, are allowed to remain in that moderate state which renders them barely sufficient for the continuation of the species.[146]

The marriages of rude peoples, Millar claims, 'are usually contracted without any previous attachment between the parties, and with little regard to the gratification of their mutual passions': a savage marries only 'when he arrives at an age, and finds himself in circumstances, which render the acquisition of a family expedient or necessary to his comfortable subsistence'.[147] For this and other reasons, in savage societies women tend to be 'deprived of that consideration and respect which, in a polished nation, they are accustomed to derive from the passion between the sexes'.[148] They are in fact 'usually treated as the servants or slaves of the men'.[149] Yet all this 'rudeness and barbarism' among the early inhabitants of the world, Millar insists, 'is not unsuitable to the mean condition in which they are placed, and to the numberless hardships and difficulties which they are obliged to encounter'.[150]

Leaving aside, with regret, a path-breaking section dealing with group marriage and matriarchy in primitive society,[151] we pass to section III of the relevant chapter, in which Millar sets out to discuss 'the refinement of the

---

[146] *Origin of Ranks*, pp. 14–15.
[147] *Ibid.*, p. 21. It is perhaps worth noting that before making this and other statements about the marriages of rude peoples Millar has given the customary bow to the ecclesiastics of his day. 'It seems unnecessary to observe', he says in a footnote on p. 19, 'that what is here said with regard to marriage, together with many other Remarks which follow concerning the manners of early nations, can only be applied to those who had lost all knowledge of the original institutions, which, as the sacred scriptures inform us, were communicated to mankind by an extraordinary revelation from heaven.'
[148] *Ibid.*, p. 32.   [149] *Ibid.*, p. 34.   [150] *Ibid.*, p. 44.
[151] Section II of the chapter, entitled 'The influence acquired by the mother of a family, before marriage is completely established'.

passions of sex, in the pastoral ages'. The invention of taming and pasturing cattle, says Millar,

which may be regarded as the first remarkable improvement in the savage life, is productive of very important alterations in the state and manners of a people.

A shepherd is more regularly supplied with food, and is commonly subjected to fewer hardships and calamities than those who live by hunting and fishing. In proportion to the size of his family, the number of his flocks may in some measure be increased; while the labour which is requisite for their management can never be very oppressive. Being thus provided with necessaries, he is led to the pursuit of those objects which may render his situation more easy and comfortable; and among these the enjoyments derived from the intercourse of the sexes claim a principal share, and become an object of attention.[152]

The virtue of chastity begins at last to be recognised; and the acquisition of property among shepherds also has a considerable effect upon 'the commerce of the sexes':[153]

The introduction of wealth, and the distinction of ranks with which it is attended, must interrupt the communication of the sexes, and, in many cases, render it difficult for them to gratify their wishes. As particular persons become opulent, they are led to entertain suitable notions of their own dignity; and, while they aim at superior elegance and refinement in their pleasures, they disdain to contract an alliance with their own dependents, or with people of inferior condition.[154]

Great families, living in the same neighbourhood, are 'frequently engaged in mutual depredations', and 'the animosities and quarrels which arise from their ambition or desire of plunder' dispose them 'to behave to one another with distance and reserve'.[155] It follows, according to Millar, that

among persons living upon such terms, the passions of sex cannot be gratified with the same facility as among hunters and fishers. The forms of behaviour, naturally introduced among individuals jealous of each other, have a tendency to check all familiarity between them . . . And thus the inclinations of individuals having in vain been smothered by opposition, will break forth with greater vigour, and rise at length to a higher

[152] *Ibid.*, pp. 57–8. [153] *Ibid.*, p. 59.
[154] *Ibid.*, p. 60. [155] *Ibid.*, pp. 60–1.

pitch, in proportion to the difficulties which they have sur-
mounted.[156]

But the passions which relate to 'the commerce of the
sexes' are raised to a still greater height when society moves
forward to the third great stage, that of agriculture: 'The
improvement of agriculture, which in most parts of the
world has been posterior to the art of taming and rearing
cattle, is productive of very important alterations in the state
of society; more especially with respect to the subject of our
present inquiry.'[157] Its most important immediate effects are,
first, that it multiplies the comforts and conveniencies of
life, and therefore excites in mankind a stronger desire of
obtaining those pleasures to which they are prompted by
their natural appetites'; and, second, that it 'obliges men to
fix their residence in the neighbourhood of that spot where
their labour is chiefly to be employed, and thereby gives rise
to property in land, the most valuable and permanent species
of wealth'.[158] Millar goes on to trace the manner in which
these circumstances affected the relations between the sexes
in ancient Greece, and then in the barbarous nations which
invaded the Roman Empire. In the latter connection the
rise of romantic love and the notion of chivalry are of course
his main themes.

Finally, Millar moves on to modern society, beginning
with a consideration of 'changes in the condition of women,
arising from the improvement of useful arts and manufactures'. 'When agriculture has created abundance of provisions', he argues,

people extend their views to other circumstances of smaller importance. They endeavour to be clothed and lodged, as well as
maintained, in a more comfortable manner; and they engage in
such occupations as are calculated for these useful purposes. By
the application of their labour to a variety of objects, commodities
of different kinds are produced. These are exchanged for one
another, according to the demand of different individuals; and
thus manufactures, together with commerce, are at length introduced into a country.

These improvements are the source of very important changes
in the state of society, and particularly in relation to the women

[156] *Ibid.*, p. 61.　　　　[157] *Ibid.*, p. 67.　　　　[158] *Ibid.*, p. 67.

. . . While the fair sex become less frequently the objects of those romantic and extravagant passions, which in some measure arise from the disorders of society, they are more universally regarded upon account of their useful or agreeable talents.[159]

And as society becomes more affluent, refined, and luxury-loving, we gradually arrive at a state of affairs in which

there is the same free communication between the sexes as in the ages of rudeness and barbarism. In the latter, women enjoy the most unbounded liberty, because it is thought of no consequence what use they shall make of it. In the former, they are entitled to the same freedom, upon account of those agreeable qualities which they possess, and the rank and dignity which they hold as members of society.[160]

But at this stage an important countervailing force begins to operate:

In a simple age, the free intercourse of the sexes is attended with no bad consequences; but in opulent and luxurious nations, it gives rise to licentious and dissolute manners, inconsistent with good order, and with the general interest of society . . . The natural tendency, therefore, of great luxury and dissipation is to diminish the rank and dignity of the women, by preventing all refinement in their connection with the other sex, and rendering them only subservient to the purposes of animal enjoyment.[161]

This suggests, according to Millar, that 'there are certain limits beyond which it is impossible to push the real improvements arising from wealth and opulence'.[162]

This very selective summary of Millar's discussion of the condition of women does not do anything like full justice to its subtlety and flexibility; nor does it give any idea of the fascinating array of sources which Millar adduces in his support. But it does at least give an indication of the nature of his basic approach to the wide range of developmental problems which he brought within his orbit. It also gives some idea of his attitude towards the noble-ignoble savage debate and the associated issue of progress and perfectibility – a theme which it may be useful to enlarge upon a little before we leave him.

[159] *Ibid.*, pp. 87–9.
[161] *Ibid.*, pp. 101–2.
[160] *Ibid.*, p. 101.
[162] *Ibid.*, p. 101.

There is no doubt that Millar, in a meaningful sense of the expression, 'believed in progress'. We have already quoted his statement, in the introduction to *The Origin of Ranks*, to the effect that 'there is . . . in man a disposition and capacity for improving his condition, by the exertion of which, he is carried on from one degree of advancement to another'.[163] And a little later in the same book, at a point where he is talking about the 'mean condition' of mankind in savage societies, we find him reminding his readers

that, how poor and wretched soever the aspect of human nature in this early state, it contains the seeds of improvement, which, by long care and culture, are capable of being brought to maturity; so that the lower its primitive condition, it requires the greater exertions of labour and activity, and calls for a more extensive operation of those wonderful powers and faculties, which, in a gradual progression from such rude beginnings, have led to the noblest discoveries in art or science, and to the most exalted refinement of taste and manners.[164]

There were two important ways, however, in which Millar's attitude towards the issue of progress and perfectibility tended to differ from that of many of his contemporaries. In the first place, he frequently suggested, as we have just seen him doing in *The Origin of Ranks*, that 'there are certain limits beyond which it is impossible to push the real improvements arising from wealth and opulence'.[165] The detailed theoretical analyses which he gave (most notably in his lectures on Government) of the reasons for believing that such limits to improvement might in fact exist are always interesting and often profound, although his social and political conclusions – as was perhaps inevitable – are not always drawn very clearly. Certainly, however, one can say that Millar was by no means happy about the economic and political conditions prevailing in the Britain of his time. No one at that time warned more strongly than Millar of the dangers of the rapidly increasing influence which the Crown

---

[163] *Ibid.*, pp. 2–3. Cf. also the statement that shortly follows to the effect that there is in human society 'a natural progress from ignorance to knowledge, and from rude to civilized manners' (p. 4).
[164] *Ibid.*, pp. 45–6.
[165] *Ibid.*, p. 101.

had exercised since 1688. He warned too, in even more forthright terms than Smith and Ferguson did, that the extension of the division of labour, by stripping the worker of his mental powers and converting him into 'the mere instrument of labour', was making it possible for the common people to become 'the dupes of their superiors'.[166] And he emphasised, once again even more strongly than Ferguson, that in modern society 'the pursuit of riches becomes a scramble, in which the hand of every man is against every other'.[167] The extent to which Millar regarded these as *resistible* tendencies is perhaps debatable; but there is at least no doubt that the alterations in society which he felt would be necessary to ensure that they were resisted were much more radical than those contemplated by the great majority of his contemporaries.[168]

The second point is this. The existence in modern society of these manifest defects and dangers did not mean, in Millar's view, that one was obliged to take Rousseau's line and maintain 'that the rude and savage life is the parent of all the virtues, the vices of mankind being the proper and peculiar offspring of opulence and civilization'.[169] It was certainly true, Millar agreed, that one should not bestow *moral disapproval* upon savages on account of their 'vices': their 'rudeness and barbarism', we have just seen him affirming, 'is not unsuitable to the mean condition in which they are placed'.[170] It was also true that there was a sense in which, as Rousseau claimed, independence and the love of liberty were to be found in their greatest perfection among barbarians; but before bestowing *moral approval* upon them on account of this 'virtue', one should remember that 'their independence . . . is owing to the wretchedness of their circumstances, which afford nothing that can tempt any one man to become subject to another'.[171] What Millar objected to in Rousseau, it seems clear, was his failure to appreciate the extent to

[166] *Historical View of the English Government*, Vol. IV, pp. 152 and 156.
[167] *Ibid.*, Vol. IV, p. 249.
[168] See W. C. Lehmann, *John Millar of Glasgow* (Cambridge University Press, Cambridge, 1960), Part I, ch. VII, *passim*.
[169] *Historical View of the English Government*, Vol. IV, p. 175.
[170] *Origin of Ranks*, p. 44.
[171] *Ibid.*, pp. 240–1.

which 'the dispositions and behaviour of man are liable to be influenced by the circumstances in which he is placed, and by his peculiar education and habits of life'.[172] If one accepted this basic materialist hypothesis, Millar in effect argued, then moralising of the sort that was Rousseau's stock-in-trade was simply ruled out of court: all one could properly do was 'to examine the effects of poverty and riches, of simplicity and refinement, upon practical morality; and to compare the predominant virtues and vices of the different periods of society'.[173] The alternative methodology adumbrated by Millar in passages such as these was never fully worked out by him, and there is much that is less than satisfactory in his posthumously-published essays on this theme. But the fact that he recognised the need for such a methodology, and himself moved as far as he did along the road towards it, would surely in itself be enough to mark him out as one of the boldest spirits of the Enlightenment.

Among the letters received by Robertson after the appearance of his *History of America* in 1777 was one from Edmund Burke. We need no longer go to history, wrote Burke, to trace human nature in all stages and periods. For now

the great Map of Mankind is unrolled at once, and there is no state or gradation of barbarism, and no mode of refinement which we have not at the same moment under our view; the very different civility of Europe and of China; the barbarism of Persia and of Abyssinia; the erratick manners of Tartary and of Arabia; the savage state of North America and of New Zealand.[174]

Turgot, of course, had said much the same as this, in suspiciously similar words.[175] But by Burke's time 'the great Map of Mankind' had of course unrolled much further than it had in Turgot's day (uncovering, in particular, the Pacific), and many more travellers, philosophers, and historians had written about the lands and peoples which the map revealed.

---

[172] *Historical View of the English Government*, Vol. IV, p. 175.
[173] *Ibid.*, Vol. IV, p. 175.
[174] Robertson, *Works* (Edinburgh, 1840), Vol. I, p. xxviii. The letter is quoted in Dugald Stewart's memoir of Robertson, which is reproduced at the beginning of this edition of the *Works*.
[175] See above, p. 70.

What we have in effect been tracing in the last three chapters is the way in which, coincident with the progressive unrolling of the map, a new way of looking at society and its history was developed. The new view gradually assumed the form of a great guiding principle, or set of principles, with the aid of which it was believed that the rapidly increasing flow of historical, anthropological, and sociological data could be organised and, if used with care, made to throw light on a number of problems concerning mankind's advance from savagery to civilisation. By 1780 this guiding principle had become so important an element in the intellectual scheme of things, so much an integral part of the social thought of the Enlightenment, that there were very few historians and social thinkers who remained unaffected by it.

The degree of its influence varied greatly, of course, from one thinker to another. If at one pole we find Millar, whose whole life-work was centred around the theory and its corollaries, at the opposite pole we find Voltaire, whom the theory seems to have affected very little. Although Voltaire was clearly interested in the Americans,[176] and was quite prepared on occasion to draw comparisons between the customs of the Americans and those of ancient peoples,[177] he stopped short of saying or implying that 'in the beginning all the World was *America*', and, indeed, showed altogether remarkably little interest in the problem of how society had come into being, and by what steps or stages it had progressed from savagery to civilisation.

Clustered near the Voltaire pole we find men like the Glasgow historian William Wight, who, though apparently a personal friend of Millar's,[178] does not seem to have made

[176] See, for example, Voltaire's comments on the Americans in his well-known *Essai sur les Moeurs et l'Esprit des Nations*. In the edition of this work which I have used (Garnier Frères, Paris, 1963), the most interesting passages are to be found on pp. 9–10, 13, 22–3, and 28–31 of Vol. I.

[177] See, e.g. *Essai*, Vol. I, p. 201. It should be added, however, that Voltaire was extremely scornful of Lafitau's efforts to trace the ancestry of the Americans to the ancient Greeks on the basis of certain cultural similarities which Voltaire evidently regarded as completely superficial: see *ibid.*, Vol. I, p. 30.

[178] Craig, in his biography of Millar (*Origin of Ranks*, p. lxiii), speaks of Wight as Millar's friend; and Alexander Carlyle seems to have met

much use of the latter's master-principle.[179] A little further
towards the Millar pole we find, for example, the baron
d'Holbach, who in his *Système Social* clearly visualises mankind as progressing from a hunting and fishing stage to an
agricultural one, but makes no mention of an intermediate
pastoral stage.[180] About this point in the scale we also –
perhaps surprisingly – find Gibbon. It is true that Gibbon
had a cast of mind which must have been rather unsympa-
thetic towards the four stages theory. But whenever in his
great work he turns to deal with barbarous peoples, the
influence of the theory is quite apparent: not only does he
very frequently attach the labels hunting, pastoral, and agricultural to different tribes and societies, but he also shows
quite a keen awareness of the influence which the mode of
subsistence exerted on the manners of (for example) the
Germans, the Picts and Scots, the 'pastoral nations', and the
Arabs.[181] And there were other contemporary historians, like
the redoubtable Robert Henry, who accepted the four stages

Millar at Wight's house on several occasions in 1768 (see Carlyle's
Autobiography, 2nd edn, Edinburgh, 1860, p. 492).
[179] Or so at least it would appear from two syllabuses of Wight's lecture-
courses which are extant: *Heads of a Course of Lectures on the Study
of History* (Glasgow, 1767), and *Heads of Lectures on the Study of Civil
History* (Glasgow, 1772). There is very little in these syllabuses which
could reasonably be construed as reflecting any concern with the four
stages theory – except perhaps that at the beginning of the sixth lecture
of Part I of the course to which the second syllabus relates Wight was
scheduled to speak about the 'influence of the improvement of the necessary arts upon government'.
[180] I have used the edition of *Système Social* which is dated 1773 and stated
to be published in London, as reproduced in facsimile by Georg Olms,
Hildesheim, 1969. In this edition the most relevant passages are to be
found on pp. 171–2 and 200–2 of Vol. I, and pp. 21–2 of Vol. II.
[181] Gibbon's comments in *The Decline and Fall of the Roman Empire* on
the Germans appear in chapter IX; on the Picts and Scots in chapter
XXV; on the 'pastoral nations' in chapter XXVI; and on the Arabs in
chapter L. In the Methuen's Standard Library edition of the book
(London, 1905), these chapters will be found in Vol. I, pp. 213–36;
Vol. III, pp. 1–68; Vol. III, pp. 69–132; and Vol. V, pp. 311–96. For
examples of Gibbon's use of the notion of hunting, pastoral, and agricultural societies, see Vol. I, pp. 218–22; Vol. III, pp. 41–4, 71–9, 82
(footnote 29), and 420–1; and Vol. V, pp. 314–16. Striking evidence of
Gibbon's awareness of the importance of the mode of subsistence is to be
found in the discussion in Vol. III, pp. 71–2ff. Attention should also be
drawn to an interesting statement about the Arabs towards the foot of
p. 314 of Vol. V in which the influence of the four stages theory seems
quite apparent.

Social science and the ignoble savage

theory but whose work covered a field which did not permit them to make a great deal of direct use of it.[182]

But, as I hope I have sufficiently shown above, many of the most influential writers on 'the history of rude nations' whose work appeared between 1760 and 1780 were much closer to the Millar pole than this.[183] By 1780, indeed, Millar's master-principle was beginning to appear as something very like orthodoxy. And in the last two decades of the century its influence spread even further. During those same two decades, however, the way was almost insensibly prepared for the arrival of a new and perhaps rather less heroic phase in its history. It is to the story of these final developments that we must now turn.

---

182 Robert Henry's massive work, *The History of Great Britain . . . Written on a New Plan*, was in 6 volumes, the first of which appeared in 1771. The 'new plan' of the title was rather similar to that which had been adopted by Goguet – whose book Henry himself had in fact helped to translate into English. At the beginning of chapter v of Book i of Henry's *History*, entitled 'The history of the arts in Great Britain' (from 55 B.C. to A.D. 449), there is a long outline of the hunting–pasturage–agriculture progression (pp. 308–11). In the next chapter, entitled 'The history of commerce, coin, and shipping in Great Britain' (once again from 55 B.C. to A.D. 449), the growth of different forms of 'commerce' through the hunting, pastoral, and agricultural stages is discussed (pp. 371–3); and there are several references back to this stadial scheme in chapter vii.

183 There are of course a number of writers coming within this category who have not been specifically mentioned above. Among these, a special mention should perhaps be made of Gilbert Stuart, author of *A View of Society in Europe, in its Progress from Rudeness to Refinement* (1778). The extensive notes appended to the text of this book are often interesting, especially those in which Stuart compares the habits and customs of the ancient Germans with those of the Americans, making frequent and on the whole perceptive use of authorities such as Lafitau, Charlevoix, and Adair (see, e.g. pp. 158, 162–3, 167, 168–9, 173–4, 180–1, 184, 187–8, 189–90, 191–2, 195, and 196–7). Although Stuart quite often criticises Millar, Robertson, and Kames, and although he never mentions the four stages theory, he makes a number of bows in the direction of the notion of the crucial importance of the mode of subsistence (see, e.g. pp. 159–60 and 169–70).

6

Revisionists, poets, and economists

During the last two decades of the eighteenth century, interest in the four stages theory reached its apogee. The ideas so magistrally expounded by John Millar – who himself continued to develop and publicise them during the whole of this period[1] – became quite widely accepted: poets even began to glorify the four stages theory in their cantos. But alongside the poets, and the dogmatists who treated the theory more or less as revealed truth, there were many revisionists who accepted it only subject to certain qualifications, or incorporated it in larger schemes of their own. And at roughly the same time, from about 1770 onwards, a number of economists began in effect to use the theory as a kind of springboard for the construction of a new system of political economy.

In order to set the stage properly for our discussion of these events, I should perhaps begin by making it clear that the use of the four stages theory during the period from 1760 to 1780 was by no means confined to those whose chief field of interest was 'the history of rude nations' – i.e. to those whose work I have considered in the previous chapter. The theory was also quite extensively used during this period by writers in a number of other fields, as the examples of Blackstone, Blair, and Du Pont will sufficiently indicate.

Blackstone's extremely influential *Commentaries on the Laws of England* was first published in 1766.[2] The opening chapter of the second book of the *Commentaries*, dealing with property in general, contains an unambiguous account of the hunting–pasturage–agriculture progression which obviously owes a great deal to the work of the pioneers of

---

[1] Millar died in 1801. The 1st edition of his *Historical View of the English Government* appeared in 1787, and the 2nd edition in 1790.
[2] William Blackstone, *Commentaries on the Laws of England* (Oxford, 1766).

177

the 1750s. In the beginning of the world, writes Blackstone, 'while the earth continued bare of inhabitants', it is reasonable to suppose

> that all was in common among them, and that every one took from the public stock to his own use such things as his immediate necessities required.

> These general notions of property were then sufficient to answer all the purposes of human life; and might perhaps still have answered them, had it been possible for mankind to have remained in a state of primaeval simplicity: as may be collected from the manners of many American nations when first discovered by the Europeans; and from the antient method of living among the first Europeans themselves, if we may credit either the memorials of them preserved in the golden age of the poets, or the uniform accounts given by historians of those times . . .[3]

But 'when mankind increased in number, craft, and ambition', Blackstone proceeds, 'it became necessary to entertain conceptions of more permanent dominion'.[4] And the gradual development of these conceptions, according to his account, was bound up with the progress of mankind through the hunting, pastoral, and agricultural stages.

The hunting–pastoral transition is described by Blackstone in the following terms:

> Such, as were not contented with the spontaneous product of the earth, fought for a more solid refreshment in the flesh of beasts, which they obtained by hunting. But the frequent disappointments, incident to that method of provision, induced them to gather together such animals as were of a more tame and sequacious nature; and to establish a permanent property in their flocks and herds, in order to sustain themselves in a less precarious manner, partly by the milk of the dams, and partly by the flesh of the young.[5]

The evidence in Genesis about 'violent contentions concerning wells', and about the right of pastoral peoples to occupy whatever ground they pleased (if not already occupied by other tribes), is surveyed by Blackstone at this point;[6] and the eventual arrival of agriculture upon the historical scene,

---

[3] *Ibid.*, Vol. II, pp. 2–3.   [4] *Ibid.*, Vol. II, p. 4.
[5] *Ibid.*, Vol. II, p. 5.   [6] *Ibid.*, Vol. II, pp. 5–6.

its effect on conceptions of property, and the consequent emergence of civil society, are described as follows:

As the world by degrees grew more populous, it daily became more difficult to find out new spots to inhabit, without encroaching upon former occupants; and, by constantly occupying the same individual spot, the fruits of the earth were consumed, and it's spontaneous produce destroyed, without any provision for a future supply or succession. It therefore became necessary to pursue some regular method of providing a constant subsistence; and this necessity produced, or at least promoted and encouraged, the art of agriculture. And the art of agriculture, by a regular connexion and consequence, introduced and established the idea of a more permanent property in the soil, than had hitherto been received and adopted. It was clear that the earth would not produce her fruits in sufficient quantities, without the assistance of tillage: but who would be at the pains of tilling it, if another might watch an opportunity to seise upon and enjoy the product of his industry, art, and labour? Had not therefore a separate property in lands, as well as moveables, been vested in some individuals, the world must have continued a forest, and men have been mere animals of prey; which, according to some philosophers, is the genuine state of nature . . . Necessity begat property; and, in order to insure that property, recourse was had to civil society, which brought along with it a long train of inseparable concomitants; states, governments, laws, punishments, and the public exercise of religious duties. Thus connected together, it was found that a part only of society was sufficient to provide, by their manual labour, for the necessary subsistence of all; and leisure was given to others to cultivate the human mind, to invent useful arts, and to lay the foundations of science.[7]

The remainder of Blackstone's argument in this part of the *Commentaries* need not concern us here. What is important in the context of our present enquiry is simply the unquestioning acceptance, in so seminal a book as this, of the hunting–pasturage–agriculture progression and the basic ideas about the development of property and society which had been associated with it in the work of the founders.

Turning now from the field of law to the field of literary criticism, one of the most influential contributions in the latter at this time was Hugh Blair's *Critical Dissertation on*

[7] *Ibid.*, Vol. II, pp. 7–8.

the Poems of Ossian, which appeared in 1763.[8] 'Among the monuments remaining of the ancient state of nations', Blair begins,

few are more valuable than their poems or songs. History, when it treats of remote and dark ages, is seldom very instructive. The beginnings of society, in every country, are involved in fabulous confusion; and though they were not, they would furnish few events worth recording. But, in every period of society, human manners are a curious spectacle; and the most natural pictures of ancient manners are exhibited in the ancient poems of nations.[9]

If we made an extensive search among 'all the most ancient poetical productions', Blair argues, it is probable that we would discover 'a certain degree of resemblance' between them. For, as he puts it,

in a similar state of manners, similar objects and passions operating upon the imaginations of men, will stamp their productions with the same general character. Some diversity will, no doubt, be occasioned by climate and genius. But mankind never bear such resembling features, as they do in the beginnings of society.[10]

And it is certainly to 'the beginnings of society' – i.e. in the main, to the hunting stage – that the Ossianic poems belong:

The compositions of Ossian are so strongly marked with characters of antiquity, that although there were no external proof to support that antiquity, hardly any reader of judgment and taste, could hesitate in referring them to a very remote area. There are four great stages through which men successively pass in the progress of society. The first and earliest is the life of hunters; pasturage succeeds to this, as the ideas of property begin to take root; next, agriculture; and lastly, commerce. Throughout Ossian's poems, we plainly find ourselves in the first of these periods of society; during which, hunting was the chief employment of men, and the principal method of their procuring subsistence. Pasturage was not indeed wholly unknown; for we hear of dividing the herd in the case of a divorce; but the allusions to herds and to cattle are not many; and of agriculture, we find no traces.[11]

---

[8] Hugh Blair, *A Critical Dissertation on the Poems of Ossian, the Son of Fingal* (London, 1763).

[9] *Ibid.*, p. 1.   [10] *Ibid.*, p. 4.

[11] *Ibid.*, pp. 16–17. 'This representation of Ossian's times', writes Blair a few lines later, 'must strike us the more, as genuine and authentick, when it is compared with a poem of later date, which Mr. Macpherson has

Here we find once again an unquestioning acceptance of the four stages theory, a number of echoes of which (together with several associated comments on the Americans) may also be found in Blair's *Lectures on Rhetoric*.[12] It is only proper to add, however, that this approach of Blair's was by no means universal among the literary critics of the time. One searches in vain for traces of it, for example, in John Ogilvie's *Essay on the Lyric Poetry of the Ancients*[13] and William Duff's *Essay on Original Genius*.[14] The fascinating chapter on 'Homer's Manners' in Robert Wood's *Essay on the Genius and Writings of Homer*,[15] however, shows clearly

preserved in one of his notes. It is that wherein five bards are represented as passing the evening in the house of a chief, and each of them separately giving his description of the night. The night scenery is beautiful; and the author has plainly imitated the style and manner of Ossian: But he has allowed some images to appear which betray a later period of society. For we meet with windows clapping, the herds of goats and cows seeking shelter, the shepherd wandering, corn on the plain, and the wakeful hind rebuilding the shocks of corn which had been overturned by the tempest. Whereas in Ossian's works, from beginning to end, all is consistent; no modern allusion drops from him; but every where, the same face of rude nature appears; a country wholly uncultivated, thinly inhabited, and recently peopled' (*ibid.*, p. 17).

12 Blair's *Lectures on Rhetoric and Belles Lettres* was first published in 1783. I have used the facsimile of this 1783 edition published by Southern Illinois University Press, Carbondale and Edwardsville, 1965, under the editorship of H. F. Harding. The most interesting references will be found on pp. 100, 108, 114–15, 140, footnote, and 283–4 of Vol. ɪ; and on pp. 288, 314–15, 316–17, 318, 321–2, and 337–8 of Vol. ɪɪ.

13 John Ogilvie, *Poems on Several Subjects, to which is prefixed An Essay on the Lyric Poetry of the Ancients* (London, 1762). On p. ix of this work Ogilvie tells us that 'as the first inhabitants of the world were employed in the culture of the field, and in surveying the scenery of external Nature, it is probable that the first rude draughts of Poetry were extemporary effusions, either descriptive of the scenes of pastoral life, or extolling the attributes of the Supreme Being'.

14 William Duff, *An Essay on Original Genius* (London, 1767). One of the things which Duff sets out to demonstrate in this book is 'that the early and uncultivated periods of society are particularly favourable to the display of original Poetic Genius' (p. viii). This demonstration occurs on pp. 260–96, but all that he really says is that the 'primeval state' (p. 271) of mankind was characterised by 'a certain innocence of manners, accompanied with that tranquillity which is its consequence' (p. 273). No indication is given as to how mankind got their living in this 'primeval state', and no savages, whether noble or ignoble, enter to disturb the happy scene.

15 Robert Wood, *A Comparative View of the Antient and Present State of the Troade. To which is prefixed an Essay on the Original Genius of Homer* (London, 1767). The copy of this work in the British Museum in

enough that Blair was not entirely alone in his adoption of this approach.

Finally, let us turn to Du Pont's *Table Raisonnée des Principes de l'Economie Politique*, which he compiled in 1773 for the Margrave of Baden, and which was published – in the form of a gigantic chart, measuring 4 feet by 4½ feet – in 1775.[16] The field covered by this unique document is very much wider than the term *Economie Politique* in its title might lead one to suspect. It actually sets out to present, in schematic form, nothing less than the whole system of interrelationships (as Du Pont and the Physiocrats then envisaged it) of 'the political, social, legal, and economic facts of mankind's existence in nature'.[17] It is intended to demonstrate how man's needs, rights, and duties give rise to society, which gradually develops through four historical stages, culminating in agriculture – or, rather, in the Physiocratic system of agricultural capitalism, to the details of the nature and operation of which Du Pont devotes the major part of the chart.

The first of Du Pont's four stages, or (as he calls them) 'natural states', is *gathering*, in which men live on vegetable products spontaneously produced by nature.[18] This state, however, 'can last only for a very short time, and is adapted only to a very small population'; moreover, it requires 'a country which is naturally fertile and in which the winter is

---

fact contains only the *Essay*, which is not paginated beyond p. xx. The British Museum also holds a later edition of the *Essay* alone (*An Essay on the Original Genius of Homer*, London, 1769) in which a number of amendments and additions have been made, some of which are extremely interesting. The chapter on 'Homer's Manners' (1767 edn, unpaginated; 1769 edn, pp. xxxviii–xlvii) contains a number of passages which are worthy of much more consideration than I have space to give them here. See, for example, the footnote added in the 1769 edition (p. xli) in which the author considers the possibility that the manners of the Americans might be adducible as confirmation of the reliability of Homer's account of the manners of ancient times.

[16] Dr J. J. McLain, of Louisiana State University, the author of a dissertation on *The Economic Writings of Pierre Samuel Du Pont de Nemours*, has kindly provided me with extensive information about the *Table Raisonnée* and its compilation, and I have also inspected the copy of this document which is held in the British Museum.

[17] The quotation is from p. 143 of Dr McLain's dissertation.

[18] The name given to this stage by Du Pont is in fact 'La recherche des productions vegetales spontanées'.

not severe'. In this state there is no authority other than that
of the father. There is some inequality, because of differences
in luck or intelligence among individuals in the search for
food, but no one is of high rank, and there is only one class
of men.

The second 'natural state' is *hunting and fishing*, which is
conceived to be brought about as the result of an eventual
insufficiency of vegetable products. In this state men are
more numerous, because they have more of the means of
subsistence. They form associations, and they elect chiefs
for their expeditions; but there is still only one class of men.

The third 'natural state' is *pasturage*, in which men,
'having taken in the hunt the young of certain domesticable
animals, and having raised them, have recognised that it was
better to gather these animals together and defend them
against the wild beasts, than to confine themselves to hunting them in competition with the latter'. In this state man
acquires usufructuary property rights over the pasture lands
of which he takes possession with his flocks and herds. In
addition, he acquires a greater degree of affluence, which
leaves him with more leisure for reflection and extends his
faculties and his ideas, thus enabling him to provide himself
with (among other things) the advances (*avances*)[19] which he
requires in order to progress to the next 'natural state'. In the
pastoral state, too, we see the emergence for the first time of
two separate classes – that of the masters, or proprietors of
flocks and herds, and that of the servants, or hired people,
who have been unable to acquire any flocks and herds and
who are therefore obliged to offer their services to the proprietors for a payment.

The fourth and last 'natural state' begins when *agriculture*
is invented. The invention of agriculture is encouraged by the
leisure afforded by the pastoral life, which allows men the
time to study botany and astronomy; and the material means
for its establishment are provided by the greater abundance
with which the pastoral life is already associated. Agriculture,
right from the beginning, requires not only labour but also

19 The nearest *modern* equivalent of the Physiocratic term '*avances*' is
'capital'.

original and annual advances;[20] and at a later stage in its development it requires in addition the permanent settlement of men in the neighbourhood of the fields they cultivate.

This fourth 'natural state', based on agriculture, marks the end of the progression which Du Pont depicts in the *Table Raisonnée*: the agricultural state does not give place to a 'commercial' state as it does in most formulations of the fully-fledged non-Physiocratic four stages theory. But 'agriculture' as Physiocrats like Du Pont envisaged it in fact partook of certain of the basic characteristics which their non-Physiocratic contemporaries assigned to 'commerce'. Du Pont's fourth state was certainly one in which agriculture was the central economic activity, and in which the owners of agricultural land played a key role; but it was also one in which it was assumed that market exchange was more or less universal and that capitalist relations of production were predominant, at any rate in agriculture.[21]

Turning now to the developments which took place during the last two decades of the century, let us begin by looking at three books – by William Falconer, John Logan, and James Dunbar respectively – which appeared almost simultaneously at the very beginning of this period. The most interesting of these books is undoubtedly Falconer's.

Falconer was a physician, and the majority of his writings dealt with medical matters – not least with the therapeutic effects of the waters at Bath, where he practised for a large part of his life. But his publications also included a dissertation on St Paul's voyage from Caesarea to Puteoli; a translation of Arrian's *Periplus*; observations on the words uttered by the centurion at the Crucifixion; thoughts on gardening among the ancients; and last but hardly least, the striking work whose somewhat elaborate title is worth reproduction in full:

---

[20] *Des avances primitives et annuelles.* The nearest *modern* equivalent would probably be 'fixed capital and working capital', but the parallel is not quite as exact as such a translation would imply.

[21] In the *Table Raisonnée* Du Pont in fact comes closer than most of his fellow Physiocrats to the notion that capitalist relations of production are predominant in manufacture and commerce as well as in agriculture.

REMARKS

on the

INFLUENCE

of

CLIMATE,	POPULATION,
SITUATION,	NATURE OF FOOD, and
NATURE OF COUNTRY,	WAY OF LIFE,

on the

Disposition and Temper, Manners and
Behaviour, Intellects, Laws and
Customs, Form of Government,
and Religion

of

MANKIND.

Falconer's *Remarks* (London, 1781) is a kind of eighteenth-century environmentalist's vade-mecum, in which the influence upon mankind of six different 'physical' causes is meticulously surveyed. Book I, containing a little less than one-third of the work's 552 pages, is devoted to the influence of climate: here the main emphasis is on the way in which heat and cold influence the human mind through the instrumentality of their effects on the human body, and much of the discussion (which as might be expected owes a great deal to Montesquieu) is somewhat fanciful. Books II, III, IV, and V (dealing respectively with the influence of 'situation', 'nature of country', 'population', and 'nature of food') are all relatively short, taking up only 87 pages between them. This leaves 296 pages – i.e. more than one-half of the work as a whole – for Falconer's very full and richly documented discussion in Book VI of the influence of 'way of life'. By the latter expression, broadly speaking, he means mode of subsistence.

The framework of the discussion in Book VI is a version of the four stages theory, of which Falconer's account is probably the most extensive and coherent (if not perhaps the most original) of the period we are now considering. 'The progress of civilisation', he says, 'may be divided into several stages; each of which, however, separately, comprehends divers degrees of improvement.'[22] The 'first and lowest' of these stages

is that generally called savage, where the people subsist by hunt-ing or fishing, and on the spontaneous produce of the earth; and are ignorant, at least in general, of the nature of private property, particularly money. Some latitude must, however, be allowed in this description, as there is scarce any people to whom it is strictly applicable.[23]

This first stage, Falconer proceeds, 'may be supposed to com-prehend . . . from the greatest degree of savageness known, to such a degree of civilisation as is produced by the general knowledge of property and money'.[24] The Americans, as usual, are adduced as the main examples of peoples living in the savage state, along with certain very primitive peoples of classical times such as 'the Fenni of Tacitus, and the Icthyophagi of Diodorus, and other writers'.[25] The ancient Germans are introduced in order to typify a people 'in a middle state, between savages and barbarians';[26] and a number of other rather more advanced nations are also brought into the picture, in so far as they are claimed by Falconer to have certain characteristics in common with peoples like the Americans, the Fenni, and the Germans. Falconer's authorities in this section include a great number of those whose work we have considered above – not only a wide range of classical authors, but also many eighteenth-century writers such as Charlevoix, Lafitau, Goguet, Hel-vétius, Blackstone, Robertson, Gibbon, Millar, Kames, and Stuart. Falconer was evidently very well versed in the litera-ture of the four stages theory, and this section of his book consists in effect of an extensive summary and evaluation of the main conclusions about the savage state which this literature had reached.

The second stage or state which Falconer distinguishes – sometimes described by him as the 'barbarous' and sometimes as the 'pastoral' state – is assumed by him 'to comprehend the period from the invention of property and money, to the general use of agriculture and cultivation of lands. This divi-

---

[22] *Remarks*, p. 257.   [23] *Ibid.*, p. 258.   [24] *Ibid.*, p. 258
[25] *Ibid.*, p. 258.   [26] *Ibid.*, p. 267, footnote.

sion, as well as the former, admits of several intermediate stages or degrees.[27] The basic criterion of distinction between the first and second states, as Falconer goes on to make clear, is that in the first the 'mode of gaining subsistence' is hunting or fishing, whereas in the second it is 'pasturage and feeding cattle'.[28] There is a classificatory difficulty here, however, in that 'the two conditions are not distinctly separated, but many nations partake of both at the same time'. Thus, Falconer says, 'I have been obliged to comprehend [the pastoral state], in some measure, in the foregoing division . . . At present, however, I mean to express a state wherein the feeding of cattle is the means of subsistence; and hunting or fishing are not practised with that intention, in a national view at least.'[29] The main examples of pastoral peoples which he adduces are of course the Arabs and the Tartars; and once again there is nothing really surprising – apart from its length – about his discussion of the different ways in which pasturage, considered as a mode of subsistence, influences various elements of the 'superstructure'.

The third stage or state is unequivocally defined as that in which 'men betake themselves to agriculture as a way of life, and general mode of subsistence'.[30] The fourth, 'commerce', is not specifically defined at all. Falconer is careful to explain, however, in an interesting footnote at the beginning of his chapter on 'the effects of a commercial life upon mankind', that

commerce . . . must not be considered as superseding agriculture, as agriculture did a pastoral life, and that a life of hunting. On the contrary, agriculture is often, though not constantly, cultivated to the highest degree in commercial states. This was the case formerly in Egypt, and is at present in China and Holland. On the other hand, the people of Athens, and of Marseilles, were but little addicted to agriculture; and the latter were even driven to trade by the barrenness of their country, which rendered it unapt for cultivation, as we are told by Strabo.[31]

The next subject of which Falconer treats is 'the effects of literature and science'. He recognises that this is a kind of odd man out, since 'it cannot be said to form an employment

---

[27] *Ibid.*, p. 321.   [28] *Ibid.*, p. 322.   [29] *Ibid.*, p. 322.
[30] *Ibid.*, p. 352.   [31] *Ibid.*, p. 404, footnote.

for the people in general, as the ways of life above described'
but he justifies its inclusion on the grounds that it produces
'even when introduced among a part of them only, the mos'
important consequences to society in general'.[32] His discus
sion of this topic (which includes a sustained attack on
Rousseau) is followed by the final section of the work, in
which 'the effects of luxury and refinement' are dealt with
'The next, and indeed the last state under which I propose
to consider mankind', he says, 'is that of a high degree o.
refinement and dissipation, attended with luxury; which
indeed, in the usual course of human affairs, generally succeeds to that last treated.'[33]

Although there is nothing very novel in Falconer's treatment of the relationships between mode of subsistence and
'superstructure' in the different stages or states of society
and although his discussion tends at times to degenerate into
a kind of hotchpotch in which the irrelevant rubs shoulders
with the relevant[34] and the fanciful with the real, his performance as a whole has considerable merit. He shows a
healthy awareness – not always shared by those upon whose
work he drew – of the immense breadth of categories such
as 'savagery' and 'barbarism'; of the difficulty of finding
individual peoples to whom the relevant criteria of distinction are strictly applicable; of the importance of the differences which may exist between peoples with the same mode
of subsistence;[35] and of the fact that commerce did not

---

[32] *Ibid.*, p. 448.

[33] *Ibid.*, p. 508.

[34] For example, he does not always distinguish carefully enough between
the effects of a particular mode of subsistence upon mankind, and the
effects upon mankind of the general advance towards civilisation which
the introduction of that mode of subsistence produces.

[35] 'It is necessary to remark', says Falconer, 'that the style of this mode of
living [pasturage], if I may use such an expression, varies extremely,
according to the climate, nature of the country, &c. Thus the Egyptians,
at a certain period, followed this course of life, as did also the people of
Sicily. But these differed extremely from the Arabs and Tartars, both of
whom pursue this course of life, and who likewise differ greatly from one
another. As the causes which I have before mentioned, as operating upon
the minds and actions of men, modify and temper each other; so, in the
present instance, we must consider the effects of the way of life, as
subject to be directed and altered in a great measure by similar circumstances' (*Remarks*, p. 322).

supersede agriculture in the same way as agriculture did pasturage and pasturage hunting.

At the same time, however, whatever his intentions, Falconer's manner of treatment did involve some weakening of the basic idea lying behind the traditional four stages theory. I am referring here not simply to his attempt to redefine the hunting and pastoral stages; his inclusion of 'literature and science' with the other 'ways of life'; his treatment of 'luxury and refinement' as a new and apparently separate stage; and his propensity to introduce material of doubtful relevance into his discussions – important though all of these things may be. What I am mainly referring to is the fact that in Falconer's book the 'way of life' is only one out of six 'physical' causes which are separately and successively considered, and that there is no real indication that he regards this as the most important of the six – apart, of course, from the fact that he devotes more space to it than to any of the others. When it comes to the question of the way in which the different causes interact with one another, all that Falconer gives us is a very vague and general statement, which says little more than that 'the effects of each of the causes here described, when combined together, overpower, temper, and modify one another in many instances; but have each of them a separate existence and action, however they may concur with one another in the general effect'.[36] Nowhere is it suggested that any one of the potential causes – whether the mode of subsistence or any other – should in any meaningful sense be regarded as having priority over the others.

The two other works in this group – John Logan's *Elements of the Philosophy of History* (Edinburgh, 1781) and James Dunbar's *Essays on the History of Mankind in Rude and Uncultivated Ages* (London, 1780) – need not detain us very long. Logan's book is actually not much more than a set of lecture-notes, based on lectures which he gave at Edinburgh under the patronage of Robertson, Blair, and others.[37] It is interesting for a rather fine formulation of the law of

[36] *Ibid.*, p. vi.
[37] See the biography of Logan in the *Dictionary of National Biography.*

unintended consequences,[38] for a statement of the principle that 'power naturally follows on property';[39] and for a recognition of the fact that there are 'three remarkable stages in the History of Property', which Logan describes as follows:

1. That which takes place among savages, when it respects present rather than permanent possession.
2. That which takes place among barbarous tribes, who have adopted the idea of permanent possession in their flocks or herds; but who, as they still continue to migrate, have no private property in land.
3. That which obtains among nations when they forsake their roving life, and, settling in the soil, appropriate land.[40]

But it is also noteworthy for a succinct statement of the view that similarities of manners as between modern and ancient nations are to be construed as evidence not of the genetic descent of the former from the latter, but of the fact that similar causes produce similar effects:

Similar situations produce similar appearances, and, where the state of society is the same, nations will resemble one another.
The want of attention to this hath filled the world with infinite volumes. The most remote resemblances in language, customs, or manners, has suggested the idea of deriving one nation from another.[41]

The implied reference to the American origins literature is of course unmistakable.[42]

Dunbar's book is rather more difficult to assess. He too, like Logan, puts forward a version of the law of unintended

---

[38] 'The arrangements and improvements which take place in human affairs result not from the efforts of individuals, but from a movement of the whole society . . . No constitution is formed by a concert: No government is copied from a plan. Sociability and policy are natural to mankind. In the progress of society, instincts turn into arts, and original principles are converted into actual establishments. When an inequality of possessions takes place, the few that are opulent contend for power, the many defend their rights: from this struggle of parties a form of government is established' (*Elements*, pp. 14–15).

[39] *Ibid.*, p. 133.   [40] *Ibid.*, pp. 21–2.   [41] *Ibid.*, pp. 16–17.

[42] Logan was also the author of a later book entitled *A View of Antient History* (Vol. I, London, 1788; Vol. II, London, 1791), which he published under the curious pseudonym of 'William Rutherford, D.D., Master of the Academy at Uxbridge', and for which he solicited Adam Smith's contribution (see W. R. Scott, *Adam Smith as Student and Professor*

consequences;[43] there is a vaguely materialist bias in his thinking, which shows itself in particular when he is discussing the influence of climate;[44] and he is quite prepared to recognise the importance of changes in 'subsistence' and 'modes of life' – although his emphasis here is on the way in which men may consciously bring about such changes rather than on the effect which such changes, once they have been brought about, may have on mankind.[45] But the main argument of the book is clearly outside the tradition of the four stages theory: the 'stages' through which society is conceived to develop[46] have nothing to do with the mode of subsistence, and the author quite happily maintains that 'degeneracy, as well as improvement, is incident to man'.[47] One interesting passage towards the end of the book, however, contains yet another example of the way in which the contemplation of the Americans was leading contemporary thinkers towards the crucial idea that similarities of manners are evidence not of genetic descent but rather of similarities in the mode of subsistence. Dunbar is talking in this passage about the ancient Germans, among whom, he says, 'the uniformity of individuals was as astonishing as the diversity of all from every other people' – a fact which led Tacitus to suppose them 'a pure and distinct race'. The New World, Dunbar proceeds,

presented appearances exactly similar. The astonishing resemblance which was there observed among mankind, seems to evidence that it was peopled originally by the same race, and at an aera of no high antiquity. The branches, though widely spread, had probably not been long separated from the common stock, *or perhaps a similarity in the modes of life contributed, more than any other cause, throughout that immense continent, to exclude variety in the human species.*[48]

(Glasgow, 1937), p. 304). *A View of Antient History* contains a large number of passages which clearly reveal the influence of the four stages theory and its methodology. See, e.g. Vol. I, pp. 1–9, 37–9, 60–3, 199–201, 207, 274, 280–1, 325–6, 361–2, and 382–3; and Vol. II, pp. 474–5.
[43] Dunbar, *Essays*, p. 60.
[44] See, e.g. *ibid.*, pp. 112–13, 207–8, and 232.
[45] See, e.g. *ibid.*, Essay X (pp. 335ff.), *passim*, and in particular p. 343.
[46] *Ibid.*, pp. 1–3.
[47] *Ibid.*, p. 3.
[48] *Ibid.*, pp. 428–9. (My italics.)

Herder

Between 1784 and 1791 there appeared in Germany Johann Gottfried von Herder's great four-part work *Ideen zur Philosophie der Geschichte der Menscheit*.[49] In this many-sided and richly ambiguous book, Herder attempted (as Professor Krieger has aptly put it)[50] 'to unify the effects of God, nature, and culture in history' and 'to reconcile the claims of humanity as a whole with the claims of its several nations in the depiction of man's earthly destiny'. In a sense, of course, these were also the problems with which men like Turgot had wrestled; and the particular brand of progressivism which Herder seems finally to have embraced in the *Ideen* – however idiosyncratically it may have been expressed and however seriously it may have been qualified – is not quite as different from Turgot's as has sometimes been claimed.[51] But if in certain respects Herder is clearly an heir to the tradition of the Enlightenment, in certain other respects he clearly transcends that tradition – and it is this latter side of his work, of course, which attracts particular attention today. His reaction against the prevailing Europocentrism of his time; his frequent emphasis on the distinctive, the unique, and the unrepeatable; his ubiquitous use of an evocative version of the principle of plenitude; and his notion that every people and every culture has worth and deserves respect – all these themes, and more, have been disentangled by modern commentators from his diffuse narrative and re-examined in the light of our present problems and preconceptions.

When we are considering Herder's attitude towards the four stages theory and the basic idea which underlay it, our starting-point must be his own principles of historical interpretation as he expressed them in the *Ideen*. The history of mankind, he argues, is characterised by an 'endlessly complicated machinery of causes mutually acting upon each

[49] An English translation by T. Churchill of Herder's *Ideen* was published in London in 1800 under the title *Outlines of a Philosophy of the History of Man*. An abridged version of this translation, edited by F. E. Manuel, was published by the University of Chicago Press, Chicago and London, in 1968, under the title *Reflections on the Philosophy of the History of Mankind*. Most of the references below are to the latter edition.

[50] In his preface to the University of Chicago Press edition, p. vii.

[51] See the interesting essay on 'Herder and the Enlightenment Philosophy of History' in A. O. Lovejoy, *Essays in the History of Ideas* (Johns Hopkins Press, Baltimore, 1948), pp. 166–82.

other'.[52] It is useless, therefore, to employ 'the philosophy of final causes' when one is examining (for example) the rise and decline of Rome. One ought properly to contemplate this series of events 'like any other natural phenomenon, the causes and effects of which we would investigate freely, without any preconceived hypothesis'.[53] But statements of this kind, which abound in the *Ideen*, must not be taken to mean that according to Herder the historian has to approach every new analytical problem empty-handed. There are in fact certain analogies, and certain broad organising principles, which the historian can usefully employ.

The main analogy at the historian's disposal, according to Herder's account, is that between the growth of a nation and the growth of a living creature. Just as the growth of a living creature is conditioned by the 'concatenation of circumstances' which surrounds it, so the growth of a nation is similarly conditioned.[54] In the case of a nation, the most important circumstances in the 'concatenation' are usually the genetic constitution of the people and the 'climate' – taking the latter to include not only the degrees of heat and cold, the character of the air, etc., but also 'the elevation or depression of a region, its nature and products, the food and drink men enjoy in it, the mode of life they pursue, the labours in which they are employed, their clothing, even their ordinary attitudes, their arts and pleasures, with a multitude of other circumstances, which considerably influence their lives . . .[55] 'Climate' in this very broad sense is of course 'a chaos of causes, very dissimilar to each other',[56] which means that the precise effects of the interaction of these causes with one another, and with the genetic constitution of the people, cannot be predicted in advance. Nor is it possible to pick out any one of these causes as *the* cause, since all of them are determined as well as determining. But it may sometimes be useful. Herder seems to suggest, to take one of the more important of the causes, hold it constant (as it were), and analyse the different effects which normally spring from it in all the different forms it may assume. It is precisely in this

[52] *Reflections*, pp. 266–7.   [53] *Ibid.*, pp. 266–7.
[54] *Ibid.*, p. 264.   [55] *Ibid.*, p. 16.
[56] *Ibid.*, p. 28; and cf. p. 16.

way that Herder analyses the effects of different modes of subsistence upon the minds of men. And the categories which he employs in this analysis are those of the four stages theory – hunting, fishing, pasturage, agriculture, and (by implication) commerce.

Herder does not, however, accept these categories unreservedly. 'It has been customary', he notes, 'to divide the nations of the Earth into hunters, fishermen, shepherds, and husbandmen; and not only to determine their rank in civilization from this division, but even to consider civilization itself as a necessary consequence of this or that way of life.'[57] This would be very excellent, he proceeds, 'if these modes of life were determined themselves in the first place'. But, as had already been observed by Falconer (whose book Herder had read),[58]

they vary with almost every region, and for the most part run into each other in such a manner, that this mode of classification is very difficult to apply with accuracy. The Greenlander, who strikes the whale, pursues the reindeer, and kills the seal, is occupied both in hunting and fishing; yet in a very different manner from that, in which the Negro fishes, or the Araucoan hunts on the deserts of the Andes. The Bedouin and the Mungal, the Laplander and the Peruvian, are shepherds: but how greatly do they differ from each other, while one pastures his camels, another his horses, the third his reindeer, and the last his pacoes and llamas. The merchants of England differ not more from those of China, than the husbandmen of Whidah from the husbandmen of Japan.[59]

Nor, Herder adds, is want alone capable of producing civilisation, for 'as soon as the Indolence of man has rendered him contented under his Necessities, and both together have begotten the child he names Convenience, he persists in his condition, and cannot be impelled to improve it without difficulty'. Other causes, he insists, 'cooperate to determine the mode of life of a people'. Nevertheless, 'let us at present consider it as fixed, and inquire what active powers of the mind are displayed in its various forms'.[60]

What follows at this point in the *Ideen* is an extended

[57] *Ibid.*, p. 50.   [58] *Ibid.*, p. 15, footnote 21.
[59] *Ibid.*, p. 50.   [60] *Ibid.*, p. 50.

discussion of the various ways in which the 'mode of life of a people' in gathering, hunting, pastoral, and agricultural societies may influence 'the practical understanding of the human species'.[61] Many of the points that Herder makes in this fascinating section, and many of his illustrations (notably those relating to the Americans, which are very numerous), have obviously been derived from the four stages theory literature, with which he must have been well acquainted. As an example, let us take his treatment of the pastoral mode of life, which is worthy of extended quotation. 'Man went incomparably farther', he says,

when he attracted animals about him, and finally brought them under his yoke. The immense difference between neighbouring nations, living with or without these auxiliaries to their powers, is evident. Whence came it, that America, on its first discovery, was so far behind the old world, and the Europeans could treat its inhabitants like a flock of defenceless sheep? It depended not on corporal powers alone, as the examples of all the numerous savage nations show; in growth, in swiftness, in prompt address, they exceed, man for man, most of the nations, that play at dice for their land. Neither was understanding, as far as it relates to the individual, the cause: the American knew how to provide for himself, and lived happily with his wife and children. It arose, therefore, from art, weapons, close connexion, and principally from domesticated animals. Had the American possessed the horse . . . the conquest would have been more dearly purchased . . . But as all this is in the hand of Fate, to the same Fate must be ascribed, what was in the nature of this quarter of the Globe, that it was so long unacquainted with either horse, ass, ox, dog, sheep, goat, hog, cat, or camel . . .

In the old world, on the contrary, how many animals are domesticated: and how much have they assisted the active mind of man! But for the horse and camel, the deserts of Arabia and Africa would be inaccessible: the sheep and the goat have been aids to domestic economy; the ox and the ass, to agriculture and trade.[62]

And as another example, we may quote a shorter extract from

---

[61] The heading of chapter 3, from which I am quoting at the moment, is 'The practical Understanding of the human Species has every where grown up under the Wants of Life; but every where it is a Blossom of the Genius of the People, a son of Tradition and Custom'.

[62] *Reflections*, pp. 53–5.

another passage in which Herder deals with agriculture, and which is interesting for (*inter alia*) the Rousseauist twist in the tail:

Generally speaking, no mode of life has effected so much alteration in the minds of men, as agriculture, combined with the enclosure of land. While it produced arts and trades, villages and towns, and, in consequence, government and laws; it necessarily paved the way for that frightful despotism, which, from confining every man to his field, gradually proceeded to prescribe to him, what alone he should do on it, what alone he should be. The ground now ceased to belong to man, but man became the appertenance of the ground.[63]

It is important to note, however, that although Herder uses the basic categories of the four stages theory in order to differentiate societies from one another, he does not (at any rate in most contexts) use them to delineate temporal stages through which individual nations naturally tend to pass. The variety of different modes of life to be found in the world, Herder seems to suggest, is not much more than another demonstration of the truth of the principle of plenitude: 'The practical understanding of man was intended, to blossom and bear fruit in all its varieties: and hence such a diversified Earth was ordained for so diversified a species.'[64] An individual nation has no natural tendency to progress from a 'lower' mode of life to a 'higher' one: on the contrary, if it has any natural tendency at all it is in fact to resist any movement away from its existing mode of life, whatever this may happen to be. In particular, everyone 'dreads submission to the yoke of agriculture', as the example of the Americans shows:

Notwithstanding the fine arable lands to be found in North America; much as every nation values and defends its property; however highly some have been taught by Europeans, to prize gold, brandy, and certain of the conveniences of life: still the tilling of the ground, with the cultivation of maize, and a few garden vegetables, is left to the women, as well as the whole care of the huts; the warlike hunter could never bend his mind, to become a gardener, shepherd, or husbandman.[65]

[63] *Ibid.*, p. 57.   [64] *Ibid.*, p. 58.   [65] *Ibid.*, p. 56.

But Herder's attitude towards this problem cannot be pinned down quite as simply as this. Even in the chapter we have just been considering, where he criticises the notion that want produces civilisation, he does after all deal with the different modes of life in the order of their (alleged) temporal succession; he does, as we have seen, speak of man going 'incomparably farther' when he finally tamed animals, and of the great 'alteration in the minds of men' produced by the coming of agriculture; and he does also speak of Providence employing agriculture as 'a principal instrument for leading man to civil society'.[66] And elsewhere in the *Ideen* there are other indications which suggest that Herder may have regarded the temporal scheme of the four stages theory as applicable, up to a point, to the development of *mankind as a whole,* as distinct from the individual nations of mankind. For example, when talking of Egypt he describes how in that country the step 'from the care of cattle to husbandry' was an easy one, since 'the settled inhabitant was invited to it by Nature herself'.[67] And there is a very interesting passage in the section dealing with the Greeks in which Herder discusses the relatively favourable situation of nations inhabiting coasts or islands as compared with that of nations inhabiting the mainland. 'On the continent', he says, 'in spite of all natural endowments, and acquired capacities, the shepherd remained a shepherd; the hunter, a hunter: even the husbandman and artist were confined like plants to a narrow spot.'[68] The implication here, fairly clearly, is that there is a 'natural' progression from hunting to pasturage and from pasturage to agriculture which favourable geographical conditions will encourage but which unfavourable geographical conditions may obstruct.

This is a proposition with which few of the eighteenth-century adherents of the four stages theory would have wished to disagree: as we have seen, many of them in one way or another tried to tackle the problem of how to sort out the respective effects of mode of subsistence on the one hand and 'climate' (in the broad sense) on the other. But while Herder paid due deference to their efforts, and was perhaps more influenced by their basic approach than he

---

[66] *Ibid.*, p. 57.   [67] *Ibid.*, p. 125.   [68] *Ibid.*, p. 167.

himself realised, he must of course be regarded primarily as a revisionist rather than as a follower. In his system, the mode of subsistence is certainly one of the more important of the interacting causes which shape our lives and history, but it is only one of them: if his system as a whole can be said to be 'materialist' in orientation, it is 'materialist' in a much less precise sense than Millar's or even Ferguson's. And Herder's emphasis on the individuality of different nations and peoples, on the danger of using any 'preconceived hypothesis' in the study of history, and on the folly of Europocentrism, points much less towards the nineteenth century, when the employment of a stadial methodology was sometimes regarded as a substitute for fact-finding, and much more towards the first half of the twentieth century, when the inevitable reaction against this misuse of stadialism took place.

In 1793, shortly after the appearance of the last part of Herder's *Ideen*, two further revisionist works appeared – William Russell's *History of Ancient Europe*,[69] and the second volume of James Beattie's *Elements of Moral Science*.[70] These two books may conveniently be considered together. In neither of them does the four stages theory occupy a central place, but the authors' attitudes towards it are not without interest.

Beattie's discussion of the theory occurs in the course of his treatment of occupancy. At first, he appears to accept the theory without question:

Property in food, being at all times necessary, must take place even in the rudest forms of society. That would probably be appropriated first, which is most easily come at, as the fruit of trees and bushes, and other vegetables; then perhaps men would think of preying on beasts, and fishes, and fowls; and, in many countries, this must have been their first provision, and, consequently, hunting, fishing, and fowling their first employments. Afterwards, finding that a provision of animal food might be secured for some length of time, by bringing the more tractable

[69] William Russell, *The History of Ancient Europe; with a view of the revolutions in Asia and Africa* (London, 1793).
[70] James Beattie, *Elements of Moral Science* (Vol. II, Edinburgh, 1793). The 1st volume had appeared in 1790.

animals together, and keeping them in flocks and herds, men would betake themselves to pasturage, in countries where it was practicable. And this we learn, from the history of the patriarchs, to have been one of their earliest vocations.

In a good soil and climate, the digging of the ground and the rearing of useful herbs, would no doubt be practised in the beginning of society, both as a recreation and as a profitable art. But agriculture, in a more enlarged sense of the word, as it depends on several other arts, especially those of working in wood and metal, could hardly take place, till after those arts were invented.[71]

So unambiguous is this statement that one is quite surprised, two or three pages further on, to find Beattie criticising the four stages theory in the following terms:

From the view of things now given, it has been supposed by some authors, that the progress of human society, from rudeness to refinement, consists of four periods or stages: that, in the first, men lived by hunting or fishing, or on such fruits and plants as the earth produces without culture; in the second, by pasturage; in the third, by both these, in conjunction with agriculture; and, in the fourth, by all these, in conjunction with commerce, which gives rise to arts and sciences, and every other elegance of life. In some countries, particularly our own, this may have happened, but could not in all: some being so barren as not to admit of agriculture; many so peculiarly situated, as to be incapable of commerce with the rest of the world; and some so destitute of territory, and so beset with the sea, as to oblige the natives, from the beginning, to live by fishing, or practise commerce. Examples will readily occur to those who are conversant with history and geography.[72]

None of the more sophisticated four stages theorists would ever have denied that the 'natural' progress of societies through the stages had often been impeded or prevented by geographical and climatic factors: clearly Beattie is criticising a vulgarised version of the theory which most of its progenitors would have disowned. What is more interesting is that in Beattie's account of this vulgarised version the different modes of subsistence are, as it were, conceived to be cumulative: as we go from stage to stage, the old modes of

[71] *Elements*, Vol. II, pp. 249–50.
[72] *Ibid.*, Vol. II, pp. 253–4.

subsistence do not disappear but are found 'in conjunction with' the new one.[73]

Russell's performance, by and large, is on an appreciably higher level than Beattie's. For example, Beattie, in order to get round the objection that 'one of Adam's sons was a tiller of the ground', simply reproduces the time-honoured – but by now rather time-worn – reply to the effect that the developmental story must be conceived to begin after the Flood.[74] Russell is not content with this. If we accept in a literal sense the Mosaic history of the Creation, the antediluvian world, and 'the dispersion of mankind, after the Flood, at Babel, or Babylon', he argues, we shall be at a loss to account for the very early peopling and improvement of Egypt, India, and China, since (as he puts it) 'the two latter countries were very distant from the scene of dispersion, and the former separated from it by almost impassable deserts'.[75] But if, he continues,

we consider that mysterious narrative of the Hebrew legislator, as a *mythical* and *political apologue*, composed for the *introduction* and *support* of the *Jewish theocracy*; or if, conformable to the opinion of many learned writers, we suppose that, in consequence of the confusion of tongues and the dispersion of mankind, the great body of the human species degenerated, during their emigration, into a state of savage barbarity; and, in that state, spread themselves widely over the face of the earth, the causes of such population and improvement may be deduced in a satisfactory manner.[76]

The first of these two alternatives was of course a comparative newcomer on the scene: even Millar, it will be recalled, had felt obliged to pay lip-service to the second, if only in a brief footnote.[77]

The proper starting-point, then, Russell proceeds, is the state of nature, about which we now know a great deal more than our predecessors did because we have 'a more perfect acquaintance with rude nations'.[78] Since (as Aristotle said) a progress in knowledge and civility is natural to man, we must

[73] We should not leave Beattie without noting his interesting statement (*ibid.*, Vol. II, pp. 358–9) of the relationships between government, property, and power.
[74] *Ibid.*, p. 251.   [75] Russell, *History*, p. 4.   [76] *Ibid.*, p. 5.
[77] See above, p. 167.   [78] *History*, p. 6. Cf. p. 9, footnote.

investigate the 'advances toward refinement' which man has made.[79] These advances, says Russell, are very different in different regions of the earth:

In northern countries, where the soil is rugged, the climate severe, and the spontaneous productions of the earth, fit for the support of human life, few and of small value, the progress of society is slow. Hunting is there long the sole employment of Man, and his principal means of subsistence. He feeds upon the flesh, and clothes himself with the skins of wild animals.

But in southern latitudes, where the earth is more bountiful, the soil more susceptible of culture, and the use of animal food less necessary, the savage state is of shorter continuance. Little inclined, in such climates, to active exertions, mankind soon relinquish the pursuit of wild beasts, or cease to consider the chace as their chief occupation. They early acquire the art of taming and rearing the more docile and useful animals, and of cultivating the most nutritive vegetable productions.

In proportion as food becomes more plentiful men are enabled to indulge more freely the appetite for society. They live together in larger bodies. Towns and cities are built. Private property in land is ascertained, and placed under the guardianship of laws. Agriculture is prosecuted; metals are discovered, and mines worked. Genius is called forth by emulation, and arts and sciences are invented. The political union among the members of the same community, is rendered more close, by an apprehension of danger from abroad; and the intercourse between them more general, from a sense of mutual conveniency. Hence patriotism and internal traffic, the two great sources of national happiness and prosperity.[80]

The leading ideas in this synoptic view of the progress of society, as two very interesting footnotes at this point show, were the product of a by no means unperceptive critique by Russell of the traditional four stages theory, particularly in the form in which it had been put forward by Kames. The latter, according to Russell, had given the impression 'that men never betake themselves to the taming or rearing of animals, until the wild breed becomes too scarce to furnish them with food; and [that] their aversion against labour [is]

[79] *Ibid.*, p. 10.
[80] *Ibid.*, pp. 11–12. In the following paragraph Russell discusses the rise of commodity exchange and money.

so great, that they do not apply themselves to agriculture, while they can find sufficient room to pasture their herds and flocks'. But this reasoning, Russell argues, founded on the practice of the North American savages and Asiatic Tartars,

> though plausible in theory, is contradicted by facts; and, therefore, cannot be of universal application; because unsupported by general observation or experience, in the history of ancient or modern nations, inhabiting the milder climates of the earth. Such of the ancient Scythian tribes, as had seized upon fertile districts, cultivated the ground; and several of them had attained, by these means, to a considerable degree of civility; while those tribes, less fortunately situated, were utterly rude and barbarous. (Herodot. lib. iv. passim.) The same observation may be extended to some North American tribes, on the banks of the Ohio, Mississippi, &c. and to every people inhabiting such districts over the face of the globe. See *Hist. Gen. des Voyages*, passim.[81]

At any rate in the case of peoples dwelling in 'southern latitudes', therefore, the four stages theory requires amendment to take account of this kind of possibility.

The other respect in which Russell felt that the traditional four stages theory was unsatisfactory was that it laid too much emphasis on the transition from one mode of subsistence to another, and too little emphasis on the emergence of *private property in land*. The latter, Russell went so far as to say,

> may be considered as the first great stage in the progress of civil society: the advance from *hunting* to *herding*, or even from *herding* to *rude agriculture*, such as is found among pasturing nations, being comparatively small. For while men pasture their cattle, or cultivate the ground *in common*, their industry is languid, and the product of their flocks and fields scanty. *Personal Property* in *Land*, and the prospect of reaping *exclusively* the fruits of his labour, can alone give activity and perseverance to the labours of the husbandman, or fertility to the earth.[82]

The fact that the introduction of agriculture was not neces-

---

[81] *Ibid.*, pp. 10–11, footnote 12. The *Histoire Générale des Voyages* was a series of accounts of voyages which appeared volume by volume in Paris from 1746 onwards. This remarkable collection, the greater part of which was edited by the Abbé Prévost, was increasingly referred to as a source of evidence about savage peoples as the century proceeded.

[82] *Ibid.*, p. 11, footnote 13.

sarily or immediately followed by the introduction of private property in land had of course already been noted by other writers. Herder, for example, had drawn attention to the fact that 'many small Negro nations', although they culti-vated their land, still treated it as common property, and had presented this as evidence of the reluctance of early peoples to submit to the yoke of agriculture 'combined with the enclosure of land'.[83] The moral which Russell draws from the fact in question, however, is a radically different one. As he sees it, private property in land is one of the most vital institutions of modern European society, so that when we are looking back at the historical origins of this society and the progressive fulfilment of the essential preconditions for its emergence, we should place our main emphasis on the intro-duction of private property in land rather than on the introduction of agriculture. This is a significant change of approach: as we shall soon see, there were others besides Russell at this time who were beginning, as it were, to pro-ject back into the earlier stages of society a number of the basic socio-economic categories which were characteristic of the 'commercial' society of contemporary Europe.

Two other revisionist writers – Lord Monboddo and Con-dorcet – remain to be considered before we proceed to the poets and the economists. Monboddo and Condorcet are in many respects strange bedfellows, of course, but the parallels which can be drawn between them are more instructive than may appear at first sight.

The six volumes of Monboddo's first great work, *Of the Origin and Progress of Language*, appeared at various dates between 1773 and 1792, and the six volumes of his second work, *Antient Metaphysics*, between 1779 and 1799. There is much talk in these discursive, repetitive, and sometimes bril-liant books about 'the several states of Society'[84] through which men have passed; and Monboddo throughout shows himself very interested in 'the Savages, as we call them, of North America, concerning whom I have been at a great deal of pains to inform myself'. The main reason for this interest

[83] Herder, *Reflections*, pp. 56–7.
[84] *Antient Metaphysics*, Vol. III (1784), p. 102.

in the Americans, of course, is that the author wants to use them 'to show what men were in the first ages of society'.[85] It turns out, however, that Monboddo is much more interested in what led up to these 'first ages' than in what followed them: his main concern is with the transition from the beast to man, from the solitary state to the herd state, and from gathering to hunting. His views on man's later stages of development tend to be expressed rather sporadically, and have to be disentangled from his long and amorphous discussions of other matters.

'At first', Monboddo argues in Volume IV of *Antient Metaphysics*, '. . . men lived upon the herbs and roots which the earth produced'. But when men increased very much in number, 'which they certainly did in the first ages of society, the natural fruits of the earth could not maintain them. And therefore . . . then, and not till then, they took to hunting and fishing; for a flesh or fish diet I hold to be unnatural to man, as unnatural as to an horse or ox . . .'[86] The fact that man, 'before he took to agriculture', lived upon the natural fruits of the earth, and by hunting and fishing, is 'well known to those who have studied the history of man in antient books' (e.g. Diodorus Siculus).[87] But, says Monboddo, there is no need to go to books to learn that men can live in this way, since we have before us the living example of the Americans, who 'practice very little agriculture, but live almost intirely by hunting and fishing',[88] and the Tartars, who 'live intirely by hunting'.[89] But in this 'nomad life', Monboddo claims,

men could have no regular polity, nor be governed by laws. For that purpose it was necessary that they should have a fixed habitation, and live together, in considerable numbers, in one place, for which agriculture is absolutely necessary; and therefore Ceres was very properly said, not only to be the goddess of agriculture, but of laws . . . Without such a life, by which men have the closest intercourse and communication, they could not have invented any arts and sciences worth mentioning . . .[90]

[85] *Ibid.*, Vol. III, pp. 206–7.
[86] *Ibid.*, Vol. IV (1795), pp. 38–40.
[87] *Ibid.*, Vol. IV, p. 40.
[88] *Ibid.*, Vol. VI (1799), p. 302.
[89] *Ibid.*, Vol. VI, p. 302; and cf. Vol. IV, p. 40.
[90] *Ibid.*, Vol. IV, pp. 40–1.

It will be noticed that Monboddo, rather curiously, cites the Tartars here as an example of a hunting rather than a pastoral people. In another place, however, this time in *Of the Origin and Progress of Language,* he seems to envisage 'the pastoral life' as naturally succeeding hunting – although only, he hastens to explain, in countries where the flocks and herds can live through the winter on the natural produce of the earth:

One natural consequence of hunting would be, that in process of time they would think of the expedient of catching certain animals alive, taming them, and breeding out of them, which would greatly add to their stock of provisions. This produced the pastoral life, which is the only means of subsistence of whole nations at this day. But it may be observed, that, unless in countries where flocks and herds can live through the winter upon the natural produce of the earth, it is impossible that men can be supported in that way, without the assistance of other arts, and particularly agriculture. And this is a good reason why the Indians of North America, not having the art of agriculture, have never attempted the pastoral life, or to tame any animals other than dogs that live upon flesh.[91]

At this point, and with this somewhat idiosyncratic attempt at a solution of the American problem, Monboddo abruptly ends his discussion of 'the progress of men in the arts of subsistence' and goes on to another theme.

In one of the few places where Monboddo sets out to deal specifically with 'the progress of civil society' and attempts to delineate the main 'stages' of this progress, the picture he presents is very different. First, he says,

we see men living together in herds, like cattle or horses, without even coupling together, or pairing, as we see the males and females of certain other species do; but, nevertheless, carrying on some common business, such as fishing or hunting, or whatever else may be necessary for their sustenance, though without any thing that can be called government or rule; and of this kind are the instances that I have quoted from Diodorus Siculus, Herodotus, and modern travellers. Next, we see them submitting to government, but only upon certain occasions; and particularly

[91] *Origin and Progress of Language,* Vol. I (1773), pp. 258–9. Cf. *Antient Metaphysics,* Vol. VI, p. 266.

for the purpose of self-defence . . . Under this kind of occasional government certain inhabitants of the Caribbee islands were when we first discovered those islands. They had chiefs and generals in time of war; but in time of peace, they lived under no government at all.[92]

The 'next stage of civil society', he proceeds,

is that of the Indians of North America, who have a government in time of peace as well as war, and may be said to form a state. This government is administered by their sachems, or old men, who meet together in council to deliberate upon public matters . . . But in other matters, every man is his own master, subject to no controul, not even that of his parents. For though they have all separate and distinct families, there is no domestic government among them; neither have they any laws or judges: so that every man defends his own rights, and revenges the injuries done him.[93]

The next stage is exemplified by 'a stricter and more regular form of government' which obtains in 'the several countries of Europe', and which 'is administered by certain magistrates, known under different names in the different countries, according to certain rules and regulations, to which every member of the state is obliged to submit, under certain pains and penalties'.[94] And 'the last stage of civil society, in which the progression ends', is

that most perfect form of polity, which, to all the advantages of the governments last mentioned, joins the care of the education of youth, and of the private lives of the citizens; neither of which is left to the will and pleasure of each individual, but both are regulated by public wisdom. Such was the government of antient Sparta, and such were all the plans of government devised by Plato and other philosophers.[95]

What comes through all this more than anything else is an immense *eclecticism*: the idea of a succession of different modes of subsistence (largely taken over from the traditional four stages theory) is juxtaposed with the idea of a succession of different forms of civil government which are connected

[92] *Origin and Progress of Language*, Vol. i, pp. 240–1.
[93] *Ibid.*, Vol. i, pp. 241–2.
[94] *Ibid.*, Vol. i, p. 242.   [95] *Ibid.*, Vol. i, p. 243.

only in the very early stages, and even then only loosely, with different modes of subsistence. It is in this respect (*inter alia*) that there is an interesting parallel with Condorcet's influential book *Sketch for a Historical Picture of the Progress of the Human Mind*,[96] which was first published in 1795, the year of the appearance of Volume IV of Monboddo's *Antient Metaphysics*. For Condorcet, too, reveals himself as a great eclectic: the ten successive 'stages' through which he conceives human society as passing are by and large so unlike one another in kind that there is little basis for comparing one with another. The first three 'stages', it is true, correspond roughly to the hunting, pastoral, and agricultural stages of the traditional four stages theory, from which Condorcet has obviously taken them over. Even here, however, a certain disparateness is apparent, since in Condorcet's description of the first stage the main emphasis is placed on the tribal form of organisation rather than on the mode of subsistence adopted by the tribes,[97] and many of the characteristics and developments which he discusses under the headings of the other two stages are not shown to be logically connected with the mode of subsistence concerned.

After this, what Condorcet presents us with is really nothing more (or less) than a condensed account of 'the history of man from the time when alphabetical writing was known in Greece to the condition of the human race at the present day in the most enlightened countries of Europe'.[98] The leading events in 'the march and progress of the human mind' during this period are dealt with (roughly in chronological order) under six successive headings, which are described as 'stages' and conceived to follow on consecutively after the tribal, pastoral, and agricultural stages. It is clear, however, that the tribal, pastoral, and agricultural stages are quite different *in kind* from the six which are supposed to follow on after them. And the tenth 'stage', the

[96] The references below are to the English translation of this work published by Weidenfeld and Nicolson, London, 1955, in their 'Library of Ideas' series. The translator is June Barraclough, and there is an introduction by Stuart Hampshire.

[97] In the summary of his argument which Condorcet gives in his introduction, this difference in emphasis is less noticeable.

[98] *Sketch*, p. 9.

last in Condorcet's sequence, is different in kind yet again, since it is concerned with 'the future progress of the human mind' and contains Condorcet's famous vision of the way in which, in times to come, 'truth alone will obtain a lasting victory' and all men will work together for the perfection and happiness of humanity.[99]

C'est magnifique – but it stands well outside the broad tradition of the eighteenth-century four stages theory. Condorcet certainly begins with the conventional hunting–pasturage–agriculture sequence, or something like it. But after this, in the remaining five-sixths of the book, there is no emphasis whatever on the mode of subsistence, and very few references back to the first three stages.[100] Condorcet uses the traditional three stages scheme merely as a convenient starting-point from which to branch out into a new sequential scheme of an entirely different character.[101]

It seems to me to be quite mistaken, therefore, to regard Condorcet as having given 'a final splendid expression to the comprehensive eighteenth-century conception of a science of man'.[102] Splendid indeed were his vision and his faith; and splendid too, in a sense, was the remarkable array of developmental 'stages' which he produced. But surely, on any reasonable interpretation of what we ought to mean by 'the comprehensive eighteenth-century conception of a science of man', Condorcet did *not* give a 'final splendid expression' to it. What he did, in effect, was to take the developmental scheme in which that conception had typically been embodied and incorporate it in a much wider scheme of his own – a scheme characterised by an eclecticism of a rather

[99] *Ibid.*, p. 10.

[100] One of the most conspicuous of these will be found on p. 79.

[101] Another important distinction between Condorcet's approach and that of the four stages theorists relates to the considerable emphasis which Condorcet places (*Sketches*, pp. 8–9) on the 'theoretical', 'conjectural', and 'hypothetical' character of his description of the progress of mankind through the tribal, pastoral, and agricultural stages. It is only after the third stage, Condorcet says, that the picture becomes 'truly historical'. Most of the four stages theorists would have regarded this as selling the pass: rightly or wrongly, they believed that the application of their new methodology would greatly *reduce* the area in which 'conjecture' had to be resorted to. Cf. below, pp. 236ff.

[102] K. E. Bock, *The Acceptance of Histories* (University of California Press, Berkeley and Los Angeles, 1956), p. 81.

similar character to Monboddo's, and an arbitrariness fore-
shadowing that of certain much later developmental schemes
in the fields of sociology and anthropology.

'Revisionist' tendencies, such as those we have been considering in the present chapter, presuppose the existence of
something 'orthodox' to revise. Striking evidence of the rise
of the four stages theory to the status of orthodoxy at this
time is to be found in two long didactic poems written by
Henry James Pye and Richard Payne Knight in 1783 and
1796 respectively. These two men, it should be noted, were
quite well-known figures in their time: Pye, however strange
it may seem, did manage to hold down the job of Poet
Laureate for twenty-three years; and Knight, although his
occasional ventures into verse did not exactly win him universal acclaim, at least had a high and deserved reputation as a
connoisseur and authority on ancient art.

Pye's poem, entitled *The Progress of Refinement*,[103] is a
long socio-historical tract in very dull verse, which, together
with Knight's later effort in the same genre, would surely find
a place in any anthology of the worst poetry of the century.
It is prefaced with a handy summary of contents, reading
exactly like the chapter-headings in a conventional prose
history of civil society, and it begins with an account of man
in a state of nature:

> Man, ere by rules of civil compact taught,
> (Uncouth his form, and unimproved his thought),
> O'er the rude waste a selfish savage goes,
> Nor mutual cares, nor mutual kindness knows,
> How to subsist his being's sole employ,
> Strength all his art, and rapine all his joy.[104]

Pye then goes on to elucidate the 'difficulties of improvement in unfavourable climates', his thesis here being that
'warm climates [are] the first scenes of [man's] emerging from
barbarism'.[105] In 'unfavourable climates', man will be a
hunter and his powers of reason will develop very slowly – a
situation which Pye describes in verse as follows:

[103] Henry James Pye, *The Progress of Refinement: A Poem in Three Parts*
(Oxford, 1783).
[104] *Ibid.*, p. 4.   [105] *Ibid.*, list of contents, p. 1.

> And where a steril soil, and frowning heaven,
> Are to his race by ruthless Nature given,
> Compell'd by chace his scanty food to gain,
> Pierced by sharp winds, or drench'd by chilling rain,
> While from the assailing climate, rigid grown,
> The alter'd fibres lose each nicer tone,
> Long is the torpid soul by want oppress'd,
> And dawning Reason slowly lights the breast.[106]

But when man lives in 'kindly regions' and under 'more genial skies', then

> Press'd by no want, in leisure's vacant hours
> The expanding Mind perceives her latent powers[107]

and he comes to live a pastoral life:

> Then as reclining on the fertile soil,
> Unknown the want of culture's stubborn toil,
> His grazing charge the gentle herdsman tends,
> And o'er the vale his eye delighted bends.[108]

With equal verve, the poet goes on to describe the manner in which Arabia, Asia, and Egypt became 'the first seats of the arts', and how, when these arts 'migrate into Greece',[109]

> Improvement spreads to life's more humble cares,
> And Industry the happy influence shares:
> Down the steep cliff, and o'er the craggy brow
> Strong Agriculture drives his laboring plow,
> And to the currents of the rising gale
> Adventurous Commerce trusts her swelling sail.[110]

The history of Greece and Rome is then deftly traced; the rise of the feudal system follows; and then the whole history of modern Europe. Apart from a rather splendid account of the way in which differences between various 'savage' peoples reflect differences in their 'climate' and 'soil',[111] and a warning about certain dangers to mankind which are implicit in the commercial stage, however, there is nothing more in the poem which is of particular interest from our present point of view.

[106] *Ibid.*, pp. 4–5.   [107] *Ibid.*, p. 5.
[108] *Ibid.*, pp. 5–6.   [109] *Ibid.*, list of contents, p. 1.
[110] *Ibid.*, p. 12.   [111] *Ibid.*, p. 71.

Knight's poem[112] is rather similar in form to Pye's (both clearly owing more than a little to Pope's *Essay on Man*), but it is altogether a much more ambitious piece of work. The 'general design' of the poem is said in the preface[113] to have been taken from Lucretius (to whom there are indeed a number of footnote references), but it is obvious from its arrangement and content that the author's main inspirational sources are much more modern. The titles of the six books are in fact

Book I: Of Hunting
Book II: Of Pasturage
Book III: Of Agriculture
Book IV: Of Arts, Manufactures, and Commerce
Book V: Of Climate and Soil
Book VI: Of Government and Conquest

And, as if this were not sufficient to indicate the leading sources of Knight's ideas, the poem is studded with numerous footnote references not only to Lucretius, but also to Ferguson's *History of Civil Society*, Robertson's *History of America*, Caesar and Tacitus on primitive tribes, Cook's *Voyages*, Smith's *Moral Sentiments*, Adair's *History of the American Indians*, Charlevoix, and many similar authorities.

There is so much in this singular poem which is germane to our subject that we shall have to ration our quotations very severely. Let us concentrate on three passages in which certain aspects of the *transition* from one developmental stage to the next are discussed. Take first the transition from hunting to pasturage, which is explained as follows:

> As growing numbers claim'd increase of food,
> In smaller herds the cattle browsed the wood:
> The hunter's labours less productive grew,
> And pale-faced famine slowly rose to view;
> Bidding each stream of social comfort flow
> In troubled tides of sympathetic woe.
>
> Hence want inventive, and prospective thought,
> More certain sources of nutrition sought;

[112] Richard Payne Knight, *The Progress of Civil Society: A Didactic Poem in Six Books* (London, 1796).
[113] *Ibid.*, p. v.

Directed man his genius to employ
To guard and save, as well as to destroy;
Bade him in wiles the youthful brood ensnare,
And train the captives with parental care;
The sturdy spirit of the headstrong break;
Restrain the restless, and entice the meek;
Teach them familiar round his hut to feed;
And for his use, to copulate and breed.[114]

When it comes to the transition from pasturage to agriculture, Knight assumes (with Lucretius – and up to a point with Rousseau) that the change takes place in close association with the discovery of metals. The basic cause of this transition, as of the earlier one from hunting to pasturage, is a growing population and a consequential shortage of food:

As o'er the earth the growing race of man,
With social influence still extending, ran,
More numerous herds required increase of food,
And bade him thin the o'ershadowing wilds of wood.[115]

But man could not 'thin the o'ershadowing wilds of wood' very effectively until he learned how to use fire. And the discovery of fire led in its turn to the discovery of metals and their working:

Thus more effective implements were found
To raise the building, and to till the ground;
Labour by art was methodized and fed;
And man's dominion over nature spread.[116]

The chief importance of this lay in the fact that it enabled man to develop tillage:

With rude design, he join'd the crooked bough,
And pointed beam, to form the rugged plough;
And made the beasts, he tamed, submissive toil
To trace the furrow, and to turn the soil.[117]

Finally, in Book iv of the poem, the rise of commerce is traced, with particular reference to the way in which, following upon the institution of agriculture, a bigger social surplus was realised and the division of labour was greatly extended. In this new situation, writes Knight,

[114] *Ibid.*, pp. 28–9.   [115] *Ibid.*, p. 49.
[116] *Ibid.*, p. 51.   [117] *Ibid.*, p. 51.

Each found the produce of his toil exceed
His own demands, of luxury or need;
Whence each the superfluity resign'd,
More useful objects in return to find:
Each freely gave what each too much possess'd,
In equal plenty to enjoy the rest.

Hence the soft intercourse of commerce ran,
From state to state, and spread from clan to clan;
Each link of social union tighter drew,
And rose in vigour as it wider grew.[118]

With this rendering into verse of one of the basic themes of *The Wealth of Nations* we must take our leave of the poets of the four stages theory – resisting the temptation to include in their company the redoubtable C. F. Volney, whose *Les Ruines, ou Méditations sur les Révolutions des Empires,* although written in prose, was perhaps sufficiently poetical in inspiration to qualify, and which contains an impressive dithyramb on the hunting–pasturage–agriculture progression.[119] It is perhaps worth noting, however, that Knight's poem received the honour of an extensive parody in the *Anti-Jacobin* in 1798.[120] This is extremely funny, but since its main targets are Knight's appalling style and (alleged) primitivism – i.e. since the four stages theory as such is left unscathed by the satirist – I must once again exercise self-denial and move on.

It is now time to tie some of the ends together, and to see the four stages theory on its way into the nineteenth century. The first task here is to bring the ignoble savage a little more to the forefront of the picture than I have so far had the opportunity of doing in the present chapter, and to say a little

118 *Ibid.,* pp. 77–8.
119 Volney's *Les Ruines* was first published in Paris in 1791. An English translation, under the title of *The Ruins, or A Survey of the Revolutions of Empires,* was published in London a little later: the British Museum copy has no date, but in the catalogue it is ascribed to c. 1795. Chapter VII, entitled in the English translation 'Principles of Society', contains the account of the hunting–pasturage–agriculture progression which I have referred to in the text. It appears on pp. 41–4.
120 This extended over three issues – those of 19 February, 26 February, and 2 April 1798.

about the way in which the proliferating voyage literature was associated with the analytical developments about which we have been talking.

Almost all the writers whose work we have considered in this chapter used the example of the Americans to illustrate the characteristics of the 'first' or 'earliest' state of mankind. Blackstone, as we have seen, drew upon 'the manners of many American nations when first discovered by the Europeans' to exemplify the 'general notions of poverty' in the early days of human society;[121] Blair frequently referred to the Americans when he wanted examples of the style of 'the most early Languages, among nations who are in the first and rude periods of Society';[122] and Du Pont, in the *Table Raisonnée*,[123] cited 'some savages in America' (together with 'some peoples in the north of Europe') as examples of nations still cultivating only a very small amount of land and abandoning it as soon as any difficulties were encountered. Falconer drew very extensively upon the literature about the Americans.[124] Logan, in his lectures at Edinburgh, talked at length about 'the History of the Aborigines of America' – interpreting this history 'not as the annals of the new world, but as it belongs to the antiquities of mankind, and delineates the picture of all nations in the rude state'.[125] And Dunbar, as we have already seen, was led to an interesting conclusion as a result of his contemplation of the 'astonishing resemblance' which was observable among the different peoples of America.[126]

Herder's references to the Americans in the *Ideen* were very frequent indeed, not least in the section where he discussed the four stages theory; and he devoted a separate chapter to the Americans – of some interest in itself – in an earlier part of the book.[127] Beattie's *Elements of Moral Science*, it is true, contains little about the Americans that is of any real relevance; but the argument at the beginning of

---

[121] Above, p. 178.
[122] *Lectures on Rhetoric and Belles Lettres*, Vol. I, p. 114; and see above, p. 181.
[123] Above, pp. 182–4.   [124] Above, p. 186.
[125] Logan, *Elements*, p. 19.   [126] Above, p. 191.
[127] In the Churchill translation of 1800 this chapter appears on pp. 154–61. It is omitted from the University of Chicago Press edition of 1968.

Russell's *History of Ancient Europe* owed much to the recent
voyage literature, which had brought (as Russell himself put
it) 'a more perfect acquaintance with rude nations' – including, of course, the Americans.[128] (Russell was in fact the
author of a lengthy *History of America* which had appeared
in 1778, the year after Robertson's).[129] Of Monboddo's interest
in the Americans there is nothing I need add to what has
already been said above;[130] and it remains only to confirm
that Pye and Knight duly referred to the Americans in their
verses. Let Pye speak for them both with the following
quatrain:

> And where the immeasurable forests spread
> Beyond the extent of Ocean's western bed,
> Unsocial, uninform'd, the tawney race
> Range the drear wild, and urge the incessant chase.[131]

In the last two decades of the century, Charlevoix and
Lafitau still remained among the most frequently cited
authorities on the Americans, but Robertson soon began to
run them close, and other comparatively new accounts –
notably those of James Adair[132] and Jonathan Carver[133] – also
came to be frequently referred to in the footnotes. Much
more important, however, was the impact of the new information about primitive peoples which the exploration of the
Pacific was bringing to light. Professor Bernard Smith, in his
monumental book *European Vision and the South Pacific*,

---

[128] Above, pp. 200 and 202.
[129] William Russell, *The History of America* (London, 1778). This work is
not remarkable for very much except the extent to which it plagiarises
Robertson and Ferguson. On p. iv of Vol. i, for example, Russell says:
'That savage and simple state, which was known only in our continent
by the fanciful descriptions of poets, actually existed in the other. Man,
in the New World, appeared under the rudest form in which we can
conceive him to subsist.' Compare this with the second paragraph of
the passage from Robertson's *History* quoted on p. 142 above.
[130] Above, pp. 203–4.   [131] *Op. cit.*, p. 71.
[132] James Adair, *The History of the American Indians* (London, 1775).
Adair's main thesis in this book was that the Americans were descended
from the Jews. Although it is completely irrelevant, I cannot resist drawing the reader's attention to the ingenious reason given by Adair on
p. 137 for the disuse of circumcision by the Americans – viz., that their
knives were worn out on the long journey over.
[133] Jonathan Carver, *Travels through the Interior Parts of North America*
(London, 1778).

1768–1850 (Oxford 1960), has described the European
reactions to the new discoveries so admirably and exhaus-
tively that there is very little for me to add. Monboddo had
already remarked in 1773 that the manners of the Americans
had been so altered during the long period of their communication and intercourse with the Old World that it was
now to countries of the South Seas rather than to the Americans that we ought to look for examples of 'people living in
the natural state'.[134] What is interesting, as Professor Smith's
book demonstrates, is the fact that when writers actually
began to look to them for this purpose, they tended to reach
conclusions very similar to those which had been reached
earlier by their predecessors when the latter had looked to
the Americans for the same purpose. The manners and customs of some of the new peoples evoked the same kind of
comparisons with classical antiquity as the manners and
customs of the Americans had evoked: Bougainville and
Banks, for example, both compared the Tahitians to the
ancient Greeks.[135] J. R. Forster, who sailed on Cook's second
voyage, assiduously collected 'parallel customs', as he called
them, 'not always with a view to prove that nations, which
chance to have the same custom, owe their origin to one
another; but rather to convince ourselves that this similarity
does not always give sufficient foundation for such a belief'.[136]
William Hodges, the landscape-painter who also sailed on
Cook's second voyage, later wrote a remarkable essay on
architecture in which he argued that this art, more than any
other, was 'influenced and modified by the nature of the
climate and materials, as well as by the habits and pursuits
of the inhabitants'.[137] And the English translator of Labillardière's *Relation du Voyage à la Recherche de la Pérouse*
spoke in his preface of the value of books such as this one to
the moral philosopher who 'loves to trace the advances of his

---

[134] *Origin and Progress of Language*, Vol. i, p. 231. Cf. Bernard Smith,
op. cit., p. 91.
[135] Smith, *op. cit.*, pp. 24–6.
[136] J. R. Forster, *Observations made during a Voyage Round the World*
(London, 1778), p. 586. Cf. Smith, *op. cit.*, pp. 64–5.
[137] William Hodges, *Travels in India during the years 1780, 1781, 1782,
and 1783* (London, 1793), p. 64. Cf. Smith, *op. cit.*, pp. 67–9.

species through its various gradations from savage to civilized life'.[138]

But although the Americans now had to share the stage
with the Tahitians and New Zealanders, they still remained
the main actors in the drama. Perhaps one of the reasons for
this was that the 'moral philosopher', seeking to trace the
various gradations of his species from savage to civilised life,
could in America get several, as it were, for the price of one.
Claret de Fleurieu, at the close of the century, put this point
very picturesquely:

Read what travellers and historians have related to us of the
inhabitants of the New World; you will there find the man of
the Old one in his infancy; among the small scattered nations,
you will fancy that you see the first Egyptians, wild and savage
men, living at random, ignorant of the conveniences of life, even
of the use of fire, and not knowing how to form arms for defending themselves against the attack of beasts: in the *Pesserais* of
TIERRA DEL FUEGO, the savage Greeks, living on the leaves of trees,
and, as it were, browzing on grass, before PELASGUS had taught
the Arcadians to construct huts, to clothe themselves with the
skin of animals, and to eat acorns; in the greater part of the
savages of CANADA, the ancient Scythians, cutting off the hair of
their vanquished enemies, and drinking their blood out of their
skull: in several of the nations of the north and south, the inhabitant of the EAST INDIES, ignorant of culture, subsisting only on
fruits, covered with skins of beasts, and killing the old men and
the infirm who could no longer follow in their excursions the rest

---

138 The translation to which I am referring was published in London in
1800. The statement quoted in the text will be found on p. v. The moral
philosopher, we are told, 'draws from voyages and travels, the facts from
which he is to deduce his conclusions respecting the social, intellectual,
and moral progress of Man. He sees savage life every where diversified
with a variety, which, if he reason fairly, must lead him to conclude,
that what is called the state of nature, is, in truth, the state of a rational
being placed in various physical circumstances, which have contracted
or expanded his faculties in various degrees ... There is sufficient variety
in human actions to show that, though Man acts from motives, he acts
not mechanically, but freely; yet sufficient similarity of conduct, in
similar circumstances, to prove the unity of his nature ... Philosophers
should not forget, and the most respectable modern philosophers have
not forgotten, that the savage state of the most civilized nations now in
Europe, is a subject within the pale of authentic history, and that the
privation of iron alone, would soon reduce them nearly to the barbarous
state, from which, by a train of favourable events, their forefathers
emerged some centuries ago' (pp. v–vi). Cf. Smith, *op. cit.*, pp. 110–12.

of the family: in MEXICO, you will recognize the Cimbri and the Scythians, burying alive with the dead king, the great officers of the crown: in PERU as well as in MEXICO, and even among the small nations, you will find Druids, Vates, Eubages, mountebanks, cheating priests, and credulous men: on every part of the continent and in the neighbouring islands, you will see the Bretons or Britons, the Picts of the Romans; and the Thracians, men and women, painting their body and face, puncturing and making incisions in their skin; and the latter condemning their women to till the ground, to carry heavy burdens, and imposing on them the most laborious employments . . .

The picture which the New World exhibited to the men of the Old who discovered it, therefore offered no feature of which our own history does not furnish us with a model in the infancy of our political societies.[139]

And another fact which may be of relevance in this connection is that after the American Revolution of 1776 a number of white Americans began to embark on serious studies of their own 'savages',[140] thereby supplying the 'moral philosopher' with information about them which was frequently much more reliable than that which could be derived from the voyage literature. One interesting feature of a number of these early studies by white Americans was that while they did not seek to deny that the savages were in a certain sense 'ignoble', they tried to *explain* this ignobility by using the familiar notion that (as Jefferson phrased it) in forming a just estimate of the 'genius and mental powers' of the savages, 'great allowance [must] be made for those circumstances of their situation which call for a display of particular talents only'.[141] Jedidiah Morse argued similarly that

the character of the Indians is altogether founded upon their circumstances and way of life. A people who are constantly employed in procuring the means of a precarious subsistence,

---

139 *A Voyage Round the World . . . by Étienne Marchand*, translated from the French of C. P. Claret Fleurieu (London, 1801), Vol. I, pp. 353–4. Cf. Smith, *op. cit.*, pp. 112–13.

140 The best account of these studies is given in R. H. Pearce. *The Savages of America* (Johns Hopkins Press, Baltimore, revised edn, 1965), ch. III, pp. 76ff.

141 Thomas Jefferson, *Notes on the State of Virginia* (ed. W. Peden, University of North Carolina Press, Chapel Hill, 1955), p. 62. Cf. Pearce, *op. cit.*, pp. 91–6.

who live by hunting the wild animals, and who are generally engaged in war with their neighbours, cannot be supposed to enjoy much gaiety of temper, or a high flow of spirits.[142]

And this view, which was also put forward by Samuel Stanhope Smith, became more and more clearly (as Professor Pearce has shown) the 'standard opinion',[143] at any rate within America itself.

The second task is to say something about the changing role of the four stages theory in the work of the economists – Smith, Turgot, Quesnay, and their successors – during the last two or three decades of the century.

There was a certain sense, of course, in which the great eighteenth-century systems of 'classical' political economy in fact *arose out of* the four stages theory. In a surprising number of cases, the builders of these systems set out by elaborating some kind of scheme of socio-economic progression which started with an American-type society and ended with the 'commercial system' of contemporary Europe, and then spent the rest of their lives making a sustained economic analysis of the working of this commercial system. Smith propounded the four stages theory in his Glasgow lectures on Jurisprudence, and later went on to analyse the commercial system in detail in his *Wealth of Nations*. Turgot propounded the four stages theory in his *On Universal History*, and later went on to analyse the commercial system in his *Reflections on the Formation and the Distribution of Wealth*. We can observe a similar kind of transition, although not of course such a clear-cut one, in the case of Quesnay (from the *Philosophie Rurale* to, say, the *Analyse du Tableau*),[144] and also in the case of Condillac (from *Histoire Ancienne* to *Le Commerce et le Gouvernment*).[145] And in the case of certain other

---

142 Jedidiah Morse, *The History of America* (2nd edn, Philadelphia, 1795), p. 31. Cf. Pearce, *op. cit.*, pp. 96–7.
143 Pearce, *op. cit.*, pp. 97–100.
144 The relevant writings of Quesnay are translated and commented upon in R. L. Meek, *The Economics of Physiocracy* (Allen and Unwin, London, 1962), *passim*.
145 Condillac's *Le Commerce et le Gouvernment*, and extensive extracts from his *Histoire Ancienne*, are both included in Vol. II of the *Oeuvres Philosophiques de Condillac*, ed. Georges Le Roy, Presses Universitaires de

writers like Cantillon[146] and Steuart[147] we can perhaps observe an analogous kind of transition, even if only in a rudimentary form and within the covers of a single book. This is a fact which is interesting not only in itself, but also because the same kind of transition was later to be clearly observable in the case of Marx.

It was only to be expected, therefore, that the four stages theory would leave its mark in one way or another on the new systems of political economy. In Smith's *Wealth of Nations* and Turgot's *Reflections*, where the transition I am talking about is observable in what may perhaps be called its pure form, there are a number of direct references to the four stages theory. They are hardly very prominent references, however: in *The Wealth of Nations* the theory is largely relegated to the chapters on defence and justice towards the end of the book,[148] and in the *Reflections* to one or two rather isolated sections round about the middle.[149] Much more interesting than these direct references – although much less obvious – is the way in which certain crucial elements of the general ethos of the four stages theory were carried over into the economic analysis itself. In particular, the notion that *historical* processes were autonomous but law-governed led to (or was closely associated with) the notion that *economic* processes in a commercial society possessed the same characteristics. The economic 'machine', it was postulated, like the historical 'machine', worked unconsciously but in an orderly and predictable manner to produce results which could be said to be 'subject to law' and which therefore constituted a perfectly proper field of enquiry for the social scientist.

France, Paris, 1948. Although Condillac cannot really be said to have been a protagonist of the four stages theory, its influence is clearly discernible at various places in Book I, chapters III–VII of the *Histoire Ancienne* (pp. 11–19 of the 1948 edn). See in particular *ibid.*, pp. 13–14.

146 Cf. R. L. Meek (ed.), *Precursors of Adam Smith, 1750–1775* (Dent, London, 1973), pp. 1–21, and in particular pp. 3–5.

147 Cf. the discussion in A. S. Skinner's 'Analytical Introduction' to his edition of Steuart's *An Inquiry into the Principles of Political Oeconomy* (Oliver and Boyd, Edinburgh and London, 1966), Vol. I, pp. lxiiiff.

148 The main references will be found in Book V, chapter I, part I ('Of the Expence of Defence') and part II ('Of the Expence of Justice').

149 In R. L. Meek (ed.), *Turgot on Progress, Sociology and Economics* (Cambridge University Press, Cambridge, 1973), the relevant passages will be found on pp. 147–8.

And what was just as important, the penumbra of qualified approbation which was attached to the working of the historical machine was also attached to that of the economic machine. The historical machine automatically produced 'progress', which was proclaimed to be (up to a point) a good thing; the economic machine automatically maximised the rate of growth of the national product, which was also proclaimed to be (up to a point) a good thing.

The influence of the four stages theory on classical political economy is also observable in an important facet of the basic methodology of the latter – namely, the idea that if one wants to understand the way in which the economic machine operates in a commercial society, one ought to begin by analysing the way in which it operated *in some kind of society which can be conceived to have historically preceded a commercial society.* Turgot, for example, began in the *Reflections* by postulating the existence of an agricultural society in which the division of labour and the exchange of commodities were supposed to be already prevalent. He analysed the way in which the economic machine would work in such a society, and then went on to ask what alterations in its working would be brought about when a new class of capitalist entrepreneurs entered upon the historical scene. The same kind of methodological device was also used very effectively by Smith, and later by Ricardo and Marx. The only real difference between their approach and Turgot's is that whereas the preceding state of society which they postulated was one in which there were neither landlords nor capitalists, that which Turgot postulated was one in which landlords – though not of course capitalists – *did* exist.[150] This difference is admittedly quite a significant one, which in the context of another discussion one might well wish to emphasise; but in the present context it is the *resemblance* between Turgot's approach and that of Smith – and also to some extent that of Quesnay and Steuart – which I think is worth stressing.

Although the four stages theory influenced classical political economy in these different ways, the theory *as such* came to play a less and less important role in economic treatises as

150 Cf. *ibid.*, p. 20.

time went on. The main reason for this, it might at first sight be thought, was that the economists, as they settled down to analysing the present, simply became less interested in looking back into the past. And to a certain extent this was no doubt true. But more important, I think, was the fact that when the economists *did* look back into the past, they began to do so with different eyes. The point here is that the progress of society through the four stages had manifestly been associated with a gradual but eventually very substantial increase in its *wealth*. What then were the main proximate *causes* of this increase in wealth? To Smith and Turgot, generalising as they did in their economic work from the experience of relatively recent times, the answer seemed fairly clear: wealth had increased mainly as a result of the extension of the division of labour, the growth of commodity exchange, and above all the accumulation of capital. When political economy as the study of 'the nature and causes of the wealth of nations' began to separate itself out from jurisprudence, sociology, and historiography, therefore, it was only natural that the economists, when they looked back at the earlier stages of society, should tend increasingly to project back into them, as it were, these three crucial categories of division of labour, commodity exchange, and capital. We now begin to hear that even in the earliest stage the savage hunter possessed 'capital' in the form of his bow and arrows and fishing net; that he engaged in a rudimentary form of the division of labour and commodity exchange; and so on. There was an increasing tendency, in other words, for the economists to interpret development in the pre-commercial stages in terms of the economic categories appropriate to contemporary capitalism. Wealth grew, and countries developed economically, they began to suggest, not so much because society adopted successively 'higher' modes of subsistence, as because *within the framework of these changing modes of subsistence* there was a gradual increase over time in the division of labour, commodity exchange, and the accumulation of capital.[151]

---

151 Sometimes, it is true, economists examined the way in which the arrival upon the historical scene of one or another of the traditional series of modes of subsistence was associated with a change, of degree or of kind,

Thus although economists continued on occasion to use the four stages theory, right up to the third and fourth decades of the nineteenth century, it was very seldom basic to their main analysis. In Mrs Marcet's *Conversations on Political Economy*, for example, we find two separate statements of the theory[152] – but Mrs B.'s only real purpose in telling her pupil Caroline about it is to point out 'the happy effects resulting from the security of property and the division of labour'.[153] Malthus used the theory in his 1798 *Essay on the Principle of Population*, but only in order to show that his three basic propositions about population were valid in all the stages of socio-economic development.[154] McCulloch used it, but only to show the importance of labour in all the stages.[155] J. S. Mill later revived it, using it to show the differences in the origin, size, and distribution of wealth in the different stages, but once again it played only a very minor role in his analysis.[156] There were exceptions, of course

in the three basic economic categories. One thinks here, for example, of Smith's remarkable account, in the well-known 'philosopher and porter' fragment, of the way in which the division of labour is extended and changed in form as society progresses through the hunting, pastoral, and agricultural stages. (See R. L. Meek and A. S. Skinner, 'The Development of Adam Smith's Ideas on the Division of Labour', *Economic Journal*, Vol. 83, December 1973, pp. 1111–13.) The significant thing, however, is not that Smith should have made this analysis, but that he eventually decided not to include it in *The Wealth of Nations*.

[152] Jane Marcet, *Conversations on Political Economy* (6th edn, London, 1827), pp. 18–20 and 46–51.

[153] *Ibid.*, p. 88.

[154] In the 1st (1798) edition of the *Essay*, Malthus's account of the hunting, pastoral, and agricultural stages will be found in chapters III and IV. Malthus was not the first population theorist to discuss the relationship between population and the mode of subsistence: in Robert Wallace's *Dissertation on the Numbers of Mankind in Antient and Modern Times* (Edinburgh, 1753) there are a number of interesting statements about it (e.g. on pp. 15ff.). Nor was Malthus the last: see footnote 157 below.

[155] McCulloch's account will be found near the beginning of his *Principles of Political Economy*, in the section (or, in some editions, the chapter) entitled 'Definition of Production – Labour the only Source of Wealth'.

[156] Mill's account will be found near the beginning of his *Principles of Political Economy*, in the 'Preliminary Remarks'. For further examples of the use of the four stages theory by economists at this period see Lauderdale's *Inquiry into the Nature and Origin of Public Wealth* (1804), James Mill's *History of British India* (1817), Robert Hamilton's *The Progress of Society* (1830), and Nassau Senior's *Outline of the Science of Political Economy* (1836).

Social science and the ignoble savage

- the names of Weyland[157] and List[158] spring to mind – but
these were surely exceptions of the type that proves the rule.
Orthodox economics in effect went its own way, concentrating on the analysis of contemporary capitalism and be-
queathing the basic methodology of the four stages theory –
together with its problems – to the anthropologists, sociologists, and historiographers.

In what form or forms, then, was this methodology be-
queathed to them? Our third and last task is to say something about the general shape which the four stages theory
had assumed by the end of the eighteenth century.
    The four stages theory, as we have seen, was fashioned
from a number of different ingredients and associated in its
origins with a number of different intellectual currents. The
particular connection upon which we have chosen to concentrate is that which existed between the methodology of the
theory on the one hand and the contemporary literature about
the Americans on the other. The comparative studies of
primitive peoples which this literature stimulated, coupled
with the concept of the ignoble savage which was derived
from it either directly, or indirectly by way of reaction to
Rousseau, were closely associated with the emergence of the
momentous idea that the *mode of subsistence* played a key
role in determining the configuration and development of
human societies. It is true that the emergence of this idea,
and the varied applications which were made of it as the
century progressed, would hardly have been possible if certain rather more fundamental and more general notions –
notably the Lockean theory of knowledge, the concept of the
operation of 'cause and effect' in the life of society, and the
law of unintended consequences – had not already been

157 John Weyland, *The Principles of Population and Production, as they are
    affected by the Progress of Society* (London, 1816). Weyland used a
    version of the four stages theory as the framework for his discussion, and
    argued (in contradistinction to Malthus) that the behaviour of popula-
    tion was *different* in each of the stages. Cf. also G. P. Scrope, *Principles
    of Political Economy* (London, 1833), pp. 260–4.
158 Friedrich List thought in terms of a stadial progression through hunting,
    pasturage, agriculture, agriculture-plus-manufacture, and agriculture-
    plus-manufacture-plus-commerce. See, e.g. *The National System of Poli-
    tical Economy* (tr. S. S. Lloyd, London, 1885), pp. 228ff.

224

developed or had not at least been 'in the air'. But it is also true, and just as important, that something else was required, in addition to these notions, in order to generate in men's minds the idea of the determining role of the mode of subsistence, and to secure for this idea the high degree of acceptance which it very soon received.

The particular modes of subsistence in terms of which most early practitioners of the four stages theory worked were hunting, pasturage, agriculture, and commerce. As the century progressed, however, there was a growing realisation that, as Herder put it, 'this mode of classification is very difficult to apply with accuracy'[159] – partly because there might be great differences between people who formally speaking came within the same category, and partly because a particular people might partake of the characteristics of two or more of the categories at the same time. There was some concern expressed about the fact that 'commerce' did not appear to be a 'mode of subsistence' in quite the same sense as hunting, pasturage, and agriculture. And there was also a certain amount of worry over the problem of whether one could in fact maintain that one particular set of factors in society played a 'determining' role, while at the same time recognising that in society everything in a sense always depended upon everything else.[160]

The four stages theory, at any rate at the outset of its career, usually took the form of a *theory of development*, embodying the idea of some kind of 'natural' or 'normal' movement through a succession of different modes of subsistence. But there were of course many variants of this idea. Some writers seemed to imply that there was a natural tendency for each individual people to march inexorably forward through hunting, pasturage, agriculture, and commerce in that order, at any rate in the absence of any strong counteracting forces. Others, interpreting the theory in a less literal and rigorous sense, thought rather in terms of a broad general tendency for individual peoples (or society as a

[159] Above, p. 194.
[160] An interesting attempt to deal with this last problem was made in a book which just falls outside our period – Hugh Murray's *Enquiries Historical and Moral respecting the Character of Nations and the Progress of Society* (Edinburgh, 1808).

whole) to move from 'lower' modes of subsistence to 'higher' ones, and were less willing to specify the finishing-point, the order of progression, and (sometimes) even the starting-point. There were differences of opinion, too, about the extent to which 'climate' was or was not an important influence, and, in so far as it *was* conceded to be of some importance, about the proper way to bring it into the general developmental picture;[161] about the character of the mechanism which brought about the transition from one stage to another; and, last but not least, about the nature and extent of the 'progress' which was involved in the movement from 'lower' to higher stages.

In the case of a number of writers, particularly around the end of the century, the modes of subsistence of the four stages theory were used as the basis for exercises in what may perhaps be called comparative social statics, without any very specific developmental postulate being put forward. In such studies differences in the 'habits and propensities' of different peoples – the Americans and the Bedouins, for example, in the case of Volney's *Tableau du Climat et Sol des États Unis*[162] – were explained in terms of their different modes of subsistence without any tendency for 'lower' modes to give place to 'higher' ones being specifically postulated.[163] But although developmental postulates were absent from these studies, or at any rate pushed into the background, various other appurtenances of the four stages theory in its traditional form were almost always present – the Lockean theory of knowledge,[164] for example, the notion that 'the same causes produce the same effects' in the social as well as the physical world,[165] the law of unintended consequences,[166] and the tendency to play down the influence of 'climate'.[167] And at the end of our period as at the beginning, in these studies as well as in those which were developmentally

---

[161] In most cases, of course, its importance was denied or played down.
[162] C. F. Volney, *A View of the Soil and Climate of the United States of America* (tr. C. B. Brown, ed. G. W. White, Hafner, New York and London, 1968). This edition is a facsimile of that published in Philadelphia in 1804. The work was first published in 1803, in Paris.
[163] *Ibid.*, pp. 391–5.
[164] *Ibid.*, p. 377.   [165] *Ibid.*, p. 367.
[166] *Ibid.*, p. xi.   [167] *Ibid.*, p. 351.

oriented, we often find the same kind of analogies drawn between the manners of the Americans and those of (say) the ancient Greeks;[168] the same kind of warning against construing similarities between savage peoples as evidence of genetic descent;[169] and the same kind of emphasis on the ignobility rather than the nobility of those primitive peoples who, like the Americans, are confined to 'the roaming and precarious life of fishers and hunters'.[170] It was with ideas such as these that the theory of the determining role of the mode of subsistence was intimately and inextricably associated through the whole of the latter half of the eighteenth century.

Only one more point now remains to be made. In the literature of the four stages theory, as we have seen, 'commerce' did not fit very easily into the stadial scheme. It was difficult to define it as precisely as hunting, pasturage, and agriculture; and it was always apparent that it did not constitute a 'mode of subsistence' in quite the same sense as these others did – if only because (as Falconer put it) 'agriculture is often . . . cultivated to the highest degree in commercial states'.[171] Thus one could not argue that commerce had replaced agriculture in the same way as agriculture had replaced pasturage and pasturage hunting: commerce had in fact grown up within these earlier forms of society, and when it emerged to full flower in Europe in the seventeenth and eighteenth centuries the material objects with which it was concerned still largely consisted, whether directly or indirectly, of the products of agriculture and pasturage. Yet it was clear that the rise of commerce was an event of tremendous importance, which had led to great changes in men's 'habits and propensities', and that for this reason if for no other it deserved to have a special label of its own attached to it and to be incorporated into the same great stadial scheme as hunting, pasturage, and agriculture.

The trouble about this, however, was that the explanation which the four stages theorists gave of the rise of commerce in modern Europe was frequently so different *in kind* from

[168] *Ibid.*, pp. 410 and 418.
[169] *Ibid.*, pp. 364–5.
[170] *Ibid.*, p. 368. Cf. p. 187, where Volney opines that the Americans are 'far more entitled to pity and horror, than to envy or applause'.
[171] Above, p. 187.

the explanation they gave of the rise of agriculture, say, or of pasturage, that this part of their discussion tended quite often to appear as something superimposed upon the four stages theory rather than as an integral part of that theory itself. The general theory of the development of society from its 'American' beginnings through pasturage and agriculture to commerce was one thing; the economic and political history of the rise of commerce in modern Europe, it sometimes seemed, was quite another. It took the genius of Joseph Barnave, writing (like Condorcet, and at almost the same time) under the shadow of the guillotine, to suggest how the two might be reconciled.[172] Essentially, according to Barnave's account, the matter is very simple. When the agricultural stage supervenes, 'the inequality of possessions soon becomes extreme',[173] and it is not long before landed property becomes 'the foundation of aristocracy'.[174] With the rise of commerce in the broad sense – i.e. of arts, industry, and trade – a new form of property, which Barnave usually calls 'commercial property', gradually arises and begins to stand in stark opposition to landed property. For in large states, 'just as landed property is the basis of aristocracy and federalism, commercial property is the principle of democracy and of unity.'[175] The latter is destined to win out over the former: *in this sense*, therefore, there is a tendency for 'commerce' to replace 'agriculture'. Which is, it goes without saying, what Barnave believes that the French Revolution is all about.

It is not really as simple as this, of course, either in Barnave's book or in reality. Nor, in what I have just said, have

[172] The edition of Barnave's *Introduction à la Révolution Française* which I have mainly used is that edited by Fernand Rude and published by Armand Colin, Paris, in 1960. The references in the text, however, are to a new English translation published in the Harper Torchbook series, New York, in 1971, under the title *Power, Property, and History*. The translation is by Emanuel Chill, who has also contributed a very interesting introduction.

[173] *Power, Property, and History*, pp. 79–80. 'It is a definite principle', Barnave adds, 'that where the only revenue is that of land, the big holdings gradually engulf the small ones; while where there exists a revenue from commerce and industry, the labor of the poor gradually succeeds in winning for them a portion of the lands of the rich' (p. 80).

[174] *Ibid.*, p. 85.

[175] *Ibid.*, p. 93.

I really been fair to men like Smith and Millar, whose account of the rise of 'commerce' was in fact quite closely integrated with the remainder of their theory of development, and whose discussion of the conflict between 'agriculture' and 'commerce' was in some ways superior to Barnave's.[176] But it remains true that Barnave, more clearly and directly than any of his predecessors, pointed the way towards a particular kind of adaptation of the methodology of the four stages theory which was later to become the groundwork of the historical materialism of Marx. Barnave was the first to appreciate, however unclearly, that if the methodology of the four stages theory was to be made fully applicable to modern as well as to ancient times, the eighteenth-century concept of 'mode of subsistence' must be transformed into what Marx was later to call *mode of production.*[177]

[176] In particular, their treatment of feudalism was much less perfunctory than Barnave's, and they went much further than he did in recognising the existence of class conflict in a modern 'commercial' society.

[177] The point here, of course, is that the Marxian concept of 'mode of production' embraces not only the kind of living that men get but also the relations they enter into with one another in order to get it.

Afterword

The notion that the key factor in socio-economic development was the mode of subsistence, in association with some
kind of doctrine of 'progress' and some kind of attempt to
define the actual stages of development in terms of different
modes of subsistence, was, I have argued above, a very
common and very important ingredient of Enlightenment
thought in the field of the social sciences during the whole
of the period from 1750 to 1800. But if it was really as
common as this, it may be asked, why have so few modern
historians of the socio-economic thought of the eighteenth
century taken notice of its existence? And if it was really as
important as this, why have those historians who *have* taken
notice of its existence so often tended to denigrate it?

In part, no doubt, the answer to both these questions lies
in inadequacy of documentation. Robertson, for example,
has only fairly recently found his way into the relevant
histories; the work of Millar and Goguet has as yet been
mentioned in even fewer; Smith's Glasgow lectures on Jurisprudence have hardly ever been remarked upon in this connection at all; and there are several other prominent writers
– as well as a number not quite so prominent – whose
espousal (or criticism) of the four stages theory has so far as
I am aware gone completely unobserved. But this, of course,
only pushes the two questions further back. The material
has always been there for the finding, and if only a few
modern historians have in fact noticed it, or if, having
noticed it, they have tended to underestimate its quality,
there must be more fundamental reasons than this.

In the case of historians of sociology and of economics, the
reason for their neglect of the four stages theory has probably lain mainly in a feeling that detailed research into this
aspect of eighteenth-century thought would not yield results
which were relevant to their purposes. If sociology is defined
in such a way as to make it start with Comte, there would

seem to be little point in seeking among the eighteenth-century thinkers for anything much more than a few primitive anticipations. And if economics is defined in terms of the relatively narrow conception of that science which began to emerge at the beginning of the nineteenth century, there would once again seem little point in investigating, for example, the relations between Smith's *Wealth of Nations* and his lectures on Jurisprudence, or between Turgot's *Reflections* and his *On Universal History*.

The case of historiographers, historians of anthropology, and scholars interested in the development of the idea of progress, however, is rather different. Here it is not so much a failure to notice the existence of the four stages theory (although that is still surprisingly frequent) which is in question, but rather a serious underestimation of its quality. The main point here, I suspect, is that the authors of most of the relevant histories were writing them under the influence of the widespread twentieth-century reaction against the whole idea of 'laws of history', and, in particular, against the tendency (as they saw it) of many nineteenth-century sociologists and anthropologists to work in terms of preconceived and over-speculative developmental schemes rather than in terms of the actual historical facts. When the authors of these histories began seeking for the early intellectual origins of this tendency, therefore, they were under an obvious temptation to visit the sins of the children upon the fathers. Thus when they came to consider the new social science of the eighteenth century, they tended to lay great emphasis on what they regarded as its 'theoretical' or 'conjectural' quality, and, implicity or explicitly, to equate these two adjectives with 'unscientific'. The main purpose of this 'afterword' is to try to separate the elements of truth in this kind of approach from those of falsity.

The ancestry of this type of critique goes back at least as far as Dugald Stewart, who in his *Biographical Memoir* of Smith,[1] as we have already seen above,[2] coined the

---

[1] The quotations from this *Memoir* in the text are taken from the Kelley reprint of 1966, which in its turn was taken from Vol. x of Stewart's *Collected Works* (Edinburgh, 1858).   [2] Above, pp. 113–14.

expression 'theoretical or conjectural history' to describe that
new 'species of philosophical investigation' in which men
like Smith, Kames, and Millar had frequently engaged.[3]
Stewart's critical discussion of this kind of investigation has
been extremely influential – by no means least in our own
century – and it may be useful to summarise it at this point.

The argument at the beginning of his discussion is
couched in fairly general terms. When we compare our own
acquirements, opinions, manners, and institutions with those
which prevail among 'rude tribes', he says, 'it cannot fail to
occur to us as an interesting question, by what gradual steps
the transition has been made from the first simple efforts of
uncultivated nature, to a state of things so wonderfully
artificial and complicated'.[4] Whence have cultivated languages arisen? Whence the sciences, the arts, and the improvement of the human mind? Whence the different forms
which civilised society has assumed in different ages? On
most of these subjects, says Stewart,

very little information is to be expected from history, for long
before that stage of society when men begin to think of recording
their transactions, many of the most important steps of their progress have been made. A few insulated facts may perhaps be
collected from the casual observations of travellers, who have
viewed the arrangements of rude nations; but nothing, it is
evident, can be obtained in this way, which approaches to a regular and connected detail of human improvement.[5]

In this 'want of direct evidence', then, Stewart proceeds,

we are under a necessity of supplying the place of fact by conjecture; and when we are unable to ascertain how men have
actually conducted themselves upon particular occasions, of considering in what manner they are likely to have proceeded, from
the principles of their nature, and the circumstances of their
external situation. In such inquiries, the detached facts which
travels and voyages afford us, may frequently serve as landmarks
to our speculations; and sometimes our conclusions *a priori*, may

---

[3] In another place, Stewart adds the names of Condillac and Goguet to the
list of those who had engaged in 'theoretical or conjectural history'
(*Collected Works*, Vol. I, Edinburgh, 1854, p. 384).

[4] *Memoir*, p. 33.

[5] *Ibid.*, p. 33.

Afterword

tend to confirm the credibility of facts, which on a superficial view, appeared to be doubtful or incredible . . .

To this species of philosophical investigation, which has no appropriated name in our language, I shall take the liberty of giving the title *Theoretical* or *Conjectural History* . . .[6]

Stewart has been led into this discussion by Smith's essay on *The First Formation of Languages*, in which (as I have already noted)[7] Smith starts by asking how two savages *would* begin to form a language, what names they *would* eventually bestow on new objects, and so on. This essay, Stewart says, 'exhibits a very beautiful specimen of theoretical history'.[8] And the mathematical sciences, too, he now informs us, afford 'very favourable subjects for theoretical history'.[9] He refers to D'Alembert's recommendation of a passage in Montucla's *Histoire des Mathématiques*[10] 'where an attempt is made to exhibit the gradual progress of philosophical speculation, from the first conclusions suggested by a general survey of the heavens, to the doctrines of Copernicus'; and reminds us that 'a theoretical history of this very science . . . was one of Mr. Smith's earliest compositions'.[11]

But, Stewart proceeds, 'inquiries perfectly analogous to these' may also be applied 'to the modes of government, and to the municipal institutions which have obtained among different nations'.[12] He points out that

it is but lately . . . that these important subjects have been considered in this point of view; the greater part of politicians before the time of Montesquieu having contented themselves with an historical statement of facts, and with a vague reference of laws to the wisdom of particular legislators, or to accidental circumstances, which it is now impossible to ascertain. Montesquieu, on the contrary, considered laws as originating chiefly from the circumstances of society, and attempted to account, from the

---

[6] *Ibid.*, pp. 33–4. [7] Above, p. 114.
[8] *Memoir*, p. 37. [9] *Ibid.*, p. 34.
[10] J. E. Montucla, *Histoire des Mathématiques* (Paris, 1758). Montucla announces in his preface (Vol. I, p. ix) that in tracing the very early history of the mathematical sciences he will sometimes substitute 'au développement inconnu de ces Sciences, un développement fictice [*sic*] & probablement fort approchant du véritable'. ('Fictice' is presumably a printer's error for 'factice'.) Examples of this approach will be found on pp. 47, 50–3, and 53ff. of Vol. I.
[11] *Memoir*, p. 35. [12] *Ibid.*, p. 35.

changes in the condition of mankind, which take place in the different stages of their progress, for the corresponding alterations which their institutions undergo.[13]

This is hardly a very accurate statement of Montesquieu's viewpoint, but there can be no quarrel with what Stewart now goes on to say:

The advances made in this line of inquiry since Montesquieu's time have been great. Lord Kames, in his *Historical Law Tracts*, has given some excellent specimens of it, particularly in his *Essays on the History of Property and of Criminal Law*, and many ingenious speculations of the same kind occur in the works of Mr. Millar.
 In Mr. Smith's writings, whatever be the nature of his subject, he seldom misses an opportunity of indulging his curiosity, in tracing from the principles of human nature, or from the circumstances of society, the origin of the opinions and the institutions which he describes.[14]

It is this 'analogy' between Smith's essay on *The First Formation of Languages* and 'a variety of his other disquisitions'[15] which is Stewart's main object of attention in the latter part of his discussion.

 Now it is of course indisputable that a very strong 'analogy' does exist between the 'train of thinking' in Smith's essay on *The First Formation of Languages* and that in, say, his lectures on Jurisprudence; and I have already given Stewart credit for perceiving that it was largely the ubiquity of this 'train of thinking' which gave unity to Smith's thought as a whole.[16] In the case of both these types of enquiry, the basic assumption was that man's ideas and institutions were in an important sense shaped by the circumstances in which he happened to find himself, with the crucial corollary that since his physical constitution was always essentially the same he would always tend to react in a similar way to similar circumstances. It followed, then, that in the 'want of direct evidence', when one did not know for certain how men had 'actually conducted themselves upon particular occasions', one might nevertheless be able to deduce 'in what

[13] *Ibid.*, p. 35.
[14] *Ibid.*, pp. 35–6.
[15] *Ibid.*, p. 37.
[16] Above, p. 114.

manner they are likely to have proceeded'. Up to a point, in other words, as Stewart put it, the 'place of fact' in both types of enquiry could be supplied by 'conjecture'.

But there was also an important *difference* between the enquiries conducted by men like Smith and Kames into the origin of language, and those they conducted into 'modes of government' and 'municipal institutions'. In the former, the 'place of fact' had perforce to be supplied *entirely* by 'conjecture'. In the latter, this was so (in so far as it was so at all) only in the case of the very earliest institutions. As later and more complex types of society came up for consideration, the 'want of direct evidence' became progressively less; more and more 'facts' of various kinds, of an increasingly relevant and reliable character, became usable, and were indeed avidly sought after; and the role of 'conjecture' in the analytical process therefore became less and less significant.

There is no hint of this difference, however, in Stewart's discussion. He defines as 'theoretical or conjectural history' that 'species of philosophical investigation' which is exemplified by Smith's essay on the origin of language; he says that enquiries 'perfectly analogous' to this may be applied to 'modes of government' and 'municipal institutions'; and to exemplify the latter type of enquiry he instances virtually the whole of the remainder of Smith's work, together with much of that of Kames and Millar. The definite impression we are left with at the end is that in Stewart's view the latter type of enquiry depended just as much upon 'supplying the place of fact by conjecture' as the former type did; that the description 'theoretical or conjectural history' could therefore just as properly be applied to it; and that its *scientific* value, like that of the former type, was virtually nil.

Present-day critics of the eighteenth-century theories of socio-economic development often start from a very similar kind of position, although they usually add a gloss of their own to it. Professor Teggart, for example, claimed that the work of the new social scientists of the eighteenth century embodied a point of view 'from which historical events were regarded as unimportant and irrelevant for the purposes of scientific inquiry in the investigation of progress and of evolution'.[17] Professor Bock, in much the same vein, speaks of the way in which, in early modern social science, 'the resolve to seek generalizations about temporal process is accompanied by the conviction that the detailed record of temporal process cannot be utilized for such a purpose'.[18] The emphasis here, as with Stewart, is on the 'conjectural' character of the work concerned. But these modern critics go further than Stewart did. In effect, they father Comte's ideas on men like Turgot, Smith, and Ferguson, suggesting that the 'history' which these men wrote was not only wholly but also *deliberately* – i.e. by choice rather than by necessity – divorced from the historical facts.

Unless they are heavily qualified, however, such statements as these are simply a travesty of the truth. In the case of most of the eighteenth-century authors whom we have considered above, it is fairly evident, at any rate when we look at the work of each of them as a whole, that their desire to make their theories and generalisations correspond with the historical facts (so far as this was humanly possible) amounted to something of a passion. There were not really very many of them, I believe, who delighted in 'conjecture' for its own sake: most of them indulged in it only when they were obliged to do so, *faute de mieux*. We must assume, then, that able and sensitive critics such as Teggart and Bock did not intend these statements to be taken literally. They must have been meant to apply, not so much to the detailed work relating to particular periods or peoples which was carried on within the broad framework of one or another stadial scheme, but *rather to that stadial scheme* itself. Interpreted in this way, the statements are not obviously incorrect, and we must give some further attention to them.

In this connection, it may be useful to refer back to Stewart's discussion, which concludes with the following very interesting passage:

I shall only observe farther on this head, that when different theoretical histories are proposed by different writers, of the

---

[17] Frederick J. Teggart, *Theory and Processes of History* (University of California Press, Berkeley and Los Angeles, 1962), p. 93.

[18] Kenneth E. Bock, *The Acceptance of Histories* (University of California Press, Berkeley and Los Angeles, 1956), pp. 85–6.

Afterword

progress of the human mind in any one line of exertion, these theories are not always to be understood as standing in opposition to each other. If the progress delineated in all of them be plausible, it is possible at least, that they may all have been realized, for human affairs never exhibit, in any two instances, a perfect uniformity. But whether they have been realized or no, is often a question of little consequence. In most cases, it is of more importance to ascertain the progress that is most simple, than the progress that is most agreeable to fact; for, paradoxical as the proposition may appear, it is certainly true, that the real progress is not always the most natural. It may have been determined by particular accidents, which are not likely again to occur, and which cannot be considered as forming any part of that general provision which nature has made for the improvement of the race.[19]

The significant phrase here is the last one: the primary purpose of the broad stadial schemes employed by the eighteenth-century social scientists, Stewart seems to be suggesting, was to ascertain 'that general provision which nature has made for the improvement of the race'. The idea, apparently, is that the stadial schemes were intended to delineate the main landmarks on the simplest route of advancement along which it was *possible* (barring accidents or exceptional circumstances) for most peoples to progress, given the physical constitution and external situation with which nature had provided them. And Stewart clearly implies that the delineation of these 'natural' landmarks was usually arrived at *a priori*, without reference to the historical facts.

Now, the particular type of eighteenth-century stadial scheme which Stewart had mainly in mind when making these comments, I believe, was not the four stages theory at all, but Smith's theory of 'the natural progress of opulence'[20] - the theory that capital is 'naturally' directed first to agriculture, then to manufacture, and finally to commerce.[21] And as applied to *this* theory, what Stewart says is perfectly true.

[19] *Memoir*, p. 37.
[20] In his comments on Smith's *The Wealth of Nations* on p. 36 of the *Memoir*, Stewart mentions in particular 'the theoretical delineation he has given of the natural progress of opulence in a country, and his investigation of the causes which have inverted this order in the different countries of modern Europe'.
[21] The theory is set out in Book III, chapter I of *The Wealth of Nations*.

237

When Smith postulated the existence of this 'natural' order in the field of capital investment, he did *not* intend it as a generalisation of the historical facts: the most he was prepared to say about the relation between the theory and the facts was that the postulated order of things had always been 'in some degree observed' in 'every society that had any territory'.[22] Indeed, the main reason for his postulation of this 'natural order of things' was precisely that in all the states of modern Europe it did *not* correspond with the historical facts, but had been 'in many respects, entirely inverted'.[23] What Smith wanted to emphasise was that certain human institutions, stemming from the original form of government of the states of Europe, had caused a less than optimal capital investment path to be pursued, so that the growth of opulence had not been as great as it could have been. To bring this point home, he chose to talk in terms of a 'natural course of things' (i.e. the optimal investment path, as he conceived it) which had been 'disturbed' and 'inverted' by these 'human institutions. To *this* type of eighteenth-century stadial scheme, then, the comments of Stewart – and of Teggart and Bock – are by no means entirely inapplicable.

To the stadial scheme of the four stages theory, however, they are very much less applicable – if indeed they can really be said to be applicable at all. When men like Smith, Kames, and Millar postulated a 'natural' tendency for societies to pass through the stages of hunting, pasturage, agriculture, and commerce, it is true that they were still in a sense describing 'that general provision which nature has made for the improvement of the race'. But they were *not* describing this 'general provision' *a priori*, without reference to the historical facts. On the contrary, their delineation of the landmarks which lay along the 'natural' route of advancement was, at any rate in intention, a broad generalisation of the historical facts as they saw them. This, they believed, was the way in which most societies (barring accidents) had *actually* advanced in the past, and were *actually* advancing

22 The phrases quoted will be found in the penultimate paragraph of Book III, chapter I.
23 The phrases quoted will be found in the last paragraph of Book III, chapter I.

in the present. When Smith said that 'in almost all countries the age of shepherds preceded that of agriculture',[24] and Kames said that the hunting–pasturage–agriculture progression 'has, in all temperate climates of the Old World, been precisely uniform',[25] they meant what they said. They recognised, of course, that the influence of great men, of climate, and of sheer accident was often quite appreciable, and that as a result there were some countries and periods in which this 'natural' progression had been disturbed in various ways, and others in which it had been accelerated, retarded, or even more or less permanently suspended. But they believed that by and large, taking the world as a whole, and making all due allowance for disturbances, frictions, and exceptions, *this was the way in which things had actually happened in history.* When one looks at the actual work of the writers we are talking about, it is surely clear that most of them regarded the broad framework of the four stages theory, not as a kind of conjectural substitute for actual history, nor as a means of avoiding the hard work of historical research, but rather as a kind of generalised summing-up of such historical facts about the development of society as were then available – as well as, of course, a provisional conceptual framework within which to study the new facts which were then beginning to become available.

To sum up this part of our argument, then, we can say that while it may be quite proper to apply the term 'conjectural history' to Smith's account of the origin of languages, or to his theory of 'the natural progress of opulence', it is quite improper to apply it – at any rate without very careful qualification – to the four stages theory. Both the broad stadial scheme which that theory employed, and the more detailed analyses carried out within the framework of this stadial scheme, were intended to correspond so far as possible with the historical facts, at any rate up to the limit of the availability of these facts. When the relevant historical facts were not available, it is true, recourse was frequently had to 'conjecture' – i.e. to educated guesses about what had *probably* happened under certain given circumstances. But before we condemn this procedure by applying a pejorative adjective

---

[24] Above, p. 117.   [25] Above, p. 158.

Social science and the ignoble savage

to it, we should remember, first, that by and large it was adopted only when it was found to be necessary (owing to a 'want of direct evidence'), and, second, that it was found to be necessary far less often than most of the critics have assumed. To accuse the Enlightenment thinkers of *merely* substituting conjecture for history is just as unfair as it is to accuse them of merely 'temporalising the Great Chain of Being', or of merely 'making a new theodicy'.

It may plausibly be argued, however, that the area covered by 'conjecture' in the work of the Enlightenment social scientists, although *intended* to be relatively restricted, was actually much wider than the thinkers themselves appreciated, since some of the methods which they employed in order to derive or 'recreate' historical facts and sequences were seriously defective. Two points may be made in this connection. The first relates to their use – or misuse – of the alleged similarities between contemporary savage peoples like the Americans and certain peoples of the past such as the ancient Greeks and the Old Testament tribes. Such likenesses, Professor Margaret Hodgen has stated, 'were thought to have historiographical significance. They were thought to confer documentary properties upon the contemporary member of each pair of parallels, to make of it a present and accessible reflection of the past of some very early and otherwise undocumented cultural condition'.[26] Upon this notion, which Professor Hodgen claims that the Enlightenment social scientists took over more or less automatically and unthinkingly from their Renaissance predecessors, she pours out the vials of her wrath, with Adam Smith and the Scots receiving rather more than their fair share.[27] The second point, which is closely connected with the first, is related to the way in which the Enlightenment thinkers, having ranked *contemporary* cultures on some kind of scale of 'lower' and 'higher', used this ranking to assist in the derivation of

[26] Margaret T. Hodgen, *Early Anthropology in the Sixteenth and Seventeenth Centuries* (University of Pennsylvania Press, Philadelphia, 1964), p. 297.
[27] Cf. *ibid.*, p. 505, where Professor Hodgen speaks of Smith's 'usual abstractness and independence of evidence'; and p. 510, where she says of the Scots: 'Few were harassed by doubts. All were perfunctory in assembling "evidences" of their logically derived "historical" findings. None made substantial departures in methodological ideas.'

240

chronological relationships between the types of culture concerned. This procedure, according to Professor Bock, involved a very old and very grave fallacy – that of 'seeking a short-cut around historical empiricism by attempting to derive process from analysis of structure'.[28] The chronological progression through hunting, pasturage, and agriculture, it is implied, had no evidential foundation other than the fact that contemporary cultures based on these different modes of subsistence were ranked in this order on the scale of 'lower' and 'higher'.

There is of course an element of truth – and as applied to one or two individual Enlightenment thinkers rather more than an element of it – in this kind of criticism. It is quite true that the procedures complained of by Professor Hodgen and Professor Bock were sometimes insufficiently thought out; that they often embodied a 'Europocentric' attitude; and that they occasionally reflected something of a contempt for the savage peoples on the lowest rung of the evolutionary ladder. It is also quite true, as I have noted above,[29] that a number of the pioneers were for various reasons predisposed in favour of the notion that 'in the beginning all the World was *America*'. Given the times in which the new social scientists were writing, the narrow range of the conceptual tools which were available to them, and the limited information at their disposal, it could hardly have been otherwise. But the point is, surely, that there is nothing inherently invalid or morally wrong in the use of these procedures *as such*: everything depends upon whether they are used with the appropriate safeguards, and upon whether the appropriate qualifications are made when drawing conclusions from them. Professor Hodgen and Professor Bock, I believe, gravely underestimate the extent to which the Enlightenment thinkers themselves appreciated the necessity for these safeguards and qualifications. Were these thinkers really quite as blind to the dangers involved in the 'similarities' procedure as Professor Hodgen makes out? Did they really derive their chronological progression from their

[28] Kenneth E. Bock, *op. cit.*, p. 99.
[29] Above, pp. 128–30.

ranking of contemporary cultures quite as directly and unthinkingly, and with quite so little regard for the rules of historiographical practice, as Professor Bock makes out?[30] Were
they really quite as contemptuous of savage peoples, and
quite as 'Europocentric', as they have often been accused of
being? If the account of their work as a whole which I have
given above is regarded as a reasonably fair and complete
one, to ask these questions is to answer them.

If we look at the work of the Enlightenment social scientists directly, then, rather than in the distorting mirror provided by the work of some of their nineteenth-century
successors, surely what shine out are its virtues rather than
its vices, its brilliant intuitions rather than its occasional
logical lapses, its adventurousness and novelty rather than
its dogmatism.[31] After all, even if judged solely by a narrow
practical criterion, it has not come out too badly: the general
view of the development of society which the four stages
theory exemplified, if we admit a certain refinement of its
basic categories and a certain relaxation of its ordinal rigidi-
ties, is clearly recognisable as an early prototype of the view
which many scientists would wish to put forward today. But
a doctrine like the four stages theory should not of course
be judged mainly by a criterion of this sort. Rather, we
should look upon it as the first great theoretical embodiment
or crystallisation of a set of wider notions and attitudes – the
law of unintended consequences, the idea of a social *science*,
the comparative method, the notion of techno-economic
determinism, and the principle of cultural evolutionism.
Whether these notions and attitudes can be developed and
reapplied so as to yield a more satisfactory theory of the

[30] Professor Teggart (*op. cit.*, pp. 128ff.) has drawn some very interesting
and persuasive parallels between the new methodological techniques
employed in the field of the social sciences in the eighteenth century and
those employed at about the same time in the fields of astronomy, geology,
and biology.

[31] Recent commentators who would seem to have recognised this include
Sidney Pollard, *The Idea of Progress* (Watts, London, 1968); Marvin
Harris, *The Rise of Anthropological Theory* (Routledge, London, 1968);
Benjamin Keen, *The Aztec Image in Western Thought* (Rutgers Univer-
sity Press, New Jersey, 1971); and Alan Swingewood, 'Origins of Socio-
logy: the Case of the Scottish Enlightenment', *British Journal of Sociology*,
Vol. 21, 1970, pp. 164–80.

Afterword

development of society than either the eighteenth-century pioneers or their nineteenth-century successors were able to provide, is perhaps the most important and controversial issue facing the social sciences today.

Index

Abel, 15, 19, 21–2, 25, 67, 73
Abraham, 22, 100
accumulation of capital, 71, 109, 129, 153, 222, 237–8
Acosta, J. de, 42–9, 64
Adair, J., 176, 211, 215
Adam, 18, 58, 87, 200
Africans, 54, 166
Agamemnon, 124
agriculture, 2, 5, 7–17, 22, 25, 27, 30–3, 35, 61, 66, 69, 72, 75, 82–84, 87–90, 92–3, 95, 98, 101, 103–106, 117–21, 131–2, 134, 140, 144, 146, 148, 153–4, 157–8, 160, 163, 166, 169, 175–80, 182–4, 186–7, 189, 194–7, 199, 201–5, 207–8, 210–13, 221, 223–5, 227–9, 237–239, 241
Alembert, J. d', 233
Allen, D.C., 37
American Indians, effect of studies of, 2–3, 37–40, 64–7, 128–30, 213–19; origins of, 41–63; Grotius on, 16; Hobbes on, 16–17; Locke on, 22; Fontenelle on, 27–28; Cantillon on, 29–30; Vico on, 31; Acosta on, 42–9; Ogilby on, 49–57; Lafitau on, 57–64; Turgot on, 70, 74; Rousseau on, 80, 82, 86; Goguet on, 96; Smith on, 115, 118–22; Helvétius on, 134–5; Robertson on, 137–45; Douglass on, 137; de Pauw on, 145–50; Ferguson on, 151–4; Kames on, 159–60; Millar on, 161, 166; Voltaire on, 174; Blair on, 181; Falconer on, 186; Dunbar on, 191; Herder on, 195–6; Russell on, 202; Monboddo on, 203–6; Jefferson on, 218; Morse on, 218–19; Volney on, 226–7
anthropology, 2, 8, 37, 64, 89, 126, 133, 143, 152, 161, 174, 224, 231, 242
Apochancana, 20–1

Arabs, 34, 66, 87, 117, 146, 148, 151, 166, 175, 187–8
Aristotle, 8, 200
Arrian, 184
arts, 5, 10, 13, 15, 25–6, 30, 33, 50, 60, 66, 69, 75, 82, 85, 89, 94–6, 103, 109–10, 118, 124–6, 141, 143, 146, 151, 154, 160–2, 169, 171, 175–6, 179, 190, 193, 195–6, 199, 201, 204–5, 210, 212, 216, 228, 232
astronomy, 26, 113–14, 183, 233, 242

Bacchus, 13, 58
Bacon, F., 12–13
Baden, Margrave of, 182
Banks, Sir J., 216
Barnave, A.P.J.M., 228–9
Barraclough, J., 207
battle of the ancients and moderns, 26–8
Beattie, J., 198–200, 214
Beccaria, C.B., 30
Bedouins, 98, 194, 226
Bergin, T.G., 31
Blackstone, W., 177–9, 186, 214
Blair, H., 177, 179–82, 189, 214
Boas, G., 7, 10, 11, 83
Bochart, S., 139
Bock, K.E., 37, 208, 236, 238, 241–242
Bodin, J., 12
Bolingbroke, Lord, 30
Bonar, J., 137
Bossuet, J.B., 23–6, 35, 41, 127, 136
Bougainville, L.A. de, 216
bourgeois optimism, 130
Briggs, H.E., 145
Brown, A.H., 5
Brown, C.B., 226
Brumfitt, J.H., 76
Buffon, G.-L.-L., comte de, 143, 145, 159
Burke, E., 173

244

Index

Caesar, Julius, 5, 11, 34, 66, 138, 151, 211

Cain, 15, 19, 21–2, 25, 67, 73, 87

Callender, J., 110, 138

Canadians, 148–9, 217

Cannan, E., 16, 126

cannibalism, 55, 145

Cantillon, R., 29, 220

Carlyle, A., 112, 174–5

Carver, J., 215

cause and effect, 1, 24, 224

Ceres, 13, 15, 204

Champailler, Y., 23, 41

Charles V, 134, 136, 138, 150

Charlevoix, P.-F.-X. de, 120–2, 139, 153, 161, 176, 186, 211, 215

Chill, E., 228

Chinese, 54, 65, 149

Churchill, T., 192, 214

circumcision, 45, 52, 145, 215

climate, 7, 12–13, 27, 32, 34–5, 43, 69, 85, 89, 94, 134–5, 141, 144–5, 147, 153, 158, 164–5, 180, 185, 188, 191, 193, 197, 199, 201–2, 209–11, 226, 239

Cole, G.D.H., 77

Cole, T., 8, 11

commerce, 2, 5, 17, 30, 32, 35, 51, 66, 71, 75, 95, 98, 101–2, 104, 109, 117–19, 121, 125–6, 132, 143, 154–5, 158, 160, 163, 166, 169, 176, 180, 184, 187–8, 194, 199, 210–13, 219–20, 224–5, 227–229, 237–8

Comtaeus, R., 51

Comte, A., 26, 230, 236

Condillac, Abbé E.B. de, 219–20, 232

Condorcet, Marquis de, 76, 203, 207–9, 228

confusion of tongues, 15, 23, 70, 73, 94, 96, 200

contract(s), 104–6, 121

Cook, J., 211, 216

Copernicus, N., 233

couvade, 62

Craig, J., 107–8, 162, 174

Craigie, T., 108, 111

Creation, 18, 23, 56, 77, 200

crime(s), 89, 103, 106, 139, 234

Cullen, W., 108

custom(s), 2, 5, 12, 31–2, 43, 50–1, 53, 57, 59, 61, 63, 92, 115, 151, 164, 174, 176, 185, 190, 216

Dalrymple, Sir J., 99–102, 106, 112, 126

degeneration, of society, 7, 26, 155, 191; of Americans, 40, 47, 51, 128; of mankind after the dispersion, 151, 200

Democritus, 8

Derrida, J., 90

Descartes, R., 12

Desnitsky, S.E., 5, 7, 12

Deucalion's Flood, 8

Dicaearchus, 8, 10–12, 14–16

Diderot, D., 97

Dio of Prusa, 14

Diodorus Siculus, 157, 186, 204–5

division of labour, 29, 71, 75, 82, 111, 155, 172, 212, 221–3

Douglass, W., 136–8

Duchet, M., 37, 89–90, 133–4

Duff, W., 181

Dunbar, J., 184, 189–91, 214

Du Pont de Nemours, P.-S., 68, 76, 133, 177, 182–4, 214

economics, 2, 132, 177, 219–24, 230–231

Edwards, H.J., 11

Egyptians, 61, 149, 188, 217

Elliott, J.H., 38

Ellis, R.L., 13

Enlightenment, 1, 4, 7, 20, 23, 91, 161, 173–4, 192, 230, 240–1, 243

Epicurus, 67

Eskimos, 97–8, 147

Europocentrism, 192, 198, 241–2

Falconer, 184–9, 194, 214, 227

Ferguson, A., 1, 4, 131, 150–5, 172, 198, 211, 215, 236

feudalism, 100–1, 138, 210, 229

Fisch, M.H., 31

fishing, 8, 19–20, 31, 61–2, 64, 66, 81, 83–4, 94–5, 97–8, 100–1, 103, 133, 140, 143–4, 147–9, 152, 156–157, 159–60, 166, 168, 175, 183, 186–7, 194, 198–9, 204–5, 227

Fleurieu, C.P. Claret de, 217

Flood, 23, 54, 56, 60, 73, 79, 86, 94, 96, 147, 200

Fontenelle, B. le B. de, 27–8, 127

Forster, J.R., 216

four stages theory, description of, 2;

245

Index

prehistory of, 5–36; 'causes' of, 126–30; influence of, 173–6; its relation to American studies, 64–67, 213–19; its history from 1780 to 1800, 177–229; Desnitsky's version of, 5; Dicaearchus's version of, 10–11; Montesquieu's anticipations of, 33–4; Turgot's version of, 72–6; Rousseau's version of, 84–91; Helvétius's versions of, 92–4, 133–4; Goguet's version of, 94–7; in the *Encyclopedia*, 97–8; Dalrymple's version of, 99–102; Kame's versions of, 103–6, 156–160; Smith's version of, 116–26; Quesnay's oral and written versions of, 91–2, 132; Robertson's version of, 138–45; de Pauw's version of, 146–50; Ferguson's version of, 150–5; Millar's version of, 160–73; Blackstone's use of, 177–9; Blair's use of, in literary criticism, 180; Du Pont's version of, 182–4; Falconer's use of 185–9; Herder's attitude towards, 192–198; Beattie on, 198–200; Russell's critique of, 200–3; Pye's poetic version of, 209–10; Knight's poetic version of, 211–13; Volney's use of, 213; and the development of classical political economy, 219–224; place of commerce in, 227–9; critique of, 230–43

Garcia, G., 141
Genesis, 20–1, 25, 40, 56, 60, 64, 79, 128, 178
geography, 7, 12, 38, 42–3, 56–7, 68, 72, 199
geometry, 26, 104
Germans, 11–12, 31, 34, 53–4, 67, 134–5, 138–40, 142, 152, 166, 175–6, 186, 191
Gibbon, E., 175, 186
Glasgow University, 5, 16, 68, 99, 107, 116, 165
Goguet, A.Y., 91, 94–8, 131, 176, 186, 230, 232
golden age, 82, 86, 178
Goldsmid, E., 53
government, 2, 5, 16–17, 27, 34, 38–39, 42, 58–9, 82, 89, 103–4, 106–7, 109–10, 121–3, 125–6, 137, 143, 152–3, 158, 160–3, 165–6, 171, 175, 179, 185, 190, 196, 200, 205–206, 211, 219, 233, 235

Graffigny, Madame de, 70–2
Grange, H., 84
Greeks, 27–8, 49, 62–3, 74, 149, 174, 197, 216–17, 227, 240
Green, T.H., 30
Greenlanders, 147, 194
Grimston, E., 42
Grose, T.H., 30
Grotius, H., 12–17, 19, 29, 35, 52–4, 56, 101, 127, 153

Hall, J.C., 76
Hamilton, Duke of, 165
Hamilton, R., 223
Hampshire, S., 207
Harding, H.F., 181
Harris, M., 143, 242
Heath, D.D., 13
Hebrews, 14, 45–6
Hellenians, 61–3
Helvétius, C., 91–4, 98, 127, 129, 132–6, 139, 186
Henry, R., 175–6
Herder, J.G. von, 192–8, 203, 214, 225
Herodotus, 11, 105, 202, 205
Hesiod, 7, 67
Higgs, H., 29
Hildebrand, G.H., 7
historiography, 2, 222, 224, 231, 240
Hobbes, T., 16–17
Hodgen, M.T., 37, 63, 240–1
Hodges, W., 216
Holbach, P.H.D., baron d', 175
Homer, 161, 181–2
Hottentots, 20, 79, 98
Hubert, R., 97–8
Huddleston, L.E., 37
Hume, D., 30–1, 102
hunting, 2, 5, 7–9, 11–12, 19–20, 22, 25–6, 30–4, 47–8, 53, 61–2, 64, 66, 69, 72–4, 81, 83–4, 86, 88–95, 97–8, 100–1, 103–5, 117–24, 131–3, 135, 137–8, 140–1, 143–4, 147–9, 152–4, 156–60, 163, 166, 168, 175–80, 183, 186–7, 189, 194–9, 201–2, 204–5, 207–13, 215, 219, 223–5, 227, 238–9, 241
Hurons, 61–3
husbandmen, *see* agriculture
Hutcheson, F., 29, 35

Index

ignoble savage(s), 3, 129, 138, 145, 155, 170, 181, 213, 218, 224, 227
Indians, *see* American Indians
Iroquois, 27, 29, 61–2, 97–8, 121

Jefferson, T., 218
Jews, 45–6, 52, 65, 215
Justi, J.H.G. von, 131
justice, 102, 109, 119, 126, 163, 220

Kaiser, W., 13
Kames, Lord, 14, 99, 102–7, 112, 126, 132, 155–60, 162, 176, 186, 201, 232, 234–5, 238–9
Kaye, F.B., 29
Keats, J., 145
Keen, B., 242
Kelsey, F.W., 13
Knight, R.P., 209, 211–13, 215
Krieger, L., 192
Kuhn, T.S., 68

Labillardière, J.J. Houtou de la, 216
Laet, J. de, 53–4, 56
Lafitau, J.-F., 42, 57–64, 66, 121–2, 128, 141, 153, 161, 174, 176, 186, 215
Lamy, B., 73–4, 88
language(s), 9, 31, 52–3, 59, 61, 69, 73, 113–14, 122, 190, 203, 205–6, 214, 216, 232, 234–5, 239; Rousseau's essay on, 76ff.
Lapps, 27, 146, 148, 158, 194
Laslett, P., 3, 21
Lauderdale, Lord, 223
law(s), 2, 5, 7, 15, 31–5, 39, 42, 48, 52, 57–8, 86, 89, 93–4, 96, 102–4, 107, 109–10, 119, 123, 126, 138, 140, 152, 158, 161–4, 177, 179, 185, 196, 201, 204, 206, 233–4
law of unintended consequences, 1, 153, 224, 242; providential version of, 24; Vico on, 31; Turgot on, 75; Ferguson on, 150; Logan on, 190; Volney on, 226
Lehmann, W.C., 172
Le Roy, G., 219
Le Roy, L., 14
Lindgren, J.R., 112
Lipsius, J., 31
List, F., 224
Lloyd, S.S., 224

Locke, J., 1, 3, 14, 20–2, 29, 35, 37, 70, 101, 126, 153, 224, 226
Logan, J., 184, 189–90, 214
Lot, 22, 100
Lovejoy, A.O., 7, 10–11, 83, 192
Lucanus, 53
Lucretius, 8–10, 83, 211–12
luxury, 137, 159, 170, 188–9, 213

McCulloch, J.R., 223
Machiavelli, N., 12
McLain, J.J., 182
Macpherson, J., 161, 180
Malthus, T.R., 223–4
Mandeville, B. de, 29, 115
Manuel, F.E., 192
Marcet, J., 223
Markham, C.R., 42
Marx, K., 164, 220–1, 229
materialism, 3, 12, 25, 59, 125, 132, 160–1, 173, 191, 198, 229
Maupertuis, P.L.M. de, 69
Meek, R.L., 69–70, 73–5, 92, 94, 109, 132, 219–20, 223
metallurgy, 82–3, 90
Mexicans, 43, 53–4, 140, 160, 218
Mill, J., 223
Mill, J.S., 223
Millar, J., 5, 35, 107–10, 112, 160–177, 186, 198, 200, 229–30, 232, 234–5, 238
Mirabeau, Marquis de, 91–2, 132
mode of subsistence, *see* agriculture, commerce, fishing, hunting, pasturage
Monboddo, Lord, 203–7, 209, 215–216
money, 27, 29, 33, 93, 186, 201
Montaigne, M., 13, 82
Montesquieu, C.L., 3, 28, 31–5, 69, 72, 89, 91, 100, 109, 127, 135, 138, 148, 153, 162, 164, 185, 233–4
Montucla, J.E., 233
Moors, 146, 148
Morse, J., 218–19
Moses, 49, 78, 200
Murray, H., 225

Negroes, 194, 203
Nimrod, 25, 48
Noah, 25, 37, 44, 55–6, 60, 86–7
noble savage, 2, 129, 145, 155, 170, 181, 227

247

Index

Norwegians, 52–4
Nugent, T., 32
Numidians, 50–1

occupation, 15, 117, 198
Ogilby, J., 42, 49–57
Ogilvie, J., 181
Oldfather, C.H., 17
Oldfather, W.A., 17
Orpheus, 28
Ossian, 161, 180–1

pasturage, 2, 5, 8–12, 14–16, 19–20, 22, 25, 27, 32–4, 50–1, 61, 66, 69, 72, 74–5, 83–4, 86–91, 93, 95, 98, 100–1, 103–5, 117–20, 122–4, 131–2, 134–5, 138, 140, 144, 146, 148–9, 152–4, 157–60, 163, 166, 168–9, 175–81, 183, 186–90, 194–7, 199, 201–2, 205, 207–8, 210–13, 223–5, 227–8, 238–9, 241
Patriarchs, 25, 51, 66–7, 87, 101, 123, 199
Pauw, J.C. de, 65, 143, 145–50, 152
Pearce, R.H., 145, 155, 218–19
Peden, W., 218
Pelasgians, 62–3, 74
perfectibility, 3, 7, 25, 80, 129, 146, 155, 170–1, 208
Peruvians, 27, 54, 74, 140, 144, 160, 194, 218
Petty, Sir W., 30
philosophy, 13, 26, 81–2, 100
Phoenicians, 51–2
Physiocracy, 91–2, 132–3, 182–4, 219
Picts, 175, 218
Plato, 8, 44, 46, 82, 206
pleasure and pain, 93, 133
Pliny, 53
Pokrovsky, S.A., 5
political economy, *see* economics
Pollard, S., 242
polygeneticism, 155, 159
Pomeau, R., 64
Pope, A., 161, 211
population, 15, 19, 21, 25, 30, 32–3, 93, 104, 117, 133, 157–9, 178–9, 185, 200, 211–12, 223–4
Porphyry, 10, 15
Porset, C., 84
Prévost, abbé A.-F., 202
primitivism, 7, 10, 17, 70, 83

property, 2, 14–23, 29, 39, 82, 84, 86–7, 89–90, 100–2, 105–6, 109, 116, 120–1, 123, 129, 140, 142–3, 146, 152–5, 159, 163, 166, 168–9, 177–80, 183, 186, 190, 196, 198, 200–3, 214, 223, 228, 234
providential theory of history, 23–5, 136
Pufendorf, S. von, 14, 17–22, 25, 29, 35, 101, 127, 153
Purchas, S., 50
Pye, H.J., 209–11, 215

Quesnay, F., 91–2, 97–8, 132, 219, 221

Rackham, H., 8
Rae, J., 99, 108
Raphael, D., 107
religion, 9, 12, 23–4, 32, 37–40, 43, 46, 48–9, 51, 53–5, 58–9, 64, 77, 102, 106, 109, 136–7, 144, 179, 185
Renaissance, 39, 240
Ricardo, D., 221
Robertson, W., 2, 65, 67, 112, 129, 134, 136–46, 150, 152, 173, 176, 186, 189, 211, 215, 230
Romans, 31, 49, 63
Rouse, W.H.D., 10
Rousseau, J.-J., 73, 76–91, 94, 97–8, 112, 115–16, 129, 131, 143, 145, 155, 172–3, 188, 196, 212, 224
Rude, F., 228
Russell, W., 198, 200–3, 215
'Rutherford, W.', 190

Salic law, 33
Sallust, 5
Schelle, G., 69–70
sciences, 1, 5, 26, 31, 50, 66, 69, 82, 93–6, 124, 126, 156, 161, 163, 171, 179, 187, 189, 199, 201, 204, 232
Scott, W.R., 99, 108, 113, 190
Scrope, G.P., 224
Scythians, 11, 16, 19, 54–6, 60, 67, 87, 97–8, 105, 142, 148, 154, 202, 217–18
Seneca, 14
Senior, N.W., 223
sensationalist psychology, 1, 20, 70, 127

248

Index

shepherds, *see* pasturage
Skinner, A.S., 220, 223
slavery, 75, 82, 137, 167
Slotkin, J.S., 37
Smith, A., 3, 16, 29, 32, 35, 66, 68, 75, 82–3, 99, 107–27, 129, 131–2, 137–8, 162, 172, 190, 211, 213, 219–23 229–40
Smith, B., 215–18
Smith, S.S., 219
sociology, 2, 150, 174, 222, 224, 230, 242
Spanish, 28, 48, 56
Spedding, J., 13
Stair, Viscount, 101
state of nature, 17–18, 21, 72, 179, 200, 209, 217; Rousseau on, 77ff.
Stein, P., 107
Steuart, Sir J., 220–1
Stewart, D., 32, 107, 110–14, 173, 231–5
Stewart, J.B., 30
Strabo, W., 187
Stuart, G., 176, 186
surplus, 75, 104, 118, 179, 212–13
Swingewood, A., 242

Tacitus, 5, 11, 31, 34, 53, 66, 138, 151, 186, 191, 211
Tahitians, 216–17
Tartars, 29, 34, 50–1, 53–6, 66, 87, 97–8, 117, 119, 124, 146, 148, 154, 158, 166, 187–8, 202, 204–205

Taylor, A.E., 8
technology, 7, 11, 50, 82, 127, 212, 242
Teggart, F.J., 7, 235–6, 238, 242
Temple, Sir W., 26–7
'theoretical or conjectural history', 113–14, 231–3, 235, 239
theory of knowledge, 1, 3, 20, 70, 127, 224, 226
Thracians, 60, 218
Thucydides, 105, 151
Tower of Babel, 88, 156, 200
Tunguses, 148–9
Turgot, A.R.J., 3, 23–5, 29, 32, 35, 68–76, 82–3, 94, 97–8, 109, 111–112, 127, 129, 131, 173, 192, 219–22, 231, 236
Tytler, A.F., 99

Varro, 10, 15
Velat, B., 23, 41
Vico, G., 31, 35
Volney, C.F., 213, 226–7
Voltaire, F.M.A. de, 23, 35, 64, 97, 161, 174

Wallace, R., 223
Weyland, J., 224
White, G.W., 226
Wight, W., 174–5
women, 161, 166–70
Wood, R., 181

Yolton, J.W., 20